Arabs Face the
Modern World

Nissim Rejwan

Arabs Face the Modern World

Religious, Cultural,

and Political Responses

to the West

WITHDRAWN
FROM
UNIVERSITY OF PENNSYLVANIA
LIBRARIES

University Press of Florida

Gainesville Tallahassee Tampa Boca Raton
Pensacola Orlando Miami Jacksonville

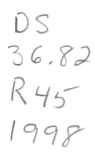

DS
36.82
R45
1998

Copyright 1998 by the Board of Regents of the State of Florida
Printed in the United States of America on acid-free paper
All rights reserved

03 02 01 00 99 98   6 5 4 3 2 1

Library of Congress Cataloging-in-Publication Data
Rejwan, Nissim.
Arabs face the modern world: religious, cultural, and political responses to the West / Nissim Rejwan.
p. cm.
Includes bibliographical references (p.   ) and index.
ISBN 0-8130-1559-6 (alk. paper)
1. Civilization, Arab—Western influences. 2. East and West.
3. Islam and politics—Arab countries. 4. Arab countries—politics
and government—1945–. 5. Arab countries—intellectual life—20th
century. I. Title.
DS36.82.R45 1998 97-39680
303.48'217492701821—dc21

The University Press of Florida is the scholarly publishing agency
for the State University System of Florida, comprised of Florida
A & M University, Florida Atlantic University, Florida Interna-
tional University, Florida State University, University of Central
Florida, University of Florida, University of North Florida,
University of South Florida, and University of West Florida.

University Press of Florida
15 Northwest 15th Street
Gainesville, FL 32611
http://nersp.nerdc.ufl.edu/~upf

UNIVERSITY
OF
PENNSYLVANIA
LIBRARIES

Video meliora proboque;
deteriora sequor

Res Pur

Contents

Preface

For nearly four centuries, between the publication of Ibn Khaldun's great *History* and the rise of the modernist movement in Arabic Islam late in the nineteenth century, the Muslim-Arab world remained in a state of intellectual and literary dearth matched only by its material and political decline. Then, toward the end of the century Muslim Arabs started to respond to the many challenges posed to them by the modern world in a new and energetic way. This book traces the various forms this response has taken and the phases through which it has passed since Jamal al-Din al-Afghani and his disciple Muhammad 'Abduh appeared on the scene with their call to revitalize Islam and adapt it to the needs of a changed world.

The first three chapters survey the four types of Muslim-Arab reaction to the new realities and bring the account up to the mid-1960s:

1. The initial theological-political teachings of Afghani and 'Abduh, the acknowledged fathers of the modernist movement in Arabic Islam.

2. The ways in which these teachings were to be translated into coherent political, social, cultural, and theological concepts, especially in Egypt. This section covers the work of such opinion-leaders as Rashid Rida, Qasim Amin, Lutfi al-Sayyid, 'Ali 'Abd al-Raziq, and Taha Husain—as well as political activists like Zaghlul and Kamil.

3. The rise of Muslim militancy, partly in reaction to the failure of many of the modernists to reconcile their religious convictions with the demands of modern life. This chapter deals mainly with the Muslim Brethren and contains a comprehensive summary of the teachings of its founders and leaders.

4. Along with Muslim militancy came another, secular, response that took the form of a nationalist movement. This, in turn, was roughly of two types—the ethnic and the territorial, depending on how the

term Arab was to be defined. This chapter is devoted to an analysis of the ideology of Pan-Arab nationalism, which reached its peak with the emergence of Jamal 'Abd al-Nasser to a position of leadership in the Arab world in the mid-1960s.

Three more chapters bring the account up to the late 1980s: The defeat of the Egyptian, Syrian, and Jordanian armies in the Six-Day War in June 1967 and the subsequent decline in the fortunes of Nasserism gave rise to a variety of violent intellectual reactions. These encompassed the literary, cultural, and religious fields, as well as the political ones. Chapter 5, "The Shock of 1967," offers a survey of these reactions in various parts of the Arab world.

A wider-ranging, deeper, and more searching set of responses followed these largely emotional reactions. In chapter 6 a number of Arab leaders of opinion examine such basic questions as the nature of Westernization and its effects, the main features of Arab civilization and the reasons why it failed to face Europe's onslaught, and the deeply ambiguous attitude toward the West this conflict brought with it—an ambivalence here illustrated in a survey of the works of Muhammad Wahbi and Hisham Sharabi, among others.

The October (Yom Kippur) War of 1973, in which the Muslim-Arab world takes pride and which served to restore some of the dignity and self-esteem lost in the Six-Day War, is taken in chapter 7 as the occasion for a comprehensive summing-up, bringing the account to the mid-1980s. A number of basic issues in Muslim-Arab intellectual history are examined: The decline and fall of the Nasserist ideology; Egypt's Arab identity; a much more relaxed literary-cultural scene; historicism versus Islamic traditionalism; and the emergence of a new Islamic militancy. Chapter 8, "The Shifting Nineties," brings the account up to our own day.

While based on solid research and much original scholarship, *Arabs Face the Modern World* can also be viewed as a work of popularization, addressed to the enlightened general reader as well as to the student of the modern Middle East.

This book has been a long time in the making, but it was only in 1995, after I joined the Harry S. Truman Research Institute for the Advancement of Peace, Hebrew University of Jerusalem, as a research fellow that I was able to give the work its final shape. My thanks are due to the Institute's directors and staff for their cooperation and encouragement. And, as always, my wife, Rachel, patiently bore with me while I made a mess of our household trying to locate a book or some obscure reference, working all around the place with the exception of my little study.

1 | The Modernist Movement in Arabic Islam

My ringing cry has urged along the road
The throng that lost their way along the plain . . .
The soul of Persia moves at my song
The caravan moves on, my call is strong:
Out of my restless spirit the flames start.
In the East's bosom I have stirred a heart.

Muhammad Iqbal, translated by A. J. Arberry

A Question of Adjustment

In *Civilization on Trial,* Arnold Toynbee reminds us that on two historic occasions in the past "Islam has been the sign in which an Oriental society has risen up victoriously against an Occidental intruder." Under the first successors of the prophet, he explains, Islam liberated Syria and Egypt from a Hellenic domination which had weighed on them for nearly a thousand years. Under Zangi and Nureddin and Saladin and the Mamluks, Islam held the fort against the assaults of the Crusaders and Mongols. "If the present situation of mankind were to precipitate a 'race war,' Islam might be moved to play her historic role once again."[1] Yet not only has Islam failed once again to take up the role of liberator of Oriental society; its whole history in modern times has so far been largely that of the modern Muslim's attempts at adjusting himself and his worldview to the situation created by his encounter with Western culture and Western ways.

The problem Muslim reformists have had to grapple with during the past century or so can be formulated in a variety of ways. Lord Cromer, British resident and consul general in Egypt from 1883 to 1907, was for all his diligence as a colonial administrator a keen and sympathetic observer of the Egyptian cultural scene. He used to quote with approval a saying of S. Lane-Poole's to the effect that an upper-class Muslim must be "either a fanatic or a concealed infidel." Cromer once wrote of Sheikh Muhammad 'Abduh, Arabic Islam's greatest theologian of modern times and leader of the modernist movement in Egypt, that he suspected him of being "in reality an agnostic . . . although he would have resented the appellation being applied to him."[2]

In this description, Cromer—who knew 'Abduh well, held him in high esteem, and used to call him "my friend"—managed to put his finger on the modern Muslim's acutest intellectual dilemma. What tended to make the educated, conscious modern Muslim something of a fanatic is the shocking discrepancy between the stupendous claims of Islam and the golden moments in its history on the one hand and its present deplorable state on the other. Indeed, the modernist movement in Arabic Islam, which started in Egypt during the last two decades of the nineteenth century, was a direct outcome of the challenge posed by European influences—a challenge that left Islam damaged and enfeebled. What tended to make a modern educated Muslim seem a concealed infidel—again in Cromer's formulation— was the difficulty of seeing how he could possibly—as 'Abduh and his followers claimed they did—believe in the compatibility of Islam and modernism: that is, the claim that the teachings of Islam and its prescriptions were fully rational and consonant with the conclusions of modern science and philosophy.

Broadly speaking, attempts on the part of modern Islam to meet the West's assault in the cultural, political, and military spheres have been of two kinds—the one showing an instinct to absorb and find compatibles, the other displaying a tendency to reject and affirm distinctions. It must be pointed out, however, that these two modes of reaction—which denote the two extreme tendencies in the struggle of the assaulted culture against the dominant one—do not exhaust all the possibilities of dealing with the problem. If these two sharply contrasted reactions of absorption and rejection can be likened—as has been done by Toynbee—respectively to those of the Herodians and the Zealots in Hellenic times, there then must be a third way, namely, that of the Pharisees. This original, positive mode of reaction to alien cultural pressure has been called one of "withdrawal and return." It is perhaps to this third tendency that we have to refer the main body of the great reform movement in Arabic Islam in modern times.

It is not easy to formulate a satisfactory definition of the term "modernism" in its Islamic context—or in any other context for that matter. Roughly speaking, the modernist movement in Arabic Islam can be described as an expression of the necessity of an intellectual response, within the religious faith, to the pressure of new circumstances and ideas as they bear upon traditional dogma and behavior. The movement's driving force, insofar as it had one such distinguishable force, was the desire to demonstrate, in practical terms and in response to particular concrete issues, that Islam was equal to the needs and demands of the modern world. Its protagonists and leading exponents were informed by a desire to rid Islam of a backward-looking mentality that they thought disqualified its followers from participation in a progressive, forward-looking mode of life. They sought to destroy the spirit of obscurantism, which encouraged authoritarian loyalties to old schools of law and custom and barred the introduction of reasonable change.

Yet, contrary to what might seem both logical and desirable, Islamic modernism did not seek any far-reaching theological reconstruction. The basic theological and orthodox doctrines of Islam have not, except in very rare cases, been involved in the debates of the modernists. Their main emphases have fallen on institutional adaptation and adjustment to new situations and on the liberation of the minds and ways of men from the paralyzing restrictions imposed by *taqlid,* the slavish imitation of traditional interpretations. Though it is true that some of the positive achievements of the movement have had important doctrinal implications, these have tended to be only indirect and sometimes unconscious. One can conclude with fairness that the modern reform movement in Islam, especially where the Arabic-speaking world is concerned, has not attempted any radical intellectual reexamination of Islam or sought a revision of its basic precepts.

As a matter of fact, the directions in which the exponents of the movement have expressed themselves were for the most part practical rather than speculative, adaptive rather than creative—with the notable exception of the Indian school of Islamic modernism led by Muhammad Iqbal. The modernist Muslim strives, in fact, to evoke an Islam that takes cognizance of all its duties in the present without inhibition from the past—an Islam which does not, as a religion, resist the pressure of social morality but rather encourages and adopts it to itself.[3]

This reluctance on the part of the modernists to deal with issues of basic doctrine was no accident. By concentrating on practical rather than speculative aspects of the subject, the exponents of Islamic reform managed, at least for a time, to avoid the main issue, which was simply how to modernize Islam itself and not merely its followers. But only for a time. This is why their work was left uncompleted and is likely to remain so for a long time. The dilemma has been formulated with considerable concision by one student of the Egyptian intellectual scene. Drawing on the disciplines of sociology and political science, the writer elaborates three main propositions:

1. A political community cannot be viable and stable unless it is founded upon a more or less generally stated set of ideas, modes of thinking, norms, and values, which one can variously call a belief system, a worldview, or a Weltanschauung.
2. There is an intimate connection between material realities and economic, social, and political conditions on the one hand, and modes of thinking and belief systems on the other. A drastic change in the former may make a particular belief system obsolete and require its modification or replacement.
3. The impact of modern science and technology makes it incumbent on most societies — "starting from a position of adherence to a theologically oriented belief system" — to reformulate their belief systems in such a way as to give them a humanistic rather than a theological orientation.[4]

The relevance of these propositions to the reform movement in Arabic Islam, whose center has been Egypt, is self-evident. Egypt—and what is said about Egypt is almost wholly applicable to Muslim Arabs elsewhere— was heir to a belief system based on Islamic doctrine, a belief system that served as the foundation of her political community and evolved over a period of many centuries parallel to the evolution of her material conditions. For three centuries after the beginning of the Ottoman occupation, both belief systems and material conditions changed very little. By the beginning of the nineteenth century, however, "the basic character of Egyptian government and the structure of the economy and society began to undergo very rapid change under the impact of renewed contact with Europe."

Despite this rapid and far-reaching change, the belief system remained frozen. "An increasingly widening gap developed between reality and ideology that undermined the existing political community and threatened to condemn Egyptian society to a permanent state of instability and tension." The situation called for the bridging of the gap by means of a readjustment of the traditional belief system "or the formulation of a new one capable of serving as the foundation of a new political community."[5]

Jamal al-Din al-Afghani and the Revolt of the East

The challenge Islam faced in the modern age, whose nature and dimensions have been sketched in the previous few pages, was duly—if never effectively—taken up. The initial response originated, however, not in Egypt or the Arab lands of the Middle East but in the teachings and activity of a dynamic, almost legendary, personality—Jamal al-Din al-Afghani, born 1838 or 1839. In recent years, Afghani's place of birth became a topic of controversy among scholars. He himself usually claimed that he had been born in a townlet near Kabul in Afghanistan. However, he is also known to have "admitted" while in Iran that he was of Iranian origin. Nikki Keddie, who was the first Western scholar to make the discovery, maintains that Afghani's main reason for later claiming Afghan birth "was probably to avoid identification with the minority, Shi'i branch of Islam, since virtually all ethnic Persians from Iran were known to be born Shi'is."[6] Keddie makes the significant point that the place-of-origin name "Afghani" was adopted by Jamal al-Din only in 1869, after he had been expelled from Afghanistan and began to claim an Afghan birth and upbringing. Evidence gathered by Iranians and others, however, establishes that Afghani was born in a large village called Asadabad near the city of Hamadan in northern Iran.[7]

By the time he was forty, having spent 1871–79 in Egypt, Jamal al-Din became the chief agent in the inception of the modernist movement there. We know comparatively very little about his childhood. From the age of ten onward he pursued his studies in various parts of Afghanistan and Iran. By the time he was eighteen he had studied practically the whole range of the Islamic sciences and acquired a remarkable familiarity with all branches of knowledge. He mastered Arabic grammar and philology, Islamic history and theology, Sufism, logic, philosophy, physics, mathematics, medicine, and various other subjects.

Afghani's long and active career began when he was eighteen. He went to India for about a year and a half and learned of the European sciences and their methods, as well as acquainted himself with the English language. Returning to Afghanistan, Jamal al-Din entered the service of the ruling emir, Dust Muhammad Khan, one of whose successors eventually promoted Afghani to the position of prime minister. When a rival emir, Shir 'Ali, supported by British arms and funds, succeeded in overthrowing the regime, Afghani—then twenty-seven—decided to leave the country. In 1869, he was permitted to make the pilgrimage to Mecca. He proceeded by way of India, where he was received with honor by the Indian government, but he was not permitted to engage in any political activity or to hold conferences with Muslim leaders. Seeing that he was rendered inactive by his inability to make contacts in India, he was conveyed in an Indian government ship to Suez a month later. Some authorities maintain that he was expelled by the British. From Suez he went to Cairo for forty days. During this sojourn he frequented the religious Islamic university of Al-Azhar, conversed with many teachers and students, and delivered lectures in his own lodgings to those who visited him.

While in Cairo, Afghani received an invitation from Sultan Abd al-'Aziz to visit Constantinople and, deciding not to make the pilgrimage to Mecca, he arrived in the Ottoman capital early in 1870 and was received with great honor. Within six months of his arrival, he was appointed a member of the Education Council, in which capacity he worked for the introduction of far-reaching reforms in the educational system. As was to be expected, these reforms earned Afghani the hostility of Sheikh al-Islam, who saw in them something that affected his own exalted position. Moreover, losing no opportunity of making his views known and gaining considerable influence, Afghani soon aroused hostility and jealousy among other religious quarters as well.

Finally, toward the end of his first year in Constantinople, Afghani was invited to address the students of Dar al-Funun (college of arts) on the importance of crafts and the trades. Although he had taken the precaution of showing the text of his address beforehand to a number of high officials, some of the views he expressed were seized upon by Sheikh al-Islam and his friends, who accused Afghani of using terms derogatory to the dignity of Islam. The press took up the matter and Afghani replied, demanding the trial of Sheik al-Islam for calling him an atheist. Such a furor was created that he was finally ordered to leave the country.

On March 22, 1871, Afghani arrived in Cairo, where he intended to stay but for a short visit. But through the influence of Egypt's prime minister, the government allotted him a monthly allowance of ten Egyptian pounds as a mark of respect and recognition—a gesture which made him stay on in Egypt for the time being. As always, he was surrounded by friends, disciples, and admirers, to whom he expounded his then extremely advanced views on theology, philosophy, jurisprudence, astronomy, and mysticism. He also took an active interest in Egyptian political affairs and did all he could to arouse the country to the dangers of foreign domination and intervention—while his writings in the local press did not conceal his anti-British sentiments.

These activities, which continued for eight years, were bound to arouse the suspicion of the authorities and the opposition of the conservative theologians. Those years, too, happened to witness the quick deterioration of the country's financial affairs, which led to European intervention. When the Khedive Isma'il Pasha was deposed, to be succeeded by Tawfiq Pasha in June 1879, it took the new regime only three months to order the expulsion of Jamal al-Din from Egypt.

In Hyderabad in India, where Afghani went after his expulsion from Cairo, he composed in Persian the only full-length book to survive of which he was the author. It was titled *The Refutation of the Materialists* and was a defense of Islam against contemporary derogatory attacks. In 1882, while Afghani was still in India, the Young Egypt Movement with which Afghani had been identified culminated in the 'Urabi Rebellion and the subsequent occupation of Egypt by the British. During the progress of hostilities, Afghani was detained by the Indian government in Calcutta. Upon the collapse of the 'Urabi movement he was allowed to leave India, whereupon he went to London for a few days and then to Paris, where he lived and worked for the following three years. Afghani's Paris stay was a period of active international propaganda for him. His newspaper articles aroused the keenest interest. In 1883 he carried on a controversy with Ernest Renan on Islam and science, the discussion centering on the ability of Islam to reform and adapt itself to modern civilization. (Renan later described his erstwhile opponent as "the first agitator for liberty in the history of the modern East and its first martyr.")

It was in Paris in 1884 that Afghani was joined by his friend and former pupil Muhammad 'Abduh, who had been exiled from Egypt on charges of complicity in the 'Urabi Rebellion. Together they began the publication of an Arabic weekly called *Al-'Urwa al-Wuthqa* (The indissoluble bond), with the object of arousing the Muslim people to the need of joining their ranks against Western aggression and exploitation. Only eighteen numbers of the periodical were to appear, of which the first was dated March 13 and the last October 16, 1884. The weekly was the organ of a secret organization of the same name composed of Muslims from India, Egypt, North Africa, and Syria. Its purpose was "to unite Muslims and arouse them from their slumber and acquaint them with the dangers threatening them and guide them to the way of meeting these dangers." *Al-'Urwa al-Wuthqa* was banned by the British government from entering India and Egypt, the two countries chiefly to be influenced by its publication. One of Afghani's disciples expressed the opinion that, had the paper been continued, it would have occasioned a general Muslim uprising. In spite of its brief existence, the publication exerted a great influence and has been published in book form many times since its demise, the last in Cairo in 1958, for which then president Nasser himself wrote a special introduction.

The thirteen years separating the collapse of *Al-'Urwa al-Wuthqa* and Afghani's death (March 9, 1897) are shrouded in some mystery. After a brief visit to London, Afghani went to Moscow and then to St. Petersburg. His Russian sojourn extended for over four years, during which he continued writing and agitating for Islamic unity. Either before or during his stay in Russia, Afghani made an appearance in Persia, where he was appointed minister of war in 1886. His learning and eloquence, as well as his manifest zeal for the interests of the country, won him unusual influence in every quarter, so much so that the shah—who himself had invited Afghani by cable—began to be suspicious. He feared that his guest would use his influence to undermine his government and his throne.

Becoming aware of this change of attitude, Afghani asked permission to leave the country and went to Russia. In Munich in 1889, he again met Shah Nasser ad-Din, then on a visit to Europe. The shah persuaded him to return to Persia and become prime minister. After a period of smooth cooperation and mutual confidence, the shah's suspicions were revived and Afghani, again asking permission to leave the country, was refused with apparent discourtesy. He then took refuge in the shrine of a local mosque for about seven months, breaking with the shah and openly advocating his overthrow. Afghani's influence grew with all classes of the people, and among his disciples were twelve men who later became prominent in the Persian "Resergimento," or nationalist revolution. It was one of these disciples who assassinated the shah on May 1, 1896.

Sometime toward the close of 1890, however, the shah finally violated the sanctuary of the mosque and had Afghani, in poor health, arrested and conveyed to the Turkish frontier. After a brief visit to London following his recovery, Afghani returned to Turkey in 1892, where he remained until his death. Cancer of the jaw, which soon spread to his neck, caused his death. Many of his Persian friends entertained strong suspicions that he was actually poisoned. Less than a year before his death, the Turkish authorities refused the Persian government's demands to extradite Afghani following the shooting of Shah Nasir al-Din. (Three others who were suspected of complicity in the plot were returned, however, and secretly put to death in Tabriz.)

It will be seen from the above sketch of Afghani's life that his activities encompassed practically all of the lands of Islam and those European countries that were involved in the affairs of Muslim peoples. At one time or another, such countries as Afghanistan, Persia, Turkey, India, and Egypt experienced Afghani's potent contact and were influenced by his thoughts and actions. The Persian revolution, culminating in the inauguration of the Constitution of 1906, was inspired and sustained in its first stages by his advice and encouragement. The successful Young Turk Movement of 1908 was being prepared for by his agitation during his stay in Constantinople. He was also seen as the prime mover in the Egyptian nationalist movement and was the chief inspirer of the intellectual and religious awakening represented by Muhammad 'Abduh and his followers. As one of his European biographers said of him: "Wherever he went he left behind him a hotbed of contention, and it can be said without exaggeration that all the movements of national emancipation, of reaction against European enterprise, which we have been witnessing in the Orient for a score of years, have their origin directly in his propaganda."[8]

It is now commonly agreed—thanks largely to the work of Keddie, Kedourie, and a number of Iranian scholars—that Jamal al-Din's life was full of obscure and complex intrigues and ambiguities. The claim has also been made, and fairly well substantiated, that Afghani was something of an opportunist, a political activist using religion for worldly and personal ends, and that generally "he was the very type of revolutionary conspirator and activist so well-known in Europe in modern times."[9] Kedourie, who enlarges on this theme by relying on certain new evidence, maintains that "on any reckoning, Afghani and his followers must be considered subverts of Islam as the orthodox have understood and practised it." He writes, too, that Afghani and his disciples and students "have seldom if at all had their doctrines criticized, let alone refuted, by the representatives of orthodoxy." He writes that these have, on the contrary, "with a common voice sung Afghani's and 'Abduh's praises, and have described them as the initiators of an Islamic renaissance rescuing the faith from a secular stagnation."[10]

These are all fairly legitimate conclusions that can be substantiated without much difficulty. As Keddie points out, however, four factors were at play here and they must be taken into consideration if one is to arrive at a correct perspective.

To start with, Afghani was influenced by a deep-rooted tradition which taught that it was correct and proper "to use different levels of discourse according to the level of one's audience." Secondly, when Afghani on certain occasions used the word "Islam" in a strongly positive, somewhat idealized sense and praised the faith for its tolerance, scientific spirit, and so on, "he was thinking of an idealized 'Islam' different not only from the Muslim religion or civilization of his own day, but from any he imagined to have existed for more than a millennium."

Thirdly, Afghani's concern for unity and his hopes for rallying *all* Muslims against the West involved engaging in political propaganda that would appeal differently to the different elements of society—an activity that led to all sorts of contradictions. According to Keddie, Afghani seems to have been caught in an unresolved contradiction between the traditional, quietist ideas of the Muslim philosophers and more modern ideas of political opposition. As for political assassinations, these, she writes, are "typical both of certain strains of the Islamic tradition and of immature modern revolutionary movements."

Lastly, the fact that Afghani spent most of his life in political activity and less time working for religious reform indicates only "that the political unification and strengthening of the Islamic world and the ending of Western incursions there were his primary goals, while the reform of Islam was secondary."[11]

Afghani was a revolutionary and a rebel rather than a contemplative thinker. It was characteristic of the man's drive and temperament that the means he chose for the realization of his ends should be that of political revolution, since this, as Charles Adams puts it, "seemed to him the quick and sure way of securing for Islamic peoples the freedom necessary to enable them to set their own house in order." Afghani considered the overthrow of Muslim rulers who stood in the way of this salvation a legitimate means to the desired end. He once said in the course of an interview with Professor E. G. Browne: "No reforms can be hoped for till six or seven heads are cut off," and he specified by name the shah of Iran and his prime minister. Nor was he devoted to any of the existing Muslim powers; it is noteworthy that his disciple and biographer, Rashid Rida, is at pains to correct a statement by a previous biographer to the effect that Afghani was devoted to the Ottoman caliphate. His objective, Rida implies, was to raise some Muslim power that would become a rallying point for all Muslim nations. He began with Egypt; when his plans failed there, he pinned his hopes on the Mahdi uprising in the Sudan; then he tried Persia; and finally, the Ottoman Empire.

As a creative thinker and systemizer, however, Afghani did not excel; he was too busy being the man of action, the agitator, and the standard-bearer to pay much attention to theory. As mentioned above, the only substantial work he left behind was *The Refutation of the Materialists*, which he wrote while in semi-exile in India. Adams summarizes the final section of the book, entitled "The Means by Which the Happiness of Nations May Be Attained," which gives an example of the more constructive side of his teachings and contains many of his fundamental ideas. In order that the happiness of nations may be attained, Afghani maintains the following:

1. The minds of the people should be purified of belief in superstitions and foolish notions. Islam requires this, especially because the doctrine of the unity of God requires the clarifying of the mind and forbids such foolish and extravagant notions as idolatry, or incarnations and suffering of the Deity.

2. The people should feel themselves capable of attaining the highest levels of nobility of character and should be desirous of being so. The only thing that cannot be reached by him who desires it is prophecy, which God confers on whomsoever he will. If all the people were persuaded of the possibility of attaining perfection of character they would vie with one another in endeavors to attain it. Islam made possible perfection for all. It is not like Brahmanism, which divides men into castes, the limits of which cannot be overstepped. Nor like Judaism, which despised men of other religions and instituted within itself the priesthood as the caste nearest God, without the mediation of which no one could attain nearness to God.

3. The articles of belief of the religion of the nation should be the first subject taught to the people, and this should be done by teaching also the proper reasons and arguments in support of these beliefs; the religious beliefs of the people should not rest upon mere acceptance of authoritative teaching. Guizot, in his work on "Civilization," shows that the most potent element in the modern progress and civilization of Europe was the appearance of a religious party that claimed the right of investigating the sources of religious belief for themselves and demanding proof for these beliefs. Islam is almost alone among the religions of the world in addressing itself to man's reason and demanding that he accept religious belief only upon the grounds of convincing argument and not of mere claim and supposition. Contrasted with Islam are other religions, such as those requiring the belief that one can be more than one and the many can be one, a belief which its professors justify on the ground that it is above reason and cannot be grasped by reason.

4. In every nation there should be a special class whose function is to educate the rest of the people and another class whose function is to train the people in morals. One class would combat natural igno-

rance and the lack of instruction, the other would combat natural passions and the lack of discipline. These two provisions—the teacher to perform the work of instruction and the disciplinarian to command that which is good and to prohibit that which should be avoided—are among the most important provisions of Islam. Islam is thus the only religion by which the happiness of nations can be attained. If it be objected, "Why then are the Muslims in the evil state in which you find them?" The answer may be given in the words of the Koran: "Verily God will not change the state of a people until they change their own state" (XIII:12).[12]

The student will probably be struck by the remarkable similarity between Afghani's contention in point three above and the teachings of the Protestant movement in Europe. His reference, for instance, to "a religious party that claimed the right of investigating religious beliefs for themselves" is an obvious reference to that movement. Indeed, Qal'achi quotes Afghani as having told Abd al-Qader al-Maghribi that there should emerge in Islam a reform movement "akin to that of Martin Luther's Protestantism . . . to eradicate mistaken notions which have taken root in the minds of the populace and of some of the theologians alike."[13]

However, despite the fact that Afghani's ideas about religious reform were clear, well argued, and systematic, his chief appeal to the young Muslims of his time was political. This can be readily understood, since the field of political agitation offered these patriots not only a seemingly quick and easy way to national independence but also an opportunity for the expression of vociferous nationalistic sentiments. This appeal was wide. Afghani-inspired political revolutionaries and venerable scholars, in equal measure, advocated both local nationalism and Pan-Islam and agitated for liberation from both internal despotism and foreign domination.

Muhammad 'Abduh: His Life and Teachings

"I leave you Sheikh Muhammad 'Abduh," Afghani told his followers and pupils in 1879 as he was leaving Egypt for the last time, "and he is sufficient for Egypt as a scholar."[14] The influence 'Abduh was to have on his contemporaries is perhaps best illustrated by the fact that he was given the rare title of *al-ustadh al-imam,* the master and the guide. When he died in 1905, he left numerous disciples and many works of intrinsic value—and, not least, the enduring impact of his own unique personality. His energy and versatility were proverbial. One of his modern interpreters relates that the majority of the sheikhs, when confronted by his many-sided personality, used to dismiss him, saying: "What sort of Sheikh is this, who speaks French, travels about in Europe, translates Western books, quotes from Western philosophers, holds discussions with their scholars, and issues *fatwas* (religious edicts) on things that not one of the ancients would have known about, takes part in benevolent organizations and collects money for the poor and unfortunate? If he is a doctor of religion, let him spend his life between his home and the mosque. If he belongs to the secular world, we are of the opinion that he is more active in that sphere than all the rest of the Muslims."[15]

Muhammad 'Abduh (1849–1905) was a pure Egyptian. While the stream of religious reform in Egypt took its rise from a source beyond the confines of the country—in the teachings of al-Afghani—it was destined to attain its full flood through Egyptian channels. For 'Abduh was not only a pure Egyptian but also came from a family that belonged to the *fellah* class of the Egyptian Delta. He grew up after the manner of life common to lads in all small villages in Egypt. In his early years, he showed a remarkable proficiency in swimming, horsemanship, and the use of firearms, acquiring a love for an active outdoor life that he preserved until old age. Although he managed to learn to recite the whole Koran from memory when he was only twelve, he displayed no pronounced desire for learning—a fact which in later years he attributed to the anachronistic methods of learning in the kind of schools open to boys of his class. "I spent a year and a half," he relates in his unfinished autobiography, "without understanding a single thing, because of the harmful character of the method of teaching; for the teachers were accustomed to use technical terms of grammar or jurisprudence which we did not understand, nor did they take any pains to explain their meanings to those who did not know them."

Despairing of success in his studies, 'Abduh finally ran away from school and hid for three months with some of his uncles. After he was taken back to the school for a brief period, he took his belongings and returned to his village with the intention of taking up agriculture as most members of his family were doing. A new period in 'Abduh's life was opened, however, when he fell under the influence of one Sheikh Darwish Kadr, who, during two weeks of reading together with 'Abduh from a book on ethics and moral discipline, managed to convert the young boy into an enthusiastic student of Sufism. During this period Darwish retained the position of guide and mentor to the young student; but it was his second and greater teacher, the dynamic Jamal al-Din, who finally delivered him from his absorption in the world of mysticism and induced him into wider fields of scholarship and practical activities.[16]

'Abduh entered the Al-Azhar University early in 1866. There was nothing in his personal appearance to distinguish him in the eyes of the sheikhs
or the professors; but his natural energy, his intellectual acumen, his thirst
for learning, and the independence of his thought soon marked him as
different from the rest of his fellow students. 'Abduh's absorption in Sufism
did not prevent him from an eager pursuit of knowledge. In the course of
this pursuit he happened upon some traces of what he calls "the true sciences," but he could find no one to guide him. Whenever he sought help he
was told that to busy oneself with such subjects was forbidden, or that the
doctors of theology had proscribed them. "When I meditated on this," he
wrote later, "I saw that when one is ignorant of a thing, one hates it." It
was while he was in this state of perplexity that Afghani arrived in Egypt,
an event which 'Abduh used to liken to "the rise of the sun of Truth." It
was in Afghani's light that 'Abduh attained satisfaction in his quest for
knowledge and found himself entering a new world in which mystic ex-
cesses had less and less attraction for him.[17]

'Abduh met Afghani during the latter's first visit to Egypt in 1869. When
Afghani returned to Cairo from his stay in Constantinople, 'Abduh began
to study regularly with him and soon came to "follow him like his shadow."
Many of the master's attributes and opinions began to show in 'Abduh's
work and behavior, and there remained in him almost no trace of the as-
cetic attitude to life and public affairs he had acquired from his absorption
in Sufism. When he received his degree as *'alim* (religious savant) in May
1877, and passed out of Al-Azhar as a student to return to it almost immediately as a teacher, his rich and eventful public life began.

'Abduh's career as a teacher was soon to be interrupted, however. On
June 25, 1879, the Khedive Isma'il abdicated in favor of his son Tawfiq,
who soon expelled Afghani from the country and removed 'Abduh from
his post as teacher in two government institutions, ordering him to go into
retirement in his native village and not leave it. The vicissitudes of Egyptian politics, however, soon led to 'Abduh's appointment as one of the
three editors and then as chief editor of *Al-Waqai' al-Misriyya,* the
government's official organ. He was permitted to engage on the editorial
staff a number of like-minded, Afghani-trained young men. He was soon
to make of his new position an office of note and influence and, in his
capacity also as head of the Department of Publications, he exercised great
influence on all other newspapers.[18]

Events, however, were already conspiring against 'Abduh. After eighteen months with the *Official Gazette,* his connection ceased with that
publication. By that time, the nationalist movement, associated with the

name of Ahmad 'Urabi Pasha, was well underway, and 'Urabi himself was at the height of his power. 'Abduh was associated with the leaders of the uprising, which began as a protest by the Egyptian officers in the army against preference shown to non-Egyptian officers. The movement expanded into a revolt against the privileged position and dominant influence of foreigners in Egypt, and 'Abduh was tried and sentenced to exile from the country for three years and three months. Thus ended, in failure and disappointment, 'Abduh's first efforts to uplift his country.

Life in exile was extended over six years, and 'Abduh was not to return to Egypt until 1888. He first intended to take up residence in Syria; but Afghani invited him, after a year of 'Abduh's stay in Beirut, to visit Paris and collaborate with him in the publication of Al-'Urwa al-Wuthqa. The tone and spirit of this journal was much more radical and aggressive than that of the ideas advocated by 'Abduh in Egypt. This showed unmistakably the influence of Afghani's closeness to him and probably the effects of the bitterness of exile. For 'Abduh remained, in the final analysis, a reformer who depended more upon methods of reform and education than agitation and revolution. His association with the 'Urabi rebellion in its later stages sprang from the fact that he was drawn by force of circumstances to accept methods of which he did not approve, while his participation with Afghani in political agitation was dictated by considerations of policy and ends rather than by an entire approval of methods.

It is to be noted that 'Abduh actually expressed to Afghani his belief that his political methods would not result in any good, for the establishment of a just and reformed Muslim government did not depend alone on the removal of the hindrances occasioned by foreigners. He thought it would be better if the two of them would devote their energies to training men according to their own ideals, in some quiet spot remote from political influences. These men, in turn, would go out to different countries to train others. Thus, at no remote date they would have a considerable force of agents at work. "It is men," he said, "who will accomplish everything." It was significant, and quite characteristic of the man's temperament, that Afghani overruled this idea, holding that they must continue in the course they had begun until they had completed their work or had failed.[19]

'Abduh returned to Beirut at the beginning of 1885 after a period of secret agitation, leaving Afghani to continue this work alone. After three and a half years there, pardon was secured for him from the Khedive Tawfiq Pasha through the mediation of a number of influential persons, including Lord Cromer. 'Abduh returned to Egypt while still under the influence of many stimulating impressions gained from his extended period of residence abroad. In this frame of mind he entered upon the culminating period of his service to his religion and to Egypt. Honored and esteemed universally, he was appointed a *qadi* (judge) in the Courts of First Instance, where he sought to promote the ends of justice and equity. He was soon to be hailed for his ability to decide cases and his uncanny insight. Then came the reform of Al-Azhar, one of the great aims of 'Abduh's life. His plans for this reform were laid before 'Abbas Hilmi when he succeeded his father Tawfiq Pasha as 'Abbas II in 1892, and managed, some three years later, to secure the enactment of a preliminary regulation whereby an administrative committee for Al-Azhar was appointed.

The committee had a hard time of it, faced as it was with opposition from the sheikhs. When, however, the favorable attitude of the Khedive himself was changed into one of determined opposition to the proposed reforms, the reactionary forces gained the upper hand. 'Abduh, despairing of success, resigned from the committee in March 1905, together with two other members. This was the end of 'Abduh's connection with Al-Azhar, as his death occurred a few months later. Al-Azhar was left, more or less, to relapse for the time being into its accustomed and undisturbed ways.

During the time in which he was working for the reform of Al-Azhar, 'Abduh engaged in other activities as well. On June 3, 1899, he was appointed mufti of all Egypt, by virtue of which office he became the supreme official interpreter of the canon law of Islam. His fatwas, touching upon any matters that were referred to him, were authoritative and final. These legal opinions were always characterized by a spirit of liberality and a freedom from bondage to tradition and a desire to render the religion of Islam entirely adaptable to the requirements of modern civilizations. Adams quotes two of these fatwas as best known: one declaring it lawful for Muslims to eat the flesh of animals slain by Jews and Christians, the other declaring it likewise lawful for Muslims to deposit their money in the postal savings banks where it would draw interest (strictly forbidden by Islam). These fatwas spread 'Abduh's fame throughout the Muslim world and made him one of the leading figures of his day.[20]

'Abduh's career was ended with his death on July 11, 1905. With his death, too, all the virulent criticisms, violent attacks, and covert intrigues that had centered on his person were silenced amidst the widespread and general acknowledgment of his great services to the cause of Islam and the advancement of its adherents. The truth was at last being acknowledged of what 'Abduh himself had written not long before his death. "I spoke out on behalf of two great causes," he declared. "The first of these was the liberation of thought from the shackles of imitation and the understanding of religious faith as members of the early Community understood it before dissension arose. . . . The second was the reform of the Arabic language. . . . I also made an appeal [for drawing] a distinction between the government's right to the obedience of the people and the people's right to justice on the part of the government."[21]

"I was not created to be anything but a teacher," said 'Abduh of himself when he was being persuaded to accept a position outside his chosen profession. Nevertheless, when one seeks to appraise his work as a thinker and estimate the value of his accomplishments in the fields of theology and philosophy, one finds that, generally speaking, 'Abduh does not rank among the great thinkers of Islam. Still, Sheikh Muhammad 'Abduh, who was Grand Mufti of Egypt when he died, attained a degree of learning that placed him in the forefront of Muslim scholars of his day and won him wide recognition throughout the Muslim world. Among many other personal accomplishments, 'Abduh was deeply versed in all the fields of Muslim learning—philosophy, theology, Koran interpretation, jurisprudence, and traditions; he had a very wide knowledge of the Arabic language and of Arabic literature; and, although he was not a gifted philosopher, he accomplished—as Professor M. Horten, one of his most conscientious students, pointed out—"all that could have been expected in the not exactly favorable circumstances."

'Abduh's chief significance, however, lies in the field of religious awakening rather than in that of science and philosophy. Horten—who is 'Abduh's leading critic among European scholars—admits that, while he accomplished something less than could have been hoped for in reconstructing the thought of modern Islam, one of the elements of his significance is to be found in the fact that he recognized the insufficiency and nonfinality of the scholastic philosophy and saw the opportunity thereby offered for the formulation of a modern philosophy. Another extenuating circumstance for 'Abduh is that he had to reckon with his environment and was dependent upon it. The surpassing backwardness of this environment allows the work of the great Muslim reformer to appear in all the clearer light, making us forgive him his many failings. Moreover, as Horten points out, "it would be a great injustice to expect of an Oriental to show completed results in fields in which the West itself is still far from such results."[22]

Still, to do 'Abduh full justice, it must be pointed out that a vital relationship existed between the character of his thought and his activities as a reformer. For, although 'Abduh started his career as a Sufi theologian-philosopher, he soon became absorbed in the manifold activities of public life, which left him little time for study. In this he was not unlike his teacher

Afghani, although he was much more devoted to study and to writing than that great agitator. Throughout his career, his work of writing and teaching paralleled his public activities. The two spheres alike were dominated by the supreme purpose of his life—the reform and revivification of Islam and the rehabilitation of Muslim peoples.

The problem of the reform of Islam as 'Abduh conceived it was not a simple one. The backwardness of the Muslim peoples, their being subject to non-Muslim powers, made it necessary that their spirit be aroused and that they themselves be united in the consciousness of a common Islamic brotherhood and of a common heritage. As 'Abduh saw it, the many ills and weaknesses from which the Muslim peoples suffered were not part of the religion of Islam but rather the result of an ignorance of the true Islam. The cure, he decided, lay in a return to the genuine religion.

The problem facing 'Abduh was thus twofold. On the one hand, there was the difficult and essential task of reforming the religion and restoring it to the simplicity and effectiveness of its early days; on the other hand, there was the no less thorny problem of effecting the return of the masses of the people to a sincere and enthusiastic acceptance and practice of this pure religion. In short, it was a question of reviving Islam in a new power, so that the Muslim peoples might be rescued from their evil state and thus the glory of the early days might be restored. The ways through which this may be done were the leading themes of 'Abduh's joint effort with Afghani, the periodical *Al-'Urwa al-Wuthqa*. A summary of the main ideas expounded in that publication, most of which 'Abduh himself wrote, presents an adequate if brief outline of his teachings.

The religion of Islam, 'Abduh maintained, is the one bond that unites Muslims of all countries and obliterates all traces of race or nationality. Its divine law (*shari'a*) regulates in detail the rights and obligations of all, both ruler and subject, and removes all racial distinctions and occasion for competition within the body of Islam. Any Muslim ruler can win distinction and gain great influence in the Muslim world by his devotion to the *shari'a*. Islam does not concern itself only with the afterlife, as do other religions, but deals also sufficiently with this present life, thus providing for what the shari'a calls "the happiness of two abodes"—this world and the hereafter. The Muslim peoples were once united under one glorious empire, and their achievement in learning and philosophy and all the sciences are still the boast of all Muslims. It is a duty incumbent upon all Muslims to aid in maintaining the authority of Islam and Islamic rule over all lands that have once been Muslim. They are not permitted under any circumstances to be peaceable and conciliatory toward any who contend the mastery with them until they have obtained complete authority without sharing it with anyone else. Yet, this unity has been lost through the ambitions and greed of aggrandizement of Muslim rulers. The downfall of Muslim nations has been brought about by the lust of the rulers for dainties and luxuries, for titles and honors, even as we see today. The bonds binding Muslims together began to fall apart when the Abbasid caliphs became content to possess the title of caliph and ceased to be scholars trained in religious matters and in the exercise of *ijtihad*—as were the first four caliphs.

Hence, from the beginning of the third century of the *Hijra*, sects and divisions multiplied and the caliphate itself became divided. Today we see Muslim rulers giving a free hand to foreigners to carry on the affairs of their states and even of their own households, and fastening foreign rule upon their own necks. Europeans, greedy for Muslim lands, seek to destroy their religious unity and thus take advantage of the inner discords of Islam. Foreigners employed by Muslim governments, since they belong neither to the religion nor to the state, are not concerned for the honor of the state and its welfare. They look only for their pay, and think only of their own interests. But the Muslim nations themselves are not concerned about helping one another today. This is because they are ignorant of one another's state. The learned men, who should have tried to strengthen the bonds of unity by making the mosques and the schools centers for the creation of a spirit of unity, have neglected this method that was within their reach, for they have no communication with the learned men of other Muslim countries and so were ignorant of their condition; further, they have been corrupted by their rulers.

The cure of these ills of Muslim countries is not to be found in multiplication of newspapers, for these have little influence; nor in the introduction of schools modeled after those of Europe, for these can be used, together with the sciences they teach, to foster foreign influence; nor in European education and imitation of foreign customs, for imitation has only succeeded in quenching the spirit of the people and drawing down upon these countries the power of the foreigners whom they imitate. The only cure for these nations is to return to the rules of their religion and the practice of its requirements according to what it was in the beginning, in the days of the early caliphs. If they rouse themselves to their present affairs and set their feet in the way of success and make the principles of their true religion their one concern, then they cannot fail thereafter to reach in their progress the limit of human perfection. Furthermore, Muslims must learn to help one another and stand united against all foes.

These are the essential points of the teachings both of 'Abduh and Afghani. But if master and pupil were in agreement about the ends and the essentials, they were far from agreement on the means and the details of action. The reformation of Islam must be accomplished. But by what means must it be brought about? Afghani, as has already been pointed out, advocated the way of political revolution. Others believed that the only hope lay in the general adoption of Western methods and Western customs. But to Muhammad 'Abduh, the only method that held any hope of success was that of a general religious awakening in every Muslim country. A passage in Rashid Rida's *Taarikh* is illuminating in this connection. It relates that, in referring to the efforts of enlightened individuals in Persia, India, Arabia, and later in Egypt, about the middle of the last century, to discover the causes of the ills of Muslims and their remedy, 'Abduh defined the objective of all these efforts as making use of the confidence a Muslim has in his religion in setting in order the affairs of this religion. In other words, 'Abduh taught, this objective may be said to consist in "the correction of the articles of belief and the removal of the mistakes which have crept into them through misunderstanding of the basic texts of the religion in order that, when once the beliefs have been made free of harmful innovations, the activities of Muslims may become free from disorder and confusion, the conditions of the individual Muslims may be improved, their understanding enlightened by the new sciences, both religious and secular, and wholesome traits of character develop; and that desirable state may communicate itself through the individuals to the nation as a whole." This, according to 'Abduh, is the purpose which those who seek reform have in mind when they summon Muslims to a knowledge of their religion, advocate religious education, or deplore the present corrupt state of the Muslims. "For to attempt reform by means of a culture or philosophy that is not religious in character would require the erection of a new structure for which neither materials nor workmen are available. If the religion of Muslims can attain these ends and gain the Muslims' confidence, why seek for other means?"[23]

However, in order to bring all this about it was necessary—as Albert Hourani writes—"to adopt some at least of the institutions, social customs, methods of education and ways of thought of modern Europe, but it was also necessary to justify the changes in terms of the principles generally accepted, that is to say the principles of Islam." This, in turn, made it necessary to consider what the principles of Islam really were. This indeed was 'Abduh's lifework, as he set himself to reconsider what Islam really was and what the Islamic community should, ideally, be. In the process of this journey of discovery, 'Abduh, continues Hourani, made an all-important distinction between what, as he saw it, was essential and unchanging in Islam and what can be changed without damage to the truth of religion or the moral bases of the community. On the one hand stood the essential Islam, the explicit content of the Islamic revelation, contained in the Koran and the well-authenticated tradition of what the prophet said and did—certain general truths about God and the universe, the general principles of human behavior and social organization, and certain commandments about acts . . . pleasing to God; on the other, detailed rules of conduct, of the ordering of society and the organization and function of government, which had been deduced by responsible human reason from the general principles, but which could be, and indeed should be, changed in the light of social welfare as circumstances changed. In the modern world, maintained 'Abduh, circumstances had changed, and the whole body of Islamic law and social morality must therefore be modified.[24]

'Abduh's spirit of reform was all-embracing. Throughout his life, he never ceased to fight the *taqlid*, the passive acceptance of dogmas from religious authorities without asking for proof. He constantly called for the principle of *ijtihad*, thought free from all fetters. The gates of ijtihad, he said, far from being closed once and for all, are wide open to all the questions raised by the new conditions of life. He reproached intelligent Muslims for failing to do anything for the reform of a society of which they knew the defects. He was against all blind imitation, pointing out that "those who imagine that in merely transplanting to their country the ideas and customs of European peoples they will in a short time achieve the same degree of civilization deceive themselves grossly."[25] They take as their point of departure, 'Abduh argued, what is in reality the end of a long evolution; for the states of Europe did not arrive at their degree of civilization without the price of enormous suffering and sacrifice.

It must, however, be kept in mind that 'Abduh's idea of Islamic reform embraced many features of contemporary life and thought and was never confined to reform of religion itself. When Islam was accused of being hostile to the development of science and culture, 'Abduh thought that there was nothing more fallacious than such hasty and partial judgments, since Islam, which is based on the requirements of human nature and of reason, itself urges the faithful to seek and reason, to develop their knowledge and perfect their understanding. Surely, the religion which declared that "the ink of a scholar is as precious as the blood of martyrs" cannot be accused of obscurantism in its essential nature. 'Abduh also rejected vehemently the doctrine of fatalism, commonly attributed to Islam. True Islam, he insisted, was the negation of fatalism and the affirmation of free will. He takes issue with those who cite the Koranic verse, "God has created you; you and what you do," as proof of Islam's fatalism, pointing out that in the same verse, "it is a question of *what you do,* and the verse implies, all considered, the attribution to man of his own actions."[26]

The essence of Muhammad 'Abduh's reform seems to lie in a pursuit of the moral life and of ethical behavior. His theory of corporate unity and corporate morality within the Muslim community as a whole or within the individual nation was based upon the principle of mutual cooperation and encouragement in the restraint of evil and the promotion of good. One of the accepted principles of society, he wrote, is that no people can exist as an independent entity unless there is a bond that binds them together and gives them unity so that they become a living community, as though they were a single body. As Amin says in his brief study:

> More than one theological or philosophical problem is [for 'Abduh] dominated by moral considerations and every effort tends towards moral action. If he fights certain manners and customs, certain popular religious beliefs, if he denounces injustice and social and political abuses, if he strives to modify the teaching methods of Al-Azhar, it is always to reform morality in Muslim society. We can safely say that the movement of religious reform with which 'Abduh's name is associated in the Muslim world was only, in the mind of the reformer, a *means* for the realization for an *end:* moral reform properly speaking.[27]

'Abduh himself said this expressly: "The aim of religious reform is to direct the faith of the Muslim in his religion in such a way as to make him better and also to improve his social condition. To put right religious beliefs, to put an end to errors, consequences of misunderstanding religious texts, so well that once the beliefs are fortified, actions will be more in conformity with morality—such is the task of the Muslim reformer." Again: "If religion is able to raise the level of morality, to give acts a solid foundation, and to urge people to seek happiness by the most appropriate means, if the adepts of this religion are very attached to it, if finally one has less difficulty in bringing them back to this religion than in creating something new of which they are not clearly conscious, why not have recourse to the religion, and why seek other less effective means?"

Thus, although he worked at one period in close association with Afghani, the aim of 'Abduh's reform is, according to Amin, "clearly not, as has wrongly been believed, the realization of the political unity of the Muslim countries, and still less 'Holy War' against non-Muslims." 'Abduh all along expressly refrained from holding Pan-Islamic ideas, which he moreover considered as chimerical and only existing in the imagination of certain dreamers, Europeans, and others.

2 | Egypt in the Wake of Modernism

From Religion to National Politics: Rashid Rida and Al-Manar

With certain shifts of emphasis, modern movements for Islamic regeneration have expressed themselves in two directions: internal reform and external defense. The protest against external encroachment and domination was always linked, in varying degrees, with the protest against internal deterioration and decay. The problem facing these movements can, in this sense, be summed up as being one of how to arrest the un-Islamic decadence of Muslim society and how, concurrently, to resist the infidel's encroachment on the Muslim's domain.

Of the two great reform movements in modern Islam—the one originating in Egypt, the other in India—the former is considered to have been inspired chiefly by theological considerations. While the pervasive character of the Egyptian movement during the last quarter of the nineteenth century was that of religious reforms, the reforms instituted by the Indian group of nationalist reformers were aimed primarily at adjusting Islam to the conditions of modern European civilization. The Egyptian reform movement under 'Abduh's leadership constituted "an attempt to free the religion of Islam from the shackles of a too rigid orthodoxy, and to accomplish reforms which would render it adaptable to the complex demands of modern life." The two movements, however, had this in common: Both assumed that Islam is a world religion, suitable for all peoples, all times, and all cultural conditions.[1]

It is to be noted, however, that the religious reform movement in Egypt, though seen as being preoccupied chiefly with theological topics, was destined to be more instrumental in the subsequent political development of that country than the mainly cultural movement in India was in shaping the future of India's Muslims. 'Abduh, in fact, has been aptly described as one of the creators of modern Egypt. At the same time, he is considered one of the founders of modern Islam. His views have been influential in many educated Egyptian circles, religious and secular alike. The genuine awakening that took place in Egypt during the first half of this century— which expressed itself in an intellectual and literary renaissance, in movements of social reform, and in a growing spirit of nationalism—can never be adequately explained or understood without reference to 'Abduh's thought and activity.

The reason for this is not far to seek. In its classical form, the problem of modern Islam was stated by Jamal al-Din al-Afghani. The Islamic peoples, he argued, possess a great transcendental religion and have behind them a glorious imperial past; yet their present state is degraded and oppressed. This was attributable to two main causes, one material, the other spiritual. On the one hand, there is the prevalent ignorance, poverty, and superstition, which prevents the Muslims from meeting the challenge of Western technological progress and expelling Westerners from the Islamic countries. On the other hand, there is spiritual backwardness and failure to carry out the divine law, which prevents Muslims from rising from the moral slough in which they find themselves. Thus, the enemy, both on the material and spiritual levels, is tradition, inertia, and conservatism.

In trying to resolve the problem of modern Islam, however, Afghani was himself forced into an obvious inconsistency. In demanding that there be a revival of the period in Islam when individual judgment and criticism were permitted in order to modify and formulate the dogma by which the Islamic community should live, he pointed to what came to be called Islamic liberalism—the revision of Muslim doctrine in the light of modern conditions. However, his "activism" and agitation for the idea of liberation from the foreigners as an end in itself made him a forerunner of modern nationalist radicalism. Thus, he attained the rather unusual combination of the role of both harmless religious teacher and dangerous political agitator.

After Afghani's death, his successors, headed by 'Abduh and Rashid Rida (1865–1935), carried on his activities, though their main preoccupation was the criticism and reevaluation of the sources of Islam and Islamic law rather than agitation against foreign domination. However, like that of his great teacher, 'Abduh's thought had in fact two main strands to which he gave equal emphasis. The first was the need to hold fast to what was constant and unchangeable in Islam; the second was the need to change what might be changed therein. These two trends were later developed by 'Abduh's various disciples in two distinct directions—the purely theological and the secular-nationalist. This latter orientation itself embraced three categories of reform and can thus be divided into three different, though complementary, classes of reformers: the founding fathers of the modern nationalist movement, the social reformers, and the intellectuals.

The leaders of the modernist movement in Islam were the true forerunners of modern Egyptian nationalism. Afghani had laid it down that it was necessary both to renew Islam and to put an end to the foreign domination of Islamic lands. In other words, although the immediate policies of the Egyptian Islamic modernists may appear to have been ones of moderation and compromise, their long-range aims were actually the same as those of the political activists and the nationalists. "The greatest of all the *Wafd* politicians and the founder of a party of opposition to the British in Egypt, Sa'd Zaghlul (1859–1927), was a pupil of Muhammad 'Abduh."[2]

This does not mean, however, that the transfer from the Muslim religious reform movement to that of secular political nationalism was a smooth or easy one. As the two aspects of Afghani's teachings—the religious-theological and the secular-nationalist—were developed by his various disciples, a cleavage emerged between those who placed the emphasis on the purely Islamic-theological aspect of the problem and those who, eager first to rid the land of foreigners, turned to the modern doctrine of secular nationalism. This growing conflict is nowhere more forcefully illustrated than in the life and work of Muhammad Rashid Rida, founder and editor of *Al-Manar* (The lighthouse) and 'Abduh's famous biographer.

A Syrian by birth, Rida came from a family claiming descent from the family of the prophet Muhammad. Rida became acquainted with the works of Afghani and 'Abduh and immediately conceived a desire to join himself to the former, but was unable to do so as Afghani continued to reside in Constantinople until his death. He managed, however, to join 'Abduh in Cairo in 1897, and in the following year he embarked on his long venture in journalism with the appearance of the first issue of *Al-Manar*. Some of the items included within the general purpose of reform for which the periodical was launched were the following:

1. To promote social, religious, and economic reforms.
2. To demonstrate the suitability of Islam as a religious system under existing conditions and the practicability of the divine law as an instrument of government.

3. To remove superstitions and beliefs that do not belong to Islam and to counteract false teachings and interpretations of Islamic beliefs— such as prevalent ideas of predestination; the bigotry of the different schools, or rites, of canon law; and the abuses connected with the cult of saints and the practices of the Sufi orders.

4. To encourage tolerance and unity among different sects.

5. To promote general education, together with the reform of textbooks and methods of education, and to encourage progress in the sciences and arts.

6. To arouse the Muslim nations to competition with other nations in all matters essential to national progress.[3]

In its advocacy of a common Islamic brotherhood that transcended national barriers, *Al-Manar* and its editor inevitably came into conflict with influences that were then emerging in Egypt. In the early years of this century, for instance, the Nationalist Party (*al-hizb al-watani*) was rejuvenated under the leadership of Mustafa Kamil Pasha. This party had no interest in religion or religious reform, but stood on an exclusive nationalism based on racial distinctions—an idea which *Al-Manar* opposed on grounds of Islamic rules and precepts, and this despite the fact that Kamil's nationalism excluded all Egyptians who were not Muslims and sometimes even embraced Pan-Islamic ideals.

In later years, Rida again directed his fire at the *Al-Siyasa* group, because they advocated a nationalism in which religion and language would not be determining factors—"so that they count a Muslim and an Arab (who holds a foremost place in the world of Islam) as a foreigner if he does not belong to the same country as themselves. Thus the Sharif—descendent of the Prophet Muhammad—of the Hijaz or of Syria is no better to them than a heathen from China."[4] Since religion was not fundamental to their idea of nationality, the nationalists both of Egypt and of Turkey were branded by *Al-Manar* as atheists and infidels.

Despite such differences of opinion, however, the transfer from religious reform to political nationalism was a smooth and easy one. Political revolution was one of the tenets of Afghani's teachings, and he approved of resorting to political assassination if it be deemed necessary for the accomplishment of his objectives. Although 'Abduh was able to accommodate himself to the more ardent nature of his teacher during the latter's lifetime, he eventually came to entertain an extreme distrust of political action. Nevertheless, his training of his pupils included something of politics, "because he believed that a man could not be perfect without some knowledge of a matter with which the independence and freedom of his country were so closely connected."[5] In fact, when speaking of 'Abduh's pupils and friends in the context of the political and social movement in Egypt in the first years of the twentieth century, 'Abduh's biographer and disciple, Rashid Rida, usually refers to them as *Hizb al-Imam*—the Imam's Party. There was, of course, no such party in the accepted sense of the term; the reference was made to that school of thought in Islam Lord Cromer used to call "the Girondists of the Egyptian national movement."

As will become clear in the following pages, the second generation of Islamic reformists in Egypt tended to gravitate alternately between religious fundamentalism and radical ideas of reform, and between conservatism and nationalism. As Malcolm Kerr points out, between these gravitations "the great moral purpose of practical reform that characterized Islamic modernism at the turn of the century has been quite dissipated."[6] However, he remarks, since the adherents of modernism have found other homes, at either end of the spectrum, the dissipation has scarcely been noticed. Writing in the mid-sixties, when Egypt as a whole seemed thoroughly swayed by the nationalist tide under Nasser's leadership, Kerr explains:

> No one in Egypt . . . is heard today mourning the legacy of Muhammad 'Abduh: on the contrary, everyone claims it as his own. The difficulty is that the teachings of 'Abduh and his circle rested on intellectual foundations that were, on the whole, vague and unsystematic. Their social and psychological impact was immense, but it was ambiguous. 'Abduh's heirs were propelled by his impetus in a variety of directions, each divergent movement gathering its own strength and developing its own distinct character in the absence of any basis for consensus on the precise nature of his message. Such diverse individuals as the liberal constitutionalist Ahmad Lutfi al-Sayyid, the militant fundamentalist Hasan al-Banna of the Muslim Brethren, and Jamal 'Abd al-Nasser can be identified, each in a different way, as heirs of 'Abduh.

The truth is that 'Abduh's historical role was simply to fling open the doors and expose a musty tradition to fresh currents. "His intention may have been more specific, but the effect was not. His heirs were, of course, the product of various other influences as well, which sometimes combined with the ambiguity of 'Abduh's legacy to promote additional tensions and equivocations of their own."[7]

The case of Rashid Rida furnishes an excellent illustration of this state of affairs. Rida's intellectual career symbolizes in some ways the political failure of the whole Islamic modernist movement. Without any particular shifts in doctrine his position evolved, under pressure of circumstances, from that of liberal reformer to radical fundamentalist to orthodox conservative. "Among those influenced by him, as a transmitter of 'Abduh's ideas, were both the Muslim Brethren, which prepared to restore Egypt to the rule of Islamic law by revolution, and Dr. 'Abd al-Razzaq al-Sanhuri, who relegated Islamic law to a minor place in drafting the Egyptian Civil Code of 1949 while praising its adaptability and relevance to modern needs in his published writings. These writings carried the inspiration of Rida's preachings, and enabled Sanhuri to make the 1949 Code seem more or less their fulfillment, which in truth it was not."[8]

The Fathers of Egyptian Nationalism: Mustafa Kamil and Sa'd Zaghlul

Of the political theorists among 'Abduh's group, Ahmad Fat'hi Zaghlul has been described as "perhaps the most important."[9] The brother of Sa'd Zaghlul—himself one of 'Abduh's disciples—Fat'hi was the most effective translator into Arabic in an age when translating from European languages was the prime literary task. He translated a number of historical and political books, through which he exercised a great influence on the mind of Egypt: Rousseau's *Social Contract,* Bentham's *Principles of Legislation,* E. R. Demolins' *A quoi tient la superiorite de Anglo-Saxons,* Count de Castrie's *Ideas and Impressions of Islam,* Gustave le Bon's *Spirit of Society* and *Secret of the Evolution of Nations.* "He chose the works he translated with the deliberate intention of giving the Egyptians some guiding ideas through the maze of political feelings and vague aims. When he translated Rousseau, for instance, he intended to give his readers an idea of the individual's place in society and his relation to different types of social groups. . . . He hoped to arouse [Egyptians] to feel their importance, and behave with pride and dignity."[10]

Fat'hi Zaghlul used the introductions to his translations as vehicles for expressing his ideas and issuing calls to the Egyptians and to Muslims in general to wake up to the realities around them. In the preface to de Castrie's book, for example, he quotes with approval the following passage from Rida's biography of 'Abduh: "With Muslims, determinism has come to stay and has gradually suppressed action. Faith has deteriorated into a negation of reason. They call indolence trust in God and the search for truth heresy. For them this is religion, and anyone who holds different views is exposed to abuse. Unquestioning acceptance of everything old is the heart of wisdom."

In the preface to Demolins' book on the Anglo-Saxons, he again tries to stir the feelings of his readers: "We are weak compared to the nations of the West—weak in agriculture, industry, commerce, and science; in will and determination. Even our personal relations lack warmth and intimacy. There is no chivalry among us any longer. Religious solidarity has gone and so have racial bonds. Our feet are too feeble for us to stand on our rights or do our duty. We are so weak that we do nothing ourselves; we ask the government instead."[11]

Fat'hi Zaghlul's chief criticism of Egyptian society can be summed up as follows: it was too apathetic to act and it was ignorant of the new conception of nationality that had led to the creation of strong modern states in Europe. According to Fat'hi Zaghlul, Egyptians did not believe in themselves and were therefore unaware of their rights either as individuals or as a nation. They made no effort to improve themselves. Personal education and self-improvement were the secret of the progress of England, and Egyptians should educate themselves on the English model.[12]

The ferment of ideas that prevailed in Egypt during the closing years of the nineteenth century and the opening decades of the twentieth—and of which Fat'hi Zaghlul's writings and translations were a typical example—produced a recrudescence of nationalist feeling that was to find its chief expression in violent anti-British agitation. Extremist anti-British opinion was led and fostered at this time by the young leader of the Nationalist Party, Mustafa Kamil (1874–1908), whose immediate hopes for Egypt's independence were based upon possible intervention by some European country, especially France, which would bring about the termination of the British occupation. In these efforts, Kamil was supported by the Khedive Abbas II and by his money. When no European intervention proved forthcoming he turned to Turkey, counting much on the aggrandizement of the Ottoman caliphate and the strengthening of Pan-Islamic connections.

Kamil's intense anti-British sentiments were due partly to his French training, but they showed more than just a trace of Afghani's influence. For one thing, the Nationalist Party, which he founded in 1908, considered itself the direct heir and successor to the old "Nationalist Party"—the name by which Afghani's group had come to be known. It is interesting to note here that this link with Afghani's ideas and aims did not come about through 'Abduh and his group, since Hizb al-Imam, on its part, was suspicious of Kamil's motives and considered that he had been bought over by the Khedive—a charge which had its origin in the apparent coordination and identity of aims of the two men.

Kamil did not believe in the advisability of forming a political party officially, since he thought that to form a party was to divide the nation.

But he was forced into proclaiming the existence of the Nationalist Party by the formation of other, less extremist groups. He wanted "the whole world be told that there is in Egypt a party which demands immediate evacuation." On October 22, 1908, he addressed a large meeting in Alexandria, acknowledging for the first time that Egypt could look neither to Turkey nor to France for her salvation. "Of late," he said, "we have been isolated and a new spirit has been born within us. More than ever before we now realize that nations cannot rise without themselves struggling for their own cause. We cannot win independence by help from others. We have to work for it ourselves. Like an individual, a nation must be strong and well-equipped to defend its honor, its life and its property. Those who count on others to secure independence are deluded."[13]

The main theme of the program adopted by the Nationalist Party was the independence of Egypt and the Sudan and the creation of a responsible parliamentary government. In December 1908, the party's executive committee, meeting to formulate a program for the new association, pledged itself to respect and honor the financial obligations of Egypt, to bring education within the reach of all, and to promote the country's economic interests and safeguard its political independence while endeavoring to establish cordial relations between Egypt and Europe and between Egyptians and resident foreigners in the country. The program also called for association between the people and the work of the government and for strengthening bonds between the Muslims and the Copts.

Mustafa Kamil died two months after the program of the Nationalist Party was drawn up. His death deprived the party of its leader and guiding spirit. Nevertheless, Kamil left a strong and abiding influence on the Egyptian political scene that continues to be felt until this day. With him, as it has been with many of Egypt's modern rulers, extremism was not an accidental impulse but a deliberate program based on conviction and pursued with vigor. Moderation in a conquered nation, he maintained, was dictated either by fear or by hypocrisy. "It is to adopt two lines of approach to one goal at one and the same time. It is talking with two tongues. The English are not moderate in their patriotism because patriotism is the noblest of sentiments. Why should it be viewed differently in Egypt?" The reformists and gradualists, he held, based their policy on the absurd notion that they could outwit the British. "I reject this in principle and do not believe it is practical. In spite of the smooth talk of their friends, the British know that the most honorable work of a true patriot lies in the creation of a new faith in the heart. Faith moves mountains."[14]

It was to the creation of this "faith that moves mountains" that Kamil's lifework was dedicated. Ahmed quotes the Khedive's remark about Kamil to the effect that "the public believed in him more than it did in his views." He adds:

> The courage and integrity which he showed in the sick atmosphere of a recently defeated Egypt were more important than any positive achievement of his. To love Egypt moderately, his thesis ran, was to play the game of the enemy. She should be loved with the whole heart. Praise of Egypt was in every one of his speeches and in every article. To him she was "the flower of Islam," "God's Heaven on earth," "the luminous planet of the East," "the land of the Pharaohs, the cradle of civilization." But his death moved the country as did no other in recent times. . . . By 1914, although the party he founded had disintegrated, the image of Mustafa Kamil was still, for most patriotic Egyptians, the symbol of the future.[15]

It is a tribute to the potency of the ideas propagated by Afghani and 'Abduh that their followers should have taken different courses of political action. At a time in which the best and ablest of young Egyptians were gravitating toward the extreme nationalist school of Mustafa Kamil or the more discreet opposition of the Khedive, many of 'Abduh's disciples chose to take a different line. "Doubting the sincerity of the ruling family," writes Ahmed, "they saw that the British occupation offered them a chance of gradually awakening their country to their own conception of nationalism. Though unacceptable in principle, British rule was easier to get rid of than that of Khedival autocracy which confused ordinary people's ideas of nationalism because of the religious element involved." The most prominent of those who tried to turn this phenomenon into a rule of political conduct was Sa'd Zaghlul, who in the years following World War I gained an international reputation as the spokesman of Egyptian national aspirations.

Born in 1859, Zaghlul studied at Al-Azhar, where he became a pupil and disciple of Afghani and 'Abduh. After working with 'Abduh on the *Official Gazette,* he took up the practice of law. In 1906, he was appointed minister of public instruction so that he might quell the spirit of insurrection, which was rife among the students as a result of Mustafa Kamil's agitation and which was rendering all discipline in the schools impossible. In 1910, he was given the portfolio of justice and was all along the target of fierce attacks from the nationalists.

One aspect of Zaghlul's life that is typical of his tactics—and that may throw some light on the tactics of national movements in general—was the seemingly sudden and decisive change that occurred in his attitude toward the British occupation. He appeared to change his stance completely from an ostensibly sincere and capable supporter of Britain to one of her most avowed enemies. The most convincing explanation of this change lies in what 'Abbas Mahmoud al-'Aqqad, his biographer and confidant, has to say about his hero—namely that Zaghlul was deliberately pursuing a dual policy. "On the one hand he tried to keep alive patriotic feeling, but on the other hand he wished to do all he could to further the causes of education and justice."

According to this version of Zaghlul's policies and tactics, there was no place for a man of his experience and abilities in the nationalist movement of the time, oriented as it was toward the Ottoman sultan and supported by the French. "Zaghlul had seen 'Urabi's movement fail and served a term of prison in its wake—and had realized how irresolute France had proved to be at the moments of crisis, and how helpless Turkey was in the face of European power. He concluded that no good purpose would be served by militancy or dependence on outside support. He worked for the preparation of his country for independence in other ways. All his official career was devoted to this end."[16]

Another explanation of Zaghlul's alleged volte face is that in his willingness to cooperate with the British high commissioner he was following the precedent set by 'Abduh, since this cooperation became a principle of 'Abduh's party. Indeed, until the year 1913, when he finally resigned his ministerial post, Zaghlul's main aim remained to accelerate reform and to curb the Khedive's power by supporting any progressive policies advanced by the British. It was only when Lord Kitchener appeared to be willing to back the Khedive with money from the Waqf administration that Zaghlul decided to part company with him. "From that time his career led him into increasing opposition to what he regarded as the mistaken tendencies of the British administration—and when the war was over he was the first to see the possibilities inherent in President Wilson's declaration and the determination that was gathering in the country."[17]

Thus Sa'd Zaghlul, who was a true product of the preceding years of intellectual and political ferment, traveled the usual road of the nationalist leader. Despite his loyal and sincere service under the British, he began soon after his election to the leadership of the Wafd Party, in late 1918, to combine the outlook of Mustafa Kamil, the intransigent nationalist, and that of 'Abduh, the exponent of Egyptian freedom. Nothing can better illustrate this transformation than the speech Zaghlul made when he and two of his colleagues were told by the British high commissioner in November 1918 that they were not really representative of the Egyptian nation and therefore could not be given permission to submit Egypt's case for independence before the Paris Peace Conference. He stated: "Do we have to ask a nation whether it wants independence? Ours is the oldest of civilizations. Our ancestors have handed down to us undisputed social virtues. Our civic sense is there for everyone to see. One can see it in our respect for the rule of law, our even temper and our identity of outlook. To ask a nation like this whether it is agreed on independence is an affront to it."

No matter how valuable this kind of rhetoric may be as a political tactic, it leaves unanswered the question whether Zaghlul and his comrades did truly represent the Egyptian populace. It also gives no indication whatever of the kind of program of action the group had in mind. To these and other reservations, voiced at the time by a variety of opponents and competitors, Zaghlul eventually formulated a kind of answer. The Wafd, he maintained, was not a political party in the accepted sense of the term:

> They ask us: "Where is your program?" And we answer: "We are not a party—we are a delegation empowered by the nation and expressing its will in a matter which it has assigned to us. This matter is complete independence and we strive to this end alone." As for internal questions—should education be compulsory, should it be free, should interest be paid on the debt, should cotton be sown on a third or a half of the cultivable area—these are matters which I leave to men who know more about them than I do. But so far as independence is concerned, we are a nation and not a party. Anyone who says we are a party demanding independence is a criminal, for this implies that there are other parties which do not want independence. The whole nation wants independence; we are the spokesmen of the nation in demanding it; we are the trustees of the nation.[18]

This may be a far cry from the gradualist stance of the original Islamic reformists and the essence of their doctrine as a long-term educational program. The great task these reformers had set themselves was to break down the innate traditionalism of the Muslim population and address themselves to a gradual revision of Muslim law in light of modernism and progress. It was to restore to the modern educated Muslim his self-respect and to implant in him the conviction that he could face the world without a total capitulation to the values of the West and its thought patterns. This being so, the immediate policies of the various Egyptian modernist scholars and religious savants can be said to have been ones of compromise and moderation, although their eventual aims were the same as those of the political activists.

It is not possible to say, even today, that the great and difficult quest started by these scholars and leaders of religion has come to fruition. However, it may be safe to say tentatively that while Afghani was the first and greatest Muslim reformist to embody within his teachings both the gradual-educational and the revolutionary-political programs, Sa'd Zaghlul was the first Egyptian leader of modern times to be able to contribute equally to both of these aims. That this contribution was perforce limited and not final is best demonstrated by the fact that exactly a quarter of a century after Zaghlul's death in 1927, the group of free officers who brought down the Egyptian monarchy on July 23, 1952, found it necessary to invoke the struggles and upheavals of a period of Egyptian history in which Mustafa Kamil and Sa'd Zaghlul featured so prominently and effectively.

The Social Reformists: Qasim Amin and Lutfi al-Sayyid

While Mustafa Kamil, Sa'd Zaghlul, and the leaders of other nationalist groups and parties were agitating for Egypt's independence on the political plane—drawing inspiration from the teachings of Muhammad 'Abduh and the Islamic reformists—another revolution aiming at a different kind of emancipation was in progress in Egypt. The leaders of this social reform movement can best be described as Westernizers, since they were all guided by an implicit determination to meet the challenges of the West on its own terms. They were among the first to realize that the modern Muslim's foremost task was to understand the West. Far from averting their gaze from the possibilities of the new world of Europe and regarding it as a hostile force to be resisted and repulsed—as some Arab-Muslim thinkers had done before them—Westernizers tried to revive their society in such a way as to make its way of life and thought approximate, or even correspond, to those of Western societies.

The Westernizers, who were the legitimate heirs of the modernist movement in Islam, realized the two main shortcomings of that movement as it was handed down to them. As they saw them, these two shortcomings were (1) the defectiveness of the movement's knowledge and understanding of Western culture and the basic elements of Western thought, and (2) the movement's preoccupation with polemics intended to prove that the doctrines of Islam were more in accord with the discoveries of modern science than are those of Christianity. If one accepts the division of Arab-Muslim reactions to Westernization at the time into two categories—the one calling for a revival of true Islam and the other advocating secularization—then the social reform leaders who were active in Egypt during the first two decades of the century can be placed somewhere in between the two.

Few of the reform leaders went the whole length to meet the advocates of secularization—a movement based on the belief that the superior strength and stability of Western society was due to the limitations it had imposed on the influence of religion, and that Arab Muslims should no longer attempt to regulate their society in accordance with Islamic doctrine and law. Nevertheless, they went far enough in that direction to make themselves quite distinct from the Muslim revivalists who insisted on observing every precept of their religion. Thus, they were caught in a contradiction best depicted by Lord Cromer when he said that an upper-class Muslim in those days "must be either a fanatic or a concealed infidel."

The two men whose views are surveyed in this section were both Muslims, and both were thinkers rather than doers. Qasim Amin (1865–1908), who was one of the small circle of 'Abduh's followers and friends, was a judge in the court of appeals of the domestic tribunals. In addition to his training in law, which was obtained in France, he studied works in ethics, sociology, psychology, and allied subjects. In addition to the cause of the emancipation of women, which he made his lifework, he was involved in the efforts then being made to establish an Egyptian university. As vice chairman of the organizing committee, he gave the project much time during the last two years of his life, dying only a few months before the opening of the university in December 1908. It is worth noting that this university—originally named Al-Jami'ah al-Ahliyya—was a popular university, founded with the help of funds contributed by the public, services rendered by prominent public figures, and government aid. Amin summed up the aim of the university when he said: "We cannot now be content with the pursuit of knowledge for government service or the practice of a specialized profession. It is time we saw some of our sons pursue knowledge for its own rewards."

Ahmad Lutfi al-Sayyid, the second subject of this section, was born in 1872, seven years after Amin. In 1889, he entered the school of law, where his studies prepared him for many of his later activities. While on vacation in Istanbul later in the year, he was introduced to Jamal al-Din al-Afghani. Lutfi has himself recorded that Afghani's impact on him was overwhelming: "From him I learned that one's first duty in life is to cultivate oneself. He impressed on me that at the end of each day one must critically review every deed done, every word uttered and every chance thought that has passed through one's mind." For eight years after graduation he worked in the legal department. Moving in the same circle as 'Abduh, the Zaghlul brothers, and Qasim Amin, Lutfi was made editor of *Al-Jarida,* the organ of the Umma (People's) Party, in 1907. Lutfi, who lived well into the 1960s and was universally respected and revered, wrote no books; but he translated several of Aristotle's treatises into Arabic, and three collections of his newspaper essays have been published by his friends and followers, who used to call him *ustadh al-jil* (master of the generation).

One of the first spheres to which the social reformers were to give their attention was the position of women. This was no coincidence. At the turn of the century, the inferior status of women in Egypt and the East generally was deemed one of the main impediments to progress. According to Stanley Lane-Poole, for instance, "the degradation of women in the East" looked like "a cancer that begins its destructive work even in childhood, and has eaten into the whole system of Islam."[19] To those Egyptians who had been to Europe for work or study, the situation looked no less bleak.

It was a member of the 'Abduh group, Qasim Amin, who was to give the first coherent expression and explicit formulation of the problem of women in Islamic society. Amin, who at the time of his death was still relatively young, made this field of reform particularly his own and managed to arouse Egyptian public opinion to an extent unknown before. His first book, *The Emancipation of Women* (Tahrir al-mar'ah), published in 1900, provoked some thirty books and pamphlets written in opposition. The author was maligned and attacked on all sides because it was thought his teachings would undermine the very foundations of Muslim society. His second and last book, *The New Woman* (Al-mar'ah al-jadidah), followed in 1901. *Al-Manar* described his two books as having produced a greater impression on the public than any other recent book.[20]

The Emancipation of Women begins with an analysis of the degraded status of women in Muslim society—a state of affairs which, according to Amin, was at variance with the teachings of the prophet Muhammad, who gave women a higher status than they had enjoyed in pre-Islamic times. The present degradation of women in Muslim lands was in fact due to the national traits of the peoples who embraced Islam. The spirit of tyranny and oppression, Amin argued, had been perpetuated by tyrannical governments, and the men, who were themselves oppressed, had become oppressors of the weaker sex. For the uplift of women, education was the primary necessity. Egyptian society had suffered incalculable loss through the ignorance of half of the population, which, according to Amin, was responsible for a condition of family life "which, I imagine, hell itself is more tolerable."

Amin's views on the education of women, commonplace though they appear to be today even for a Muslim, were sufficiently revolutionary at the time to arouse the shrill criticism even of a man like Mustafa Kamil, then at the height of his power as a nationalist leader. The controversy around Amin's views deserves detailed consideration because the real point at issue was relegated to a secondary position and two world outlooks were pitted against each other. While ostensibly defending the use of the veil, which Amin sought to prove was contrary to the teachings of Muhammad, Amin's critics were in fact attacking Western standards of morality and emphasizing the dangers of copying them.

It was the idea of Westernization, implicit in Amin's whole approach and themes, that caused the violence of his critics' reaction. For his views did not stop at rejecting the use of the veil in a form that prevented women from carrying out their social duties, or at a call for educating women to perform their functions in society. He dealt critically with such established customs as polygamy, the repudiation of wives, and family life in general. In regard to polygamy, he held the view that the original Islamic conception had been obscured by later custom, which subjugated women's sexual life to their husbands' dictates. He quoted the Koran's injunction, "It is for the women to act as they [the men] act by them, in all fairness," to support his contention that while polygamy was admissible in some cases, such as a wife's chronic illness or barrenness, polygamy as currently practiced was a legal excuse for satisfying animal passions.

Amin also sought to prove that the arbitrary divorce of wives as practiced during his time was against the true spirit of Islam and the tradition of Muhammad. He maintained that husband and wife should be given ample opportunity (with the judge as mediator) to arrive at a reconciliation, and wives should have the right to ask for release from their husbands in special circumstances.[21]

Amin's second book, *The New Woman,* was written in reply to his critics, whose methods he described as both obsolete and harmful. By invoking false pride and working up undisciplined instincts, he charged, they made clear thinking impossible. Echoing 'Abduh's pragmatic views, he said that "of all the methods one can think of, only the rational method can fulfill the aim of the *shari'a.*" He proceeded to ask whether the emancipation of women was conducive to a better life or not. Here he presented a view of Islamic civilization that shocked the conservatives and shook the intelligentsia. The civilization of Islam, Amin explained, began and ended before science developed as it has today. Yet a great many Muslims believed that the best was already past and that their duty lay in keeping the past intact and unaltered. To say that it is impossible to better the past was a sign of failure and surrender. It showed an uncritical acceptance of a view of Islamic civilization that was presented by chroniclers and historians who wanted to prove it was perfect. However, Amin added, nothing can be further from the truth than such a view: Islamic civilization has many flaws and is inadequate for the modern world. He maintained that contemporary Muslims' past civilization should have a historical value only, teaching them valuable lessons about the factors governing the rise and fall of nations and providing the spiritual basis for their daily lives. Amin warned that anyone looking to this civilization for guidance in coping with modern problems would be disappointed.

Turning to Islam as a factor in history, Amin claimed that Islam's main historical function was to provide a simple and warlike people with cohesion and faith. It made a nation out of warring tribes, enabling them to conquer nations far superior to themselves in the arts of civilization and to give these nations a unified government and law. But, as time passed, the Muslim mind became stationary under the rigorous supervision of theology. It failed to evolve a science of political or economic institutions, though a number of theories on government were advanced by writers of note. This state of near-stagnation also left many moral problems unresolved. The laws of marriage and divorce, for instance, had remained as they were in the time of the prophet. No caliph or emir found it fit to develop or reform them in the interests of stability within the Muslim family.

To hold on to a petrified past was therefore to court disaster. Modern mechanical civilization was a unifying force in this world; governments all over the world were run more or less on the same principles, and Egypt could not stay outside the processions. Those who looked upon the West as an implacable enemy were not helping Egypt. Europe was in a position to teach the East not only about industries and the arts but also about that art which was the key to all others—civic virtues, an art almost unknown in the contemporary East.

The tide of disapproval Amin's books set in motion seems to have been provoked largely because his ideas led him far beyond the problem of women. It is plain from his assertions in the two books summarized above that Amin was advocating nothing less than a social and intellectual revolution. Today, however, Amin is hailed everywhere as the hero and founder of the feminist awakening in the Arab East.

While Qasim Amin chose to concentrate his energies on the emancipation of women, other Egyptian thinkers were busy attacking the problem of modernizing their country from other angles. Ahmad Lutfi al-Sayyid was born several years after Amin (1872) and lived to see the free officers' revolution of July 1952 enter its tenth year. He was convinced that the start of any real reform of Egyptian society was reform of the national character. More politically inclined than Amin, Lutfi al-Sayyid thought that the prime aim of all public activity should be to raise the intellectual and moral powers of the people. He constantly reminded his country's political leaders that the nation's high road to real independence was strength of character. He spoke of the "constitutional character" (al-akhlaq al-dus-turiyya) in which heads of families and villages should train their people. In discussing the defects of the Egyptian character, he maintained that a nation's character was identical with its history and that its moral constitution and its form of government reacted to one another. The standards of public morality in Egypt needed to be changed, he said. But this change could only take place gradually and on the basis of a correct estimate of the prevalent situation and the forces of change at work within it.

In diagnosing the maladies of the Egyptian character, al-Sayyid made striking use of the traditional songs and sayings of the people, which reflected the history and the daily behavior of the Egyptians. To give one example, the Egyptian popular saying *Allah yiwalli man yasluh* (Allah enthrones him who is fit) summed up the Egyptian's whole philosophy of government as something ordained by God and of which the rigors could only be made less exacting by God. This utter submission and passivity, Lutfi maintained, resulted almost in a deification of government officials. Out of fear or from the desire to ingratiate themselves with the authorities, people effaced themselves until they became nothing. There was no sense of honor and dignity except the ancient, distorted one. The members of society—beginning with the pasha, the bey, and the effendi—each expected the one lower than him to submit to him. When the effendi sat in the same room as the bey or pasha, he took the chair nearest the door; when he walked with them, he brought up the rear. Private individuals, notables, or landowners would do anything to acquire titles of honor, which were no more than vestiges of authority.

The most dangerous aspect of this worship of authority was that men were more conscious of others' faults than those of their own. The newspapers, for example, courageously exposed the faults of Britain but refrained from exposing the inner forces of decay within the Egyptian people itself. Britain could be attacked because her power was not sanctified by religion or tradition; but the forces of local authority were protected from criticism by a system of habit that had acquired something of the sanctity of religion.

Another aspect of the Egyptian character to which Lutfi took strong exception was the attitude typified by the common expression *ma'leish*, "never mind!" This turned the virtue of forgiveness and toleration into a veritable vice. People used the expression not to forgive others but to forgive themselves. When accused of indolence, the senior official would use it. The good-natured, simple-minded fellah used it when he welcomed a criminal with open arms and celebrated his release, showing a profound, traditional disrespect for the law to which he nevertheless submitted without question. From this attitude sprang a deep weakness in the face of evil. Forgiveness and toleration might in strong natures spring from a feeling that man is imperfect, but in Egyptian society it seems to be rooted in a kind of cowardice. "There is so much forgiveness in our life that one cannot say whether it is that of the strong or that of the feeble and cowardly." Every man tried to efface himself because "God forbid that I should impose myself." For this reason, Egyptians tended to have a low opinion both of themselves and of others. In short, the Egyptians lacked what Lutfi considered to be the source of all civic virtues, namely self-respect.

Lutfi's views of national character were closely linked with his idea of Egyptian history. The general level of morality in a society, he maintained, deteriorates with autocratic rule, and this was what prevailed in Egypt throughout history. In an article surveying the main epochs of Egyptian history, Lutfi argued that ancient Egypt had never known the sort of organized government the Greeks invented—and since then tyranny had found a fertile soil there. For the rulers of Egypt, the interests of the Egyptian people had never been more than secondary to their main purpose. A succession of foreign rulers, different from the Egyptians in race, language, customs, and outlook, had taught the Egyptians to be ever on the defensive. Although in their heart they might curse their rulers, they had to show their loyalty in order to survive. This habit of two-faced behavior was handed down from father to son, with disastrous results for the national character. "Freedom of thought never bloomed, the springs of morality were twisted and moral courage was stifled."

Lutfi was a liberal and a utilitarian in the best British tradition. He generally avoided discussing religious issues, concentrating on a campaign for improvement and reform in a few chosen fields. A believer in the unity of theory and practice, he took his stand on a small number of theoretical principles and explained them inasmuch as they applied to practical problems facing Egypt. Chief among these problems was that of the family, the status of women and their place in society. Lutfi's starting point was that of his friend Qasim Amin. In this, as in all spheres of life, Lutfi believed in the paramount importance of education. He placed all his hopes in the fundamental goodness and rationality of man and trusted human nature and intelligence. If men are enlightened and left free to follow the light of reason, he affirmed, the obstacles to progress put up by superstition and tyranny will automatically disappear and a happy state of society will emerge. The differences that exist between nations and individuals are due to differences in education: men are born ignorant but not stupid.

In the same way as education was linked with the problem of the family, Lutfi associated it with what he called the "end of the ends" — the independence of Egypt. Lutfi was convinced that Egypt needed above all else a collective consciousness. The first aim of education must therefore be to lessen the natural differences between individuals and increase the points of contact between them. There was only one path to real progress in Egypt — the path of the gradual development of new habits and new qualities of character.

Lutfi was primarily interested in politics. His most important work in this sphere was clarifying the ideas of Egyptian nationalism, political liberty, and constitutionalism. Since his ideas on the latter two subjects have been touched upon above, we will confine our short survey here to Lufti's views on Egyptian nationalism.

A series of five articles that Lutfi began in *Al-Jarida* in March 1907, under the general title of "Nationalism in Egypt," gives a fairly comprehensive idea of these views, particularly if they are coupled with his later writings on the subject. Lutfi's first assumption in this respect was that there was a separate Egyptian nation. He was opposed to the Pan-Islamic Ottoman sultan and the Turko-Egyptian khedive as being as foreign to Egypt as the British occupier. He admitted that religion was an element in the building of a nation, "But I emphatically reject the suggestion that religion is a suitable basis for political action in the twentieth century; our nationalism must rest on our interests and not on our beliefs."

It was inconceivable to Lutfi that an Egyptian Muslim should prefer the interests of Turkey to his own. The Egyptian, he maintained, was a distinct individual. He belonged to a race with its own peculiar characteristics, some acquired and some inborn. Regional traditions, intermarriage, and the community of interests that sprang from them had produced a particular nation. "They are all the sons of this land, whether they are brown or white. Most of us realize that we are a nation in our own right, and it is only the deluded few who would rather be Pharaonic, Arabs, Turks, or Circassians," he wrote.

Lutfi was a severe critic of both Pan-Islamists and pro-Turkish nationalists. He considered them dangerous because they engaged the public's mind with considerations irrelevant to the progress of the country. Indeed, he tended to attack them more than he attacked the British. He believed that Oriental despotism and theocratic ideas were a greater menace to the growth of the Egyptian nation than was the British occupation, which by its very nature was only temporary. Like Mill and Locke, he believed that liberty was an essential attribute of human beings. For a man to give up his liberty was to give up life itself. Although his liberalism was of purely Western extraction, in expounding it to his fellow countrymen he made use of his own interpretation of Egyptian history. "We cannot have all the liberties enjoyed by Americans or Englishmen or Frenchmen at present," he wrote in 1914. "But if we cannot attain all of what we want, it is reasonable to want what we can attain. We must do away with personal rule. . . . When a government assumes the task of thinking on behalf of its citizens and installs its institutions as barriers between men and their passions—both harmful and harmless—it kills in them the sense of responsibility for their actions."[22]

The Crisis Erupts: 'Ali 'Abd al-Raziq and Taha Husain

The Egyptian historian and scholar Ahmad Amin (1886–1954), the great chronicler of Islamic history and thought and an original thinker in his own right, once remarked that "modern education in the East has made the Muslims ashamed, in their heart of hearts, of being Muslims; it has made Muslim reformers ashamed of the mission of religion." Indeed, the inheritors of the modernist movement in Islam have been an unhappy lot in yet another sense. Seldom were the sins of the fathers visited on their sons so consistently as they were in the case of the first Islamic reformists. These reformists, with Muhammad 'Abduh in the lead, had formulated two main principles. The first narrowed and restricted the confines of what was to be considered revelation; the second was the assertion that revelation could not be in contradiction with reason.

What happened in Egypt during the three decades following 'Abduh's death was that the intellectual leaders tried to exploit these two principles to their logical limit without pausing to see where that was leading them. Thus, the point was bound to be reached where reason came up against the limitations inherent in 'Abduh's two principles, however liberally these might be interpreted.

The triumph of liberal nationalism and the emergence of the social reformers tended to make the Egyptian intellectual leaders ignore whatever
problems were left unresolved by the Islamic reform movement. Chief among
these, of course, was the evident conflict between reason and the contents
of divine revelation. It was on this rock that the intellectuals' efforts were
all but destroyed.

In its most acute form, the problem can be formulated in the following
manner: the reformists had maintained that Islam was the religion of reason and thus in no way contradicted Western scientific knowledge; but to
have maintained this was to ignore that all attempts to insert rationalism
and intellectualism into Islam had been defeated as far back as nine centuries earlier. So long as the intellectuals were occupied with social and political reform, this fundamental contradiction was not felt too acutely. But
when they started delving into historical and theological subjects, the crisis
erupted with a bang rather than a whimper. Of the intellectuals who were
to go each in his own way through this crisis, two will be dealt with in this
section.

In the mid-twenties, while the Wafd Party was changing the Egyptian
political landscape without much of a break with the tradition that upheld
the validity of Islam for the modern world, two young men from Al-Azhar
were ushering in a revolution of a rather different kind. 'Ali 'Abd al-Raziq's
book *Al-Islam wa-usul al-hukm* (Islam and the fundamental principles of
authority), which was published in 1925, was a work on the caliphate and
embodied the preliminary results of investigations pursued by the author
into the history of the Muslim judiciary.

Born in 1888, 'Abd al-Raziq came from one of the old fellah families in
a village in Middle Egypt. He entered Al-Azhar University when he was
about ten years of age, so that his early years in the institution were the
closing years of 'Abduh's association with it. Although he was influenced
by 'Abduh's ideas, he was to advance beyond them in many essential ways.
In 1912, a year after he obtained his final certificate from Al-Azhar, he
took up lecturing in that institution. That same year, he went to Oxford
for a degree in economics and political science. After a little more than a
year's residence there, however, he was compelled by the outbreak of the
war to return to Egypt, where he was appointed a judge in the shari'a
courts.

'Abd al-Raziq's book, thought to have been written when his mind was
still somewhat preoccupied with the struggle against the sultan of Turkey
and all that he stood for, presents a well and closely argued case against the
institution of the caliphate. Its chief purpose was to impress on the minds

of Muslims that Muhammad's message was purely religious, the moral being that the sultans' endeavors to rule the Islamic world by the pretense of unity in secular and spiritual affairs were not to be accepted. The unity brought about by the prophet, 'Abd al-Raziq argued, was basically a unity of faith, not of politics. Muhammad did not intend to establish an empire, nor did his mission require him to exercise authority over his followers or opponents. Whatever social and political changes he effected in the life of the Arabs were incidental consequences of the moral revolution he had worked for and achieved. "If we were to collect all his direct teachings on the question of government, we would get little more than a fraction of the principles of law and organization needed for maintaining a state."[23]

From this, 'Abd al-Raziq went on to the heart of the matter—the caliphate—asserting that that institution had had a disastrous effect on the progress of the Muslims. The caliphate was, in his view, the source of all evil and corruption in the history of the Muslims, since very early in its evolution as an institution it deteriorated into an instrument of obstruction against rational thinking on the problems of government. Only theological terms were allowed: Arab scholars who transmitted Greek philosophy and learning had never dared look into Plato's *Republic* or Aristotle's *Politics*. 'Abd al-Raziq argued that there was no valid religious reason for this obscurantism, and that the Muslims were entitled to build their respective states and evolve their own systems of government in light of their present needs and the modern ideas and experiences of humanity.[24]

It is not difficult to see the reason for the uproar created by 'Abd al-Raziq's book. The fundamental importance attributed by Muslim thought to the identity of church and state in Islam, an identity which the author rejected outright, caused the authorities of Al-Azhar to fight his doctrines tooth and nail. As Grunebaum points out, 'Abd al-Raziq's endeavors to disprove the view that the caliphate is a necessary institution are of relatively minor interest "when compared to the author's thesis that Muhammad's mission and hence his authority was spiritual rather than political . . . that political and administrative rules were merely incidental to the peculiar position of the Prophet, and that Islam was never intended to remain confined to the Arabs." The inference is that the shari'a Muhammad instituted concerned only religious affairs. Islam, the author's thesis runs, imposes a moral and religious code. This code is concerned solely with the relation of man and God, this world being of too little concern to the Most High for Him to devise for it any special set of laws over and above the general rules along which He made the human mind work. Thus, the whole structure of canon law, which holds back the progress of the Muslim community, is shown to be no more than a human system of regulations, which Islam has every right to discard and replace by such a government and legal order as appear best suited to human needs and most apt to rescue the Muslims from their present humiliation and subjugation.[25]

The irony of the situation is that, as a recent commentator has put it, though 'Abd al-Raziq's thesis was quite drastic, "he had reached it only by pursuing some of 'Abduh's ideas to their logical conclusions." It was 'Abduh who had hinted that the prophet might be fallible in his activity beyond the transmission of Allah's message, and it was he who had rejected consensus (*ijma'*) as a binding principle of Islamic doctrine.

> To 'Ali 'Abd al-Raziq these views led to three conclusions. First, if the Prophet may be fallible in his political actions, then these actions are religiously irrelevant and should be evaluated in the light of history and reason. Secondly, if there is no *ijma'*, there is no foundation for any universal interpretation of the Koran and the *Hadith* (Oral Tradition) and, therefore, these sources must have been intended to be understood individually and to bind only individual consciences. These conclusions were reinforced in 'Ali's mind by general rational speculation as to the essentially ethical and spiritual function of religion which, again, is not a view alien to 'Abduh's thought.[26]

In the event, however, 'Abd al-Raziq's thesis was rejected by the religious establishment out of hand. The disciplinary court of Al-Azhar, before which the case was brought, reaffirmed vigorously the traditional idea that Muhammad was the founder of both a political and religious system and that the shari'a, being founded on direct revelation from God, was equally binding on civil and religious life. Grunebaum, who does not subscribe to the view that 'Abd al-Raziq's ideas had their origins in certain of Muhammad 'Abduh's teachings, has written: "The lesson of 'Ali 'Abd al-Raziq's *cause célèbre* seems to be that, while the individual Muslim state or states will increasingly move away from the political and legal setting prescribed by Canon Law, the principles believed to be laid by the *shari'a* will remain unimpugned. The canonic ideas and injunctions may stay suspended for an indefinite length of time, but they will not be abrogated as there is no body that could abrogate a divine revelation. The contrast between the actual and ideal, however irksome, has been for many centuries a familiar feature in Muslim life. It is hardly to be expected that the cleavage will be felt as sufficiently painful and irreconcilable to make the faithful consent to a reconsideration of the fundamentals."[27]

The other young Azharite whose work was to create an uproar was Taha Husain, who was subsequently to get the rare title of Dean of Arabic Letters. Taha Husain was born in 1889. After securing his early education in a school in Upper Egypt he entered Al-Azhar, where he remained for a number of years. Though blinded at a very early age, he was a most brilliant student; but because of his independence of thought and his advanced ideas, he was dismissed from the university before he had obtained his final certificate. He at once entered the Egyptian University, which had just then opened its doors. In 1914 he received the degree of Doctor of Philosophy—the first student to be granted the degree by that institution. As his thesis for the degree, he presented a study of the poetry of Abul 'Alaa al-Ma'arri, which was published in 1915. Because of his brilliant work as a student, he was sent to France as a member of the university's educational mission. He spent three years at the Sorbonne, where he was awarded the doctor's degree with distinction. His Ph.D. thesis, written in French, was "The Philosophy of Ibn Khaldun: Introduction and Criticism." Upon his return to Egypt, he started teaching at the Egyptian University.[28]

Taha Husain was distinguished from the start by a fearless resolve to apply Western canons of literary criticism to the study of Arabic literature in a single-minded endeavor to free such study from the trammels of ancient methods of criticism, and to raise Egyptian scholarship to a level of scientific efficiency comparable to that of Western scholarship. At the University, where he taught classical literature before he was transferred to the faculty of Arabic letters, he translated Aristotle's *Constitution of Athens,* several plays of Sophocles, and selections from other Greek works. In addition to his teaching and research, he also served as literary editor of *Al-Siyasa,* the daily organ of the Liberal Constitutionalist Party, where he wrote two series of weekly essays made up of two sets of studies: one on Arabic culture in the first and second Islamic centuries, and one on contemporary French letters.[29]

Taha Husain's most important work, however, and the one that made him the subject of a cause célèbre, was a slim, innocent-sounding book called *Fil sh'ir al-Jahili* (On pre-Islamic poetry), published in 1926. Though perhaps not more radical in its conclusions than 'Ali 'Abd al-Raziq's book on the caliphate was in its own way, the book raised an even more violent storm of hostile criticism. While 'Abd al-Raziq's book was restrained, purposeful, dignified, and relevant, Taha Husain's was garrulous, provocative, and discursive. The book, which dealt with the understanding and background of pre-Islamic poetry, might have passed unnoticed except by specialists had it been written differently. As one observer put it, "The young Azharite from the Sorbonne was so elated by his European experience that he could not but be over-exuberant and militant." In his introduction and program of research, Husain threw down the gauntlet to his readers. He was not concerned with their reactions or feelings, he told them. As soon as they picked up his book they ought to put aside their religious sentiments. To uphold or decry Islam did not interest him. He was a student of literature and would not be disturbed in the least if his findings did not coincide with the accepted concepts of Islam. And so on and so on.[30]

The reader may wonder in what way a book on Arabic poetry of the pre-Islamic period can infringe so on basic Islamic dogmas and concepts. To answer this question we have to keep in mind a few facts. The pre-Islamic poetry has always been used as an inexhaustible source from which proof and illustration have been drawn in support of the doctrines of Islam and to demonstrate the grammatical correctness and rhetorical elegance of the language of the Koran. Now came Taha Husain who tried to show that all of this poetry—which is so abundant, he writes, that we might imagine all the ancients were poets!—has been fabricated to meet the exigencies in view. Husain reached the conclusion, in fact, that this poetry "proves nothing and tells nothing and should not be used, as it had been, as an instrument in the study of the Koran and the *Hadith*. For there is no doubt that this poetry was tailored and invented all of a piece so that the *'ulema* might prove by it what they had set out to prove." In the course of this remarkable book, moreover, Taha Husain gave expression to ideas that were taken as indications of a sinister purpose of unbelief on the author's part, as when he denies the legend of the foundation of the *Ka'bah* by Abraham and Ishmael and questions the historical existence of these two figures; denies that the seven variant dialectical readings of the Koran, which are commonly accepted as having emanated from Muhammad himself, ever came from him; and denies that the religion of Islam was primarily the religion of Abraham and existed in Arabia before the time of Muhammad. Here is a typical passage, cited by Nadav Safran:

> The Torah may speak to us about Ibrahim and Ismai'l, and the Koran may tell us about them too; but the mention of these names in the Torah and the Koran is not sufficient to establish their historical existence, let alone the story which tells us about the emigration of Ismai'l, son of Ibrahim, to Mecca and the birth of the *Arabicized Arab* there. We are compelled to see in this story a kind of fiction to

establish the relation of Jews and Arabs on the one hand, and Islam and Judaism and the Koran and the Torah on the other.[31]

So much for the views expressed in the book. But more important than the conclusions were the critical methods of approach to the study of Arabic literature that Taha Husain advocated. In his introductory chapters he severely criticized the prevalent methods of teaching Arabic letters. Throughout the book he directs his ridicule against the attitude of accepting everything the ancients said without criticism and taking everything on faith. "It is my desire," he wrote, "that we should not accept anything that the ancients said about our literature and its history, except after examination and confirmation." Further, he said, the study of Arabic literature, if it is to be developed as it should, must be freed from its connection with the theological sciences. At present, it is studied simply as a means to the understanding of the Koran and the traditions. If it were possible to understand them without it, it would not be studied at all. Arabic is regarded as a sacred tongue and is therefore not subjected to true scientific investigation. But if Arab literature is to enjoy an existence suitable to the present day, the study of it should receive the same recognition and should be conducted with the same independence and lack of interference accorded to the study of medicine or any other recognized science.

> Why should I simply repeat what the ancients said or publish what they said? Why should I spend my life in praising the orthodox Sunnis or berating the heretical Shi'ites and Mu'tazala and Khawarij, without any gain or any scientific purpose? Who can compel me to study literature to become a preacher of Islam or a guide to infidels, when I do not wish to preach nor to argue with infidels, but am content to keep my own religion as a matter between God and myself? . . . When we undertake the investigation of Arabic literature and its history, we must forget our national feelings and all their peculiar tendencies; we must forget our religious feelings and all that is connected with them.[32]

The appearance of Taha Husain's book brought sharp reactions from the traditionalists and the 'ulema. Rashid Rida, Al-Manar's editor, asserted that the author had "established his apostasy from Islam." He led a concerted effort with other 'ulema to get Husain expelled from the Egyptian University. When this failed, the fire was turned against the university for being a haven for heretics and a breeding ground for atheism. In the end, the author was tried for attacking the religion of the state, but the court dismissed the charge. The book was then withdrawn, the references to Abraham and Ishmael were deleted, and the remainder was considerably expanded and republished in 1927 under the revised title *Fil adab al-Jahili* (On pre-Islamic literature).

It would be instructive to dwell here upon Taha Husain's defense of himself, his conduct, and the way he explained his own views. During the height of the uproar, he wrote a letter to the director of the Egyptian University in which he testified that he was a Muslim, believing in Allah, His angels, His books, His prophets, and in the Day of Judgment. In the course of his trial, he affirmed further that, as a Muslim, he did not doubt the historical existence of Abraham and Ishmael and everything recorded in the Koran concerning these two figures; but, as a scholar, he is compelled to have strict regard to the methods of investigation and not assent to their historical existence except as established by scientific evidence. For the benefit of those who could not reconcile the two attitudes, the one made plain in the book and the other expressed in his subsequent pronouncements in public, he wrote in *Al-Siyasa* on July 17, 1926:

> Every one of us, if he but think a little, can discover in himself two distinct personalities: one a rational personality that investigates, criticizes, makes solutions, changes today the opinion it held yesterday, tears down today what it built up yesterday; the other is a sentient personality that feels delight, suffers, rejoices, sorrows, feels satisfaction or constraint, desires, fears, without criticism, investigation or search for solution. Both of these personalities are connected with our constitution and make-up, and we cannot escape from either of them. What, then, is to hinder the first personality from being scholarly, inquisitive, critical, and the second believing, assured, aspiring to the highest ideals?

To many, this position would seem untenable. At best, it is an individualistic solution that perhaps enabled the author to set his own and his critics' minds at rest. But it contributed nothing to the controversy raging about the borderline between reason and revelation. Taha Husain, however, took his new position seriously enough. This was evident when in 1934 he published the first volume of a trilogy on Muhammad, *'Ala hamish al-Sira* (On the margin of the prophet's life), the writing of which extended over a period of eight years. The book was admittedly based on belief in the sayings of traditional authorities in all matters referring directly to the prophet and on a completely unrestricted weaving of legends around his birth and life. In the introduction to the first volume, Husain cited his theory of dualism to justify this procedure. He went even further when he used the occasion to speak with contempt about unspecified potential critics who clung to the position that he had previously held himself. Reason, he now argued, is not everything. Men have other faculties that need to be fed and satisfied no less than the mind. "These legends and tales do not satisfy reason and are not acceptable to logic . . . but the sensibilities, emotions, and the imagination of the people, and their naivete . . . make them like and desire these legends and seek in them relief from the burdens of life."[33]

That Taha Husain was taking this position seriously—that, in fact, he had decided to make it a kind of article of faith—was evident when in 1938, while issuing another volume of his trilogy on Muhammad, he published a book denouncing the advocates of a "spiritualist Eastern" orientation for Egypt and pleaded the case for an unequivocal Western orientation. The book, *Mustaqbal al-thaqafa fi misr* (The future of culture in Egypt), is in the main a program for national instruction. In it, the author accords equal attention to the purpose, content, and implementation of a specifically Egyptian education. Such a program was deemed essential after the Anglo-Egyptian Treaty of 1936, which granted Egypt independence, and the convention of Montreux of 1937, which extended Egypt's domestic sovereignty by abolishing the capitulations and gave Egypt exclusive responsibility for developing her cultural potentialities. In this book, Taha Husain develops his concept of a specifically Egyptian education from his own idea of Egypt's place within the civilizations of the world. In the first, theoretical part of the book, the author gives his assessment of his country's culture.

Independence (*istiqlal*) and freedom (*hurriyya*) are not ultimate goals in themselves, Taha Husain argued. They are means toward evolving *hadara* (civilization), which rises on the foundations of *thaqafa* (culture) and *'ilm* (scientific knowledge). To these three, *'ilm*, *thaqafa*, and *hadara*, Egypt must devote her efforts, so that her present can come to match the glory of her past. Since only God can create *ex nihilio*, however, Egyptians have to think of the future of civilization in Egypt on the basis of the past and present. In this train of thought the problem immediately emerges: Is Egypt of the East or of the West?[34]

History will have to be our guide, Husain says. From olden times there have been two civilizations on this globe whose every encounter was a hostile clash—that of Europe and that of the East. Is the Egyptian mind (*'aql*) Eastern or Western in terms of its concept formation of imagination (*tasawwur*), perception (*idrak*), understanding (*fahm*), and judgment, *hukm 'ala al-ashyaa?* There is but one test: is it easier for the Egyptian mind to understand a Chinese or a Japanese, a Frenchman or an Englishman? The answer is obvious. There is no evidence of intellectual, political, or economic ties between Egypt and the East (that is, the Far East) in antiquity. Close ties existed solely with the Near East—Palestine, Syria, Iraq.

On the other hand, there is no need to emphasize the well-known connections between Egypt and the Aegean and Egypt and the Greeks, from the very beginnings of their civilization down to Alexander the Great. In fact, Egypt resisted the Persian invader from the East with the help of Greek volunteers and Greek cities until she was freed by Alexander. This shows that the Egyptian mind had no significant ties with that of the Far East and met that of Persia with hostility. Its real ties were all with the Near East and the Greeks. If the Egyptian mind was affected by any outside influence, this influence was Mediterranean. The Mediterranean civilizations interacted, with Egypt holding the precedence of age, but never did her *'aql* enter into contact with India, China, or Japan.

Though all this is quite well known, the Egyptians will consider themselves Easterners, closer in mind to the Indian, the Japanese, the Chinese, than to the Greek, the Italian, the Frenchman! Had the ready acceptance of Islam made the Egyptians an Eastern nation? According to Taha Husain, spiritual and political unity do not necessarily go together. The Muslims always realized that political organization and faith are matters of a different order. They conceived of government as dedicated primarily, if not exclusively, to the practical management of public affairs. Europe is organized along the same lines. Islam and Christianity show important similarities, both having influenced and having been influenced by Greek philosophy. Whence, then, the alleged difference in their effect on the mentality of their adherents?

In the modern age, Egypt has taken Europe for her model in all aspects of the material life.

> Constitutional and representative government has been adopted from Europe, but has at once become so deeply rooted in Egypt that no one would wish to return to the earlier stage of our political life. In organizing our democratic institutions, which we are borrowing from Europe, we are trying to establish that very equality which is the birthright of all members of one state. To reach these goals there is only one way: to share European civilization in its good and in its bad aspects.

Turning to the "tales" told of the spirituality of the East and the materialism of the West, Taha Husain conceded that there was a great deal of materialism in European civilization. But it would be absurd to deny that it also possessed great spiritual content. Besides, he argued, the Near East had been the cradle of all the divine religions, those adopted by Europeans as well as those followed by Near Easterners. "Can these religions be spirit in the East and matter in the West?" he asked rhetorically.

Throughout this section of the book, Taha Husain made evident his conviction that Egypt should go for an out-and-out Westernization. He warned against stopping in mid-course or attempting to go back. "The world," he wrote, "has struggled for hundreds of years to attain the present stage of progress; it is in our power to reach this same stage within a short time. Woe to us if we do not seize the opportunity."

The Roots of the Dilemma: Coming to Terms with Western Rationalism

In the years and decades that followed the publication of the views of Taha Husain and 'Ali 'Abd al-Raziq, several Egyptian and Arab Muslim thinkers took up the same challenges and tried to resolve the same sort of problems. But the essence of the dilemma remained unchanged. Taha Husain's opinions as they have been summarized above, for instance, seemed to be very far from the teachings of Muhammad 'Abduh and his immediate followers. It is extremely doubtful whether they represented Egypt's actual cultural orientation even at the time his book on the future of Egyptian culture was published. Rather than reflect the course Egypt and its culture were actually taking, the book "reflected only the deep crisis which the Western cultural orientation—and with it the intellectual development of modern Egyptian thought—had reached." The explanation is simple enough: "Fifteen years before the appearance of *The Future of Culture in Egypt*, Taha Husain's views were largely held by most of Egypt's leaders of opinion; barely three decades after, the book itself and the whole tone of its argument came to betray the fact that its author had suddenly found himself rowing upstream."[35]

A misfortune of a different kind was to befall 'Ali 'Abd al-Raziq and his ideas. It is remarkable that, though his main thesis—as propounded by him in his book on the principles of Islamic government—was in fact reached only by pursuing some of 'Abduh's own ideas, one outstanding authority on modern Islam found that in its total rejection of that thesis the Azhar court actually "found itself in agreement with 'Abduh who, while demanding its reform, had always upheld the basic validity of Canon Law for civil as well as religious matters and who also had been a staunch defender of the inseparability of civil and religious authority in Islam." In fact, according to the same authority, "there can be little doubt that the attitude taken by Al-Azhar (and later confirmed by a higher court) was in full accord with majority opinion."[36]

What Rashid Rida said in 1899 still expressed, and continues to express, the consensus of Muslim religious leaders on this point. "The assertion," Rida wrote, "that the government and the state should be separated from religion is one that necessitates the blotting of Islamic authority out of existence, and abrogating entirely the Islamic *shari'a*.... Were Muslims to adopt the Christian position on the matter, we should have laid aside half of our religion—that part which forms a protective fence around the other half."

And so we seem to come back to the same ponderous question with which we started this inquiry: How to modernize Islam without virtually rejecting its own most basic tenets. The roots of the dilemma lie in the same questions to which the Muslim reformists did not, and could not, furnish satisfactory answers. In its simplest form, the problem is that of the apparent incompatibility between Islam as a revealed religion and the premises and findings of scientific rationalism. In their search for a religious and social doctrine in keeping with their efforts to lift Islamic society out of its tradition-bound inertia, Muslim reformists could consider two alternative conceptions. The first, in Malcolm Kerr's formulation, "would be to assign separate spheres of competence to reason and revelation, along lines roughly similar to the Thomist tradition in Catholicism." According to this conception, "God's creation of the world of nature, including human nature, in keeping with an Eternal Law, provides human reason with the necessary basis for determining the principles of social morality, while revelation addresses itself to spiritual questions of personal devotion and redemption." Islamic thought has not inclined in this direction, however, "because of its own primary image of God as ever-present, ever-willing and ever-creating: God is 'wholly other' than His creation, but He cannot have withdrawn or detached Himself from it."

The second alternative presenting itself to the Islamic reformist, Kerr writes, "is to recognize the parallel competence of both reason and revelation within the same sphere, denying that there is either a separation or a conflict between them." Specific divine commands, according to this conception, may exist in matters immediately concerning ordinary social life, without the competence of reason thereby being devalued. "Similarly, reason may be capable of reaching certain conclusions regarding the nature of the Deity or of the after-life. There are gaps, to be sure, but only random ones, in the subject matter of each kind of knowledge. Thus reason can discover the existence of God and identify His most important qualities, but cannot determine the correct forms of worship; revelation prescribes all the details of the law of inheritance, but omits mention of the details of governmental organization." It was this approach, in which reason and revelation form an integrated combination, and which is more congenial to the Islamic religious outlook, that 'Abduh and many other modernists adopted.[37]

However, as we have seen earlier in this chapter, the attempt thus to reconcile reason and revelation led only to confusion. In a book that appeared in 1960, Peter Partner puts his finger on what is clearly the heart of the matter: "Matthew Arnold described Western culture as based on 'Hebraism' whose governing idea is 'strictness of conscience,' and 'Hellenism' whose governing idea is 'spontaneity of consciousness.' In Islam there is only Hebraism: only the idea of patient obedience to the law; the accent is on 'firm obedience,' and not on 'clear intelligence.'"[38]

Is the attempt to modernize Islam, then, ultimately doomed to failure? Montgomery Watt thinks that it is "far too soon to pronounce the position hopeless." Out of all this ferment "something may yet come. . . . A man with the requisite training, and above all with gifts of courage and wisdom, might transform the whole scene." But where is such a man to be found? Watt refuses to despair: "Reasons can be given to show that no Islamic *milieu* is likely to produce him; but he may nevertheless appear."[39]

Is there any way out of the dilemma? One student of the Egyptian ideological scene has maintained that in order to be viable and stable, a political community must be based on a shared set of ideas, an ideology. It is precisely this that Egypt has been in search of for the past century or so. The belief system Egypt inherited, which was based on Islamic doctrine, remained frozen after the beginning of the nineteenth century, when the basic character of Egyptian government and society began to change rapidly under the impact of renewed contact with Europe. The ensuing gap between the old ideology and the new reality widened, undermining the existing political community and threatening to condemn Egyptian society to a permanent state of instability and tension.[40]

The difficulty, of course, is how, if at all, a Muslim society is to acquire a "new" belief system without undergoing virtual de-Islamization. This is because Islam—and here it differs from both Judaism and Christianity—

recognizes no distinction between a spiritual and a temporal realm, between religious and secular activities. As we have seen, 'Ali 'Abd al-Raziq's attempt to argue that Islam was merely a religion and that Muhammad was the founder of a religious faith, not a state or an empire, was met with the 'ulema's angry disapproval and censure. There does not seem to be a way out of this impasse.

3 | Islam Takes the Offensive

Allah is our goal
The Prophet is our leader
The Koran is our constitution
Holy War is our way
Death for Allah's sake is our supreme desire
Slogan of the Muslim Brethren

In the Name of Allah: The Rise of the Muslim Brethren

The Muslim Brethren, *Al-ikhwan al-muslimun,* which can be considered the greatest politico-religious movement in modern Islam, continues until this day to capture headlines. Having been outlawed and dispersed in Egypt, its birthplace, some forty years ago, it lay dormant in Syria and showed little sign of life in countries such as Saudi Arabia, Iraq, Yemen, and the Arab countries of North Africa — as well as in several other Arab countries where it was known to have partisans and supporters. Although following the death of Jamal 'Abd al-Nasser in 1970 the movement was given some measure of freedom of action under President Anwar al-Sadat's regime, the Brethren's future remains shrouded in uncertainty. Nevertheless, there is little doubt that its essence, its message, and its teachings will remain with us as long as Islam itself does.

The reality of the impact made by the Muslim Brethren has never been contested. In its nearly seventy years of life, the movement has had an undeniable impact on the course of Islamic history and on Islamic think-ing. It has become a part of the modern history of the Middle East. Many books were written by the Brethren and their enemies, which has given Muslims a stimulus to concern themselves with spiritual issues. As an Is-lamic religious movement, moreover, the Muslim Brethren has its basis in Islam's history and culture. Its principles are easily traced to both past and recent Islamic movements, such as the Wahhabi and Sanusi movements in the Arab Peninsula and North Africa, respectively; the Salafiyya school of Rashid Rida; and, further back, the school of Ibn Taimiyya and that of Ahl al-Hadith.

Some of these principles may be listed at the outset, since they are com-mon to most of these movements:

1. The belief in the unity and perfection of the Islamic system.
2. The identification of state with religion.
3. The enforcement of the shari'a.
4. The return to the Koran and the Hadith (tradition) to the exclusion of all other sources.
5. Refraining from all scholastic theology (*'ilm al-kalam*).
6. Opposition to mystical innovations of all kinds.
7. Emulation of the early righteous ancestors.

Thus there was really nothing entirely new about the principles of the Muslim Brethren — except, of course, that the movement represents a reac-tion to the circumstances of the twentieth century. As Werner Caskel, the German Orientalist, has put it, the movement represents "something unique in Westernized Islam: the transformation of faith into action." The Mus-lim Brethren, in short, was a reaction to the West's sweeping impact. Its founder, Hasan al-Banna, relates in his memoirs how, when he was a stu-dent, he and his friends spent "God knows how many nights" discussing the general situation *"and the need to take Islamic counter-action."*[1]

This need for counteraction was and has been at the very core of the dilemma of every believing Muslim today. The West's challenge was mani-fest everywhere and was too real to ignore. In its essence, the dilemma is not entirely new. It is faced, albeit in different forms, by every old culture responding to the challenge of modern civilization. In its simplest form the dilemma can be formulated thusly: How to acquire the elements of mod-ern civilization without losing sight of religious principles. As Werner Caskel has pointed out, for a civilization to receive cultural stimuli, two condi-tions must be fulfilled: a consciousness of being inferior and contacts be-tween the two cultures at more than one point and for some length of time.

In the case of Islam, only the second condition was fulfilled. When the modernist movement emerged in Egypt during the second half of the last century, it proved too much for the conservatives. What the movement wanted was "to free Islam from the crust into which it had hardened."

What the Muslim Brethren was attempting, on the other hand, was nothing less than *to achieve a religious and social reform from the point of view of a fundamental reformism and to use for this purpose Western techniques and organizational methods.* Therein lies the Brethren's novelty: without changing anything fundamental in Islamic traditions and culture, the Brethren tried to borrow from the West only that which was in keeping with its dogma. The Brethren's idea was that "In Western civilization there is much good and much evil and to adopt what is beneficial from its industry and science is indispensable to our renaissance. Every innovation which does not destroy the personality of the nation and does not contradict its fundamental virtues is a fresh force which strengthens its being and secures its future."[2]

A brief history of the origins of the movement and the early life of its founder and supreme guide, Hasan al-Banna, will perhaps be in place here as they reflect the general situation in one Muslim country during the first three decades of this century. Born in 1906, al-Banna came from a typical Muslim milieu in a village in the Gharbia province. His father was a watchmaker and at the same time *imam* and *khateeb* of the village mosque. He had a religious upbringing and was a diligent student of the Koran, the tradition, and the *musnad* works and wrote on these subjects. After going through a preparatory school, he entered the teachers college at Damanhur when he was only fourteen. In 1923, he went to Dar al-'Ulum in Cairo, wherefrom he emerged four years later as the first in his class. After spending six years teaching elementary school in Ismailia, he was assigned to Cairo.

Equipped by his home life with the minimum prerequisites for his career, Hasan al-Banna had from the start an inclination to pedagogy and *irshad,* the religious guidance of men. In a paper he wrote while in Dar al-'Ulum, he described the office to which he felt himself called. He wrote that he would like to teach the children and the parents through talks, conversations, letters, and books, while he moved from one place to another. For this aim he considered himself to be prepared through a knowledge of the good and the beautiful, through perseverance and a readiness for self-sacrifice, through a hardened body, and through association with like-minded people.

Hasan al-Banna was confirmed in this path by what he encountered in

Cairo and in Ismailia: the estrangement from the faith and customs of Islam, the ignorance of the masses, and what has been called the "religious barbarism of the workers" in Ismailia. His concepts of reform were shaped in the spiritual battle that began in 1925 between the conservatives and the reformists. The battle agitated him until the end of the twenties. While in Ismailia, he and six of his adherents founded the *al-ikhwan al-muslimun* association in March 1928. By the time he went on his Cairo assignment in 1933, ten other groups from Suez to Port Said had been founded. The next year, forty groups of the Ikhwan were operating all over Egypt. It should be noted that the core of the movement consisted of fellahs and workers right from the start.[3]

When Hasan al-Banna founded the association, he did not provide any finished program for it. The movement was a reaction, a protest against what he encountered in Cairo and Ismailia. Al-Banna provides a description of this stage of his development in his memoirs. In the country, one gathers, he had not known the license and general laxity of Islamic morality that he observed in the towns. In some of the newspapers he saw articles that he found completely incompatible with the teachings of Islam, and he was made acutely aware of the ignorance of the common people in religious matters. He realized that the mosques alone were inadequate as a medium for the dissemination of the teachings of Islam among the broad masses. He was not narrow-minded in his teachings, and he limited his instruction to matters of general interest. He directed the attention of his listeners to those things they could sense in their environment, attempting to smooth over the points of disputation among the notables. He wrote: "I tried to make this a broad, general movement based on science, education and a spirit of militancy—which things are the pillars of the Islamic mission. He who wishes a specialized education—he, and what he chooses, is his own affair."

The teachings of the Ikhwan did crystallize into some sort of program, although that was only ten years after their association was founded. The movement's basic principle was designated by al-Banna as being *shumul ma'na al-Koran*—the all-embracing character of the Koran. He defined Islam as follows: "Islam is a creed and is service of God, fatherland and nation, religion and state, spirituality and action, book and sword." In 1938, the program was considerably enlarged. The Ikhwan now "represented a doctrine of the predecessors, a way of following the Prophet, a door to mystical reality, a political body, a sports club, an association for the advancement of science and education, an economic corporation and a social ideal." Al-Banna wrote as follows: "The Ikhwan believe that many views and sciences which have been joined to Islam and have taken on its coloring actually show the color of the ages in which they were created and of the peoples who lived in those ages . . . therefore we have to understand Islam in the way in which our pious predecessors, the Companions and the Successors, understood it and we have to stop at those limits . . . without allowing ourselves to be chained by something other than what God has chained us with."[4]

No change in this program was made between 1939 and 1945, when it was reiterated in the form of an amendment introduced in the basic regulations of the association, stipulating that the Brethren "will always prefer gradual advancement and development, productive work and cooperation with lovers of good and truth," and that they "do not wish harm to anyone no matter what his religion, race or country."[5]

The shifting fortunes of the Muslim Brethren in their relations with the authorities may be reviewed very briefly. In the beginning, the government paid very little attention to the association, but as World War II broke out this attitude changed radically. In 1940, a number of severe measures introduced under the influence of the occupying power were taken against the Brethren. In 1944, the Wafd government of Nahhas Pasha reverted to a more lenient attitude. After the war ended, all restrictions were removed.

The association's growing demands and demonstrations, however, drove the government in late 1946 to take certain countermeasures, although after the breakout of the Israeli-Arab war two years later the *katayib* (units) of the Ikhwan went into battle (as Arab League troops and not as part of the Egyptian Army) and fought stubbornly. In fact, they were considered as having fought so well in Palestine that Prime Minister Nuqrashi Pasha considered them, especially in view of the general excitement about the defeat, so dangerous that he made some acts of violence the excuse for dissolving and dispossessing their organization (December 8, 1948). Nuqrashi was assassinated by one of the Brethren only three weeks later. When al-Banna was shot to death on February 12, 1949, the material destruction of the organization was already proceeding.

After this, the fortunes of the Brethren underwent many shifts. The Wafd government again gave it a helping hand by partially lifting the reprisals in 1950, when a new supreme guide, Hasan Isma'il al-Hudaibi, was elected. The next year, at the beginning of the anti-British unrest in the Suez Canal zone, the *katayib* of the Ikhwan again showed their mettle. Their performance brought them thousands of students and members of the educated classes. When the free officers' revolution came on July 23, 1952, the view was widely held that this was a movement initiated and instigated by the

Brethren; but after a brief flirtation, it became obvious to both sides that no form of unity between them was feasible. The final blow came when a member of the Brethren's "secret organ" made an unsuccessful attempt on the life of Colonel 'Abd al-Nasser on October 26, 1954. In less than two weeks the backbone of the organization was broken, members of the secret organ were arrested, the supreme guide was sentenced to death with a number of other leaders of the Brethren, and six of them were hanged. It is estimated that at least five thousand Muslim Brethren were sent to Egyptian concentration camps. Hundreds of families were left destitute, and the country was deprived of the services of many educationalists, religious leaders, and professionals.[6]

The Brethren's whole ideology is based, of course, on the Koran. As al-Banna put it: "The Brethren believe that the fountainhead of the teaching of Islam is the Book of God and the way of His Prophet. If the nation but adheres to these it would never go astray. . . . We should look back to these two pure sources and draw upon them for the Islamic system upon which the nation shall be built."

Since Islam, as noted above, is considered by the Brethren as at once creed and worship, fatherland and nation, religion and state, politics in all its forms is an integral part of Islam and of the Brethren's program and doctrine. To their critics, who often ask them what business they have playing politics and whether they are men of religion or of politics, the Brethren answer by asking: If Islam is something other than politics, social affairs, economics, law, and culture, then what is it? Is it merely genuflections and incantations? "Is it not surprising," they ask, "that while Communism has a State which sponsors it and voices its appeal, and while other systems also have nations which contend for them, there is no Islamic Government to take up the duty of calling for Islam? — Islam, which contains all the advantages of these other systems and has discarded all their disadvantages, which offers other peoples an international system with real solutions to the problems of humanity?"[7]

The Brethren's foreign policy program was one of the most extreme among those of the anti-British groups, their attitude being determined by the Hadith: *al-aqrab awla bil-ma'ruf* (the one nearest is most worthy of your charity). In a group of thirty internal directives distributed to members in 1936 — called, respectively, the Ten Duties, the Ten Sins, and the Ten Deliverances — imperialism, foreign companies, and imitation of the West are featured among the sins, while encouragement of national enterprises and respect for nationalism are among the deliverances.

Beyond attainment of freedom and independence, the Brethren's aims in the foreign policy field were vague. They advocated a rapprochement among the Muslim countries in education, social affairs, and economy—such agreements gradually to lead to a brotherly Muslim federation and finally to a caliphate to carry Islam's mission to the world. In a memorandum submitted to the Arab kings and heads of state and subsequently published under the title *Nahwa al-nur* (Toward the light) there are fifty demands by the association, one of which reads as follows: "To strengthen relations between all Muslim countries, especially Arab ones, in preparation for serious and practical thinking about the lost Caliphate."[8]

The Brethren are at once Pan-Islamists and Pan-Arab. Al-Banna's theory in this respect is based on his reading of the words *wataniyya* (patriotism) and *qawmiyya* (nationalism). In his pamphlet, *Da'watuna* (Our mission), he explains that the European interpretation of these two terms must not be accepted and that they should be given meanings in keeping with the spirit of Islam. It transpires that patriotism means the love of the "Islamic Fatherland," including all countries inhabited by Muslims, their liberation from the foreigners who dominate them, and the achievement of a rapprochement between all of them.

As to nationalism, al-Banna sees this as the sum total of the nationalisms of the various Islamic peoples. He does not object to these nationalisms—on condition they all cooperate toward the attainment of the final aim. According to al-Banna, the content of nationalism lies merely in following in the path of the Muslim fathers and believing in holy war (*jihad*) and devotion to work. He is on record as being against any tendency to racial pride and was a critic of modern Turkey because she ignored the Islamic tradition and adopted Turanian ways. Al-Banna was also against any nationalism that despised other races and aspired to aggressive deeds—such as Italian and German nationalisms.[9]

The Brethren's attitude to Pan-Islam and Pan-Arabism raises a most interesting question as to the compatibility of these two doctrines. It is generally thought that the two are contradictory, owing, according to one authority, to an historical accident whereby Pan-Arabs acquired the reputation of being opposed to Pan-Islam. "Pan-Islam was used by the Ottomans to provide a support for their empire; when the Pan-Arabs rose, they necessarily had to emphasize the opposition between Pan-Arabism and Pan-Islam. In Egypt, of course, there was no place and no need for such opposition: the enemy was Britain, not the Ottoman Empire."[10]

That Islamic sentiment and Islamic solidarity gave body and passion to the struggle against the foreigner is aptly illustrated by the following prayer composed by al-Banna for the use of his followers:

O God, Lord of the Creation who giveth assurance to the insecure, who humbleth the vainglorious and who layeth low the tyrants, accept our prayer and answer our call. Enable us to obtain our right, and give back to us our freedom and independence. O God, those British usurpers have occupied our land and made free with our rights, they have oppressed the country and spread evil in it. O God, turn their intrigues away from us, weaken their strength and disperse their hosts; annihilate them and those who have helped them to victory, or have aided them, or have made peace with them, or have befriended them, in a manner worthy of an all-powerful and majestic One. O God, let their actions rebound on them, let calamities descend on them, humiliate their kingdom, release Your land from their power, and let them have no sway over any of the Believers. Amen.[11]

The Brethren were firmly attached to their anti-British and anti-foreigner policies. They continued, through thick and thin, to demand the liberation of the Nile valley, sometimes quietly and sometimes violently. When, at the beginning of World War II, 'Ali Mahir Pasha decided to keep Egypt out of the war, the Brethren supported him wholeheartedly. They did not concur when Ahmad Mahir later declared war on Germany and Italy, and they wrote advising him to retract the declaration. Their campaign against the British did not stop, however, and it led to the persecution and arrest of many of the Brethren. Their differences with the government reached a point where they were accused of complicity in the assassination of Ahmad Mahir. After the armistice, they demanded complete satisfaction of their demands and even rejected the principle of negotiations (they had borrowed the Watani Party's slogan: "No negotiations before evacuation").

In sum, it is possible to list the Brethren's program in foreign policy according to the phases which they envisaged:

1. The liberation of the whole Nile valley (Egypt and Sudan).
2. The liberation of Arab countries and their unification.
3. The attainment of Pan-Islamism, which defines the complete and natural boundaries of the whole Islamic homeland.
4. Worldwide unity under the Islamic mission. (For this aim they cite the well-known sura from the Koran: "We have not sent thee otherwise than as mercy unto all creatures.")

At the head of the Brethren's program, however, stands their demand for a state permeated by religion and a unified legal and judicial system based entirely on the shari'a. The organization has been very clear about

Islamic government. Hasan al-Banna declared in one of his speeches explaining the movement:

> The Brethren went to the Book of God and sought inspiration and guidance therefrom; they knew for certain that Islam is this full, comprehensive meaning and that it must have supervision over all matters of life, that it gives its tone to all things, that all things must come under its rule, conform to its rules and teachings, and draw upon it. . . . But if [the nation] is Muslim in its worship and imitates non-Muslims in all other things, then it is a nation devoid of Islam.

And again:

> The Islam in which the Muslim Brethren believe makes government one of its pillars, and relies upon execution as much as upon guidance. . . . The Prophet made government one of the bonds of Islam. . . . In our books and jurisprudence, administration is considered as one of the doctrines and tenets [of Islam] and not as casuistry and a consequence of tenets, for Islam is a system of laws and execution as much as it is legislation and teaching, law and judicature—one inseparable from the other. If the Islamic reformer satisfied himself with being a jurist-guide . . . then the natural consequence is that [his] voice will be a cry in the wilderness.[12]

What the Brethren advocated is that legislation in its entirety should be first of all Islamic and that all practical and applied laws should derive from Islamic canon law. One of the first of the fifty demands they included in the memorandum to Arab rulers reads: "Reform of the law so that it becomes in keeping with Islamic legislation especially in the criminal and personal field." And: "That all the actions of the government should be taken in accordance with the rules and teachings of Islam, so that the systems in prisons and hospitals do not contradict Islamic teachings, and working hours not collide with the times of prayer unless necessary, that official ceremonies take on an Islamic character, and so on." Finally, the request is made that "some military and administrative posts be given to graduates of Al-Azhar"—the Islamic theological school. The demands also stipulate that all the things forbidden by Islam—alcohol, cabarets, sexual license, etc.—be likewise forbidden by the governments concerned.

The special brand of patriotism that the Brethren preach emphasizes service to one's particular state rather than to the broad fatherland of all the Muslims, which comes only second in order. This is only in practice, however; in principle they maintain that Islam does not recognize geographical limits or differences of race or blood but considers the Muslims to be one nation, the Islamic fatherland, one fatherland. The Brethren preach that the Islamic fatherland is any stretch of land inhabited by Muslims and that their duty, after liberating their own country, is to work for the liberation of other countries of this fatherland.

In the Islamic religious government, Muslims will protect their non-Muslim co-citizens and give them fair treatment and equity. The status of minorities is governed by the following Koranic text: "God doth not forbid you to deal with kindness and fairness toward those who have not made war on you on account of your religion, or drive you forth from your homes; for God loveth those who act with fairness."[13]

On the position of adherents of the revealed religions, the Brethren follow another Koranic injunction: "Say ye: 'We believe in God and that which hath been sent down to us, and that which hath been sent down to Abraham and Ishmael and Isaac and Jacob and the tribes; and that which hath been given to Moses and to Jesus, and that which hath been given to the prophets from their Lord. No difference do we make between any of them; and to God we are resigned. If therefore they believe even as ye believe, then have they true guidance; but if they turn back, then do they cut themselves off from you; and God will suffice to protect thee against them, for He is the Hearer, the Knower."[14]

Those, however, whom it is necessary to oppose and with whom Muslims must have no dealings, are defined in the following verse: "Only doth God forbid you to make friends of those who, on account of your religion, have warred against you, and have driven you forth from your homes, and have aided those who drove you forth; and whoever makes friends of them are wrong-doers."[15]

As for its dealings with the outside world, the Islamic government would be guided by the principle that promises, agreements, and treaties must be honored in accordance with the following texts: "And keep the covenant. Lo, of the covenant it will be asked. . . . But this concerneth not those Polytheists with whom you are in League, and who shall have afterwards no way failed you nor aided anyone against you. Observe, therefore, engagement with them through the whole time of their treaty, for God loveth those who fear Him.[16] . . . So long as they are true to you, be ye true to them."[17]

Elaborating on this point, al-Banna wrote in *Toward the Light:* "Islam lays down these rules and acts in accordance with these methods; [this] should be considered by the Westerners as an additional guarantee, securing the observance of their treaties and the discharge of commitments made by the Islamic States towards them. We even would say that it is for the good of Europe itself to be motivated by these pertinent theories in dealings among its own countries, for this is better for them, and more enduring."[18]

It is interesting to note here that the Brethren's ideas of religious government, though based exclusively on Koranic texts, are not unanimously accepted by religious leaders of Islam. For instance, on the basic question of the legality of religious government, the Brethren differ from Sheikh 'Ali 'Abd al-Raziq, who—as we have seen in a previous chapter—concludes that the necessity of the caliphate was neither mentioned in the Koran nor indicated in the Sunna (the Way). He also maintains that the functions of government have their reference in the discretion of reason, the experience of nations, and the rules of politics—just as the building of cities and administrative centers have their reference in engineering.

It appears that there are few Muslim theologians who would agree with this view. Al-Banna has likened the Islamic state to a three-legged table that falls if any one leg is broken. The first leg is the Islamic principle, the second is the unified nation, and the third is Islamic religious government, which operates upon the unity of the nation and the unity of the principle.

Guideposts on the Road: An Ideology for Militant Islam

The Muslim Brethren have always made it clear that if and when they take power, they will tolerate no political parties or any other kind of political grouping. The very first of their fifty demands stipulates the dissolution of parties, the unification of the nation's political forces, and their direction toward a single goal. The Brethren hold that political parties were brought into being by specific circumstances and motives that were personal for the most part, and not for the general good. The programs of these parties have so far not been made clear, they say. Each claims it will work for the good of the nation in all aspects of reform. Yet the details of these reforms, the means of their realization, and the preparation for these means are not made clear by the leaders of these parties. All the parties are alike in this. They are also alike in another matter: They are greedy to take over the government, and all employ every kind of propaganda, honest and dishonest, to attain this end. Political parties, the Brethren maintain, distort all aspects of the people's life, harm their interests, corrupt their morals, destroy their loyalty, and generally have the worst effects on both their private and public life.[19]

It is idle to speak of the Brethren's attitude to parliamentary democracy, since they have only one standard to judge the fitness or otherwise of governments, parties, and men: their willingness and/or ability to further the application of the precepts of Islam. The Brethren believe that a representative system of government—even the parliamentary system—has no need of a multiparty system; otherwise, they say, there would be no coalition governments in democratic countries. It is quite possible to run a constitutional parliamentary government on the one-party system, and the argument that parties are essential to parliamentary systems is dismissed. Furthermore, coalitions based on the multiparty system are useless—a mere sedative and not a cure, since sooner or later the parties of the coalition rebel against each other. The only solution, they maintain, is to abolish all parties.

Behind this attitude to political parties is the Brethren's concept of freedom, especially freedom of expression. They make a distinction between freedom of opinion in thought, in plain speaking, and in giving advice—all of which are enjoined by Islam. They also distinguish between fanaticism of opinion, rebellion against society, and persistent effort to widen the gulf dividing the nation and weaken the authority of government—all of which Islam rejects and strongly prohibits. Such practices, they maintain, are in fact a necessary adjunct of party politics. Islam, on the other hand, calls for unity and cooperation.[20]

To substitute for political parties, the Brethren suggest a new system whereby the efforts of the nation focus on a sound and strong Islamic program. In other words, Islamic government should be the polity of Egypt, leaving no place for political partisanship. In application of this principle, the Brethren require that anyone wishing to join them must be free from all party affiliation. His political beliefs should be confined to those concepts which have their premises and teachings in the Koran itself.

It is worth noting that the Brethren did not take this drastic attitude toward parties right from the start. At first they were neutral to all other organizations, religious, social, or political, and wished them well. They changed their stand only gradually. Their final outspoken opposition to parties came after World War II, when they began to feel that they were no longer a "movement" but represented the great majority of Egyptians. They declared that there was a new movement that had transformed the nation by degrees. This movement had greatly expanded its mission, which was going to occupy its proper place now that it had become a reality and had attained such preeminence. They said this mission, and no other, was the reform mission of the entire nation.

It was this ambitious scope, this all-embracing character, that distinguished the Brethren from all other reform movements in Islam. For here was no reform movement in any of the accepted senses of the term. Ishaq Musa al-Husaini, the movement's historian, quoted one of al-Banna's biographers when he said the Brethren were

> organizing a movement, leading a generation, applying the principles of the Islamic system to government, politics and social matters, putting them into practice as a binding constitution, besides defending them as true doctrine. An Islamic movement on a scope so wide and comprehensive, with its concomitant universal revolution of thought and accompanying historic repercussions, will have grave and far-reaching effects on the future of humanity. An Islamic movement in this sense has not been known in history for a very long time—not until Hasan al-Banna raised its banner in the twentieth century, under the name of the Muslim Brethren movement.[21]

Though the Brethren have openly advocated borrowing from Western civilization what good there is in it, they hold that the West is doomed. Their views on this subject, and on the respective merits of the East and West, are summarized by al-Banna himself in *Toward the Light*, written, it must be noted, as early as 1936. Here is the relevant passage in full:

> From this study, we may arrive at the conclusion that Western civilization, which for a certain time has, through its science, been in a position to dominate and subjugate the whole world, has at the present time reached a stage of complete decadence: its organization, its bases, its systems are crumbling. Its political systems are dictatorships, its economic systems are threatened by crises—as its millions of discontented, of unemployed, of the starving—bear witness. Its countries are threatened by revolutions which break out everywhere; its nations find no remedy to that situation. Its alliances lead nowhere; its treaties are violated; its charters are mocked at and its strength is no more than a myth.
>
> Its inconceivable policy places the world in a situation which might be compared to a ship lost at sea, tossed among innumerable dangerous reefs. All of humanity is unhappy, suffering from this painful state of affairs, dominated by ambition and by materialist considerations. There is a crying need for the law of Islam—a law which could be [humanity's] only salvation, the only way to find happiness.
>
> In ancient times, the countries of the world were under the lead of the East. With the rise of Greece and Rome, power passed to the

West and it was the prophetic missions of Moses, Jesus and Mohammed which restored power to the East. Then, the East underwent a long eclipse, while the West experienced its renaissance of modern times: the Divine Will deemed that the West should assume the leadership of the world, and the West did this through a policy of oppression and tyranny. It is the duty of the Fighters of the holy Faith to work, under the protection of God and the banner of the Koran, to extend the power of the East—for then Islamic peace will reign on earth and all the banners will be raised.

That is no hallucination—it is the verdict of history.[22]

Apart from this general view of Europe and the West, the Brethren also evolved a definite policy toward the European countries that rule any of the Islamic lands. This policy was based on two premises: first, that the Islamic fatherland is one and indivisible and aggression against any part of it is therefore aggression against the whole; and second, that Islam requires that Muslims be leaders in their own countries and masters in their own lands. Moreover, Muslims are duty bound to persuade others to join their mission and accept Islam as a guide, even as they themselves have been guided by it. It is, therefore, the duty of all Muslims to act jointly to free themselves from foreign tyranny and domination. In support of this admonition, the Brethren cite the following example, given in the form of a *fatwa*: "A captive Muslim woman taken prisoner in the East must be ransomed by the people of the West even though the cost thereof be all the property of the Muslims." Jihad must be declared on the aggressors. Freedom and independence must be regained by force, even though it means bloodshed—for death is better than a life of slavery, bondage, and humiliation.

Thus far, the Brethren's attitude toward violence and the use of force seems in keeping with the precepts of Islam. But for jihad, to which Islam did indeed call and which is considered one of the foundations of the faith, rules have been laid down by the Muslim 'ulema, first among them being the precept that Muslims never start a fight but engage in it only in self-defense. The Muslim is never encouraged to carry arms and fight people on impulse or whim. "He who attacks you attack him in like fashion and know ye that Allah is with the pious" (Koran, II:194). "Fight in the name of Allah those who fight you, and aggress not for Allah likes not the aggressor" (Koran, II:160).

This notwithstanding, it is fairly certain that sometime before October 1954 the Brethren decided to use violence on a large scale inside Egypt to overthrow the free officers' regime. The point in dispute was the agreement reached with the British over evacuation of the Canal Zone, to which the Brethren took strong exception. When the agreement was initialed, it was decided that the organization must take positive steps to prevent its signing. What these positive steps were to be was indicated by the abortive attempt on Nasser in October. The attempt heralded the virtual destruction of the organization in Egypt.[23]

It is to be seen from the foregoing that the Brethren's program is extremely ambitious, far-reaching, and all-embracing. It is remarkable how elaborate and comprehensive their methods and general principles are. Pointing out that the Brethren "will always prefer gradual progress and development," Hasan al-Banna in 1945 explained that this gradual development must pass through three distinct stages:

1. A stage of propaganda—the promulgation and inculcation of the idea and its dissemination among the broad masses of the people.
2. A stage of attracting and selecting supporters, the drilling of recruits, and the mobilization of those who answer the call.
3. A stage of implementation, action, and fulfillment. (This last stage, al-Banna added, will not come about "until the propaganda has become widespread, the supporters numerous and the movement solidly established.")[24]

On various occasions, al-Banna laid it down that Islam has an all-inclusive meaning, regulating all the affairs of life and interpreting all matters, for which it lays down exact and precise rules. He claims that the peoples of the Islamic East will never find a decent life based on noble ideals except in Islam. He believes that nationalism in Islam is more complete, purer, nobler, and higher than it is on the lips of the Europeans and in their writings. In everything related to the issues worrying the world's politicians and sociologists—internationalism, nationalism, socialism, capitalism, Bolshevism, war, the distribution of wealth, relations between producer and consumer—in all of these, al-Banna says, Islam has immersed itself and laid down for the world rules which will secure for it all the benefits therein. He believes that the movement is a universal and all-embracing one. It has not passed by anything worthy in any other movement without acquainting itself thoroughly with it and reaching conclusions.

The principles of the Brethren, which are thus said to embrace every religious, political, social, and economic aspect of life, are usually summed up in six broad aims:

1. **Scientific:** To explain the Holy Koran in precise terms, interpreting it and referring back to its origins and universal elements, completely

revealing it in the spirit of the age, and defending it from falsehoods and suspicions. (In this they are said to tread the path taken fifty years earlier by Muhammad 'Abduh, who set out to prove that Islam was compatible with the spirit of the age and in harmony with all science and knowledge. He therefore dealt with matters far beyond the scope of religion.)

2. **Practical:** To rally the Egyptian nation and all the Islamic nations around these Koranic principles, to imbue the peoples with the spirit of the Koran, and to bridge differences between the viewpoints of the various Islamic sects.

3. **Economic:** To increase the national wealth, liberating and protecting it; to raise the standard of living; to achieve social justice between individuals and classes, social security for all citizens, and equal opportunity for all. This principle is aimed to serve the workers who had been the backbone of the movement, put a limit to foreign influence in the economy, animate local industries, and enable the workers to organize themselves in trade unions.

4. **Social Work:** Social welfare and social service; the fight against ignorance, disease, poverty, and vice; and the encouragement of useful, benevolent, and charitable works.

5. **Patriotic:** To liberate the Nile valley and all other Arab countries and parts of the Islamic fatherland from all foreign domination; provision of assistance to Islamic minorities everywhere to secure their rights; unqualified support for Arab unity and working for an Islamic league; sincere furtherance of world cooperation based on high and worthy ideals; and institution of a sound state that can put the rules and injunctions of Islam into practice.

6. **Universal:** The promotion of universal peace and a humanitarian civilization, both material and spiritual, on the basis of Islamic principles, proclaiming fraternity for all and providing the practical means to its attainment in a world yearning for a virtuous and spiritual life.[25]

Finally, in the Brethren's dealings with the various factors around them, certain general principles are elucidated. These pertain to the Brethren's methods of work as well as their aims. In part, these principles require the following:

1. Avoidance of theological controversies, as the Brethren belong to no one special sect in Islam. On the contrary, they seek and work for the unification of the various viewpoints in Islam.

2. Avoidance of domination by notables and men of importance, as well as political bodies and parties, since the mission of Islam is one of unity, not diversity.
3. Belief in the gradual process. This does not prevent the Brethren from seeking to realize their aims through power: the power of faith and doctrine, the power of unity and solidarity, and the power of the arm and weapon. But they would use force only when nothing else avails.
4. Setting up a religious government.
5. Arab unity and Islamic unity.
6. Revival of the caliphate as the symbol of Islamic unity.
7. Any (European) country which has attacked or is engaged in aggression against the Islamic homeland will be stopped by a holy war— *jihad*.[26]

It will be seen from the above survey that, although their aims and principles are all-embracing and cover every aspect of life, the Brethren have managed to color all their activities with a special religious tinge. That the movement came as a strong reaction to the state of affairs in Egypt at the time—and resulted largely from the inevitable processes of borrowing from the West—is apparent from a letter written by al-Banna in the early days of the Brethren in which he says: "In our Egyptian society, the norms of morality have been torn to pieces and the standards of virtue have crumbled. . . . The engines of destruction are to be noticed on all sides: young men and women, families and individuals, are shattered body and soul."[27]

That the movement was spurred by a great and genuine fervor is also clear. The memorandum *Toward the Light* concludes with the following words: "We place ourselves, our talents, and all we possess at the disposal of any organization or government which would step forward with the Islamic nation to advancement and progress. We shall answer the call and we shall be the redemption."

The failure of the Brethren to strike real roots in Egyptian society and politics can be ascribed to several other factors, though all of them seem subsidiary to the one mentioned above. One of these was their indiscriminate anti-Westernism. Concentrating on the evils, real and imagined, of the Western way of life, they condemned Western civilization as materialistic and essentially nonreligious. The Muslim Brethren, moreover, fell short of their own ideal of peace and the pursuit of their ends by peaceful means when they themselves resorted to terrorism and violence. Many of the movement's potential supporters among Egypt's Muslim intelligentsia found themselves disillusioned by the growing preoccupation with seizing political power, to the neglect of basic reforms in modern Islam.

Developments in Egypt in the early fifties also proved unfavorable to the Brethren. The rise of the free officers after the revolt of July 23, 1952, and the announcement that the new regime was prepared to implement a basic reform program robbed the organization of its main moral ground for opposing the government. The failure of the movement's leaders to grasp the full implications of the new political situation, and their subsequent refusal to cooperate with the new regime, may well have deprived them of a unique opportunity to establish the Brethren solidly in the life of the new Egypt.

A probably even more decisive failure on the part of the Brethren was the antagonism the organization managed to arouse among educated modern Muslims. Its educational philosophy was an ideal that confined its followers to a rigid Islamic fundamentalism and excluded them from the ever-expanding opportunities of secular education. The Muslim intellectual of contemporary Egypt has been thoroughly exposed to the ideas and achievements of at least one culture other than his own. He finds himself fairly at home in the intellectual worlds of both the West and Arab Islam. The Muslim Brethren, on the other hand, have, through an exclusive concentration on Arab and Islamic history and religion, virtually disqualified themselves from belonging to this elite Muslim group. Moreover, in thus circumscribing their own intellectual horizons "they fell short of the ideal of Muslim scholars, an ideal first inculcated in Islamic society during the golden age of Arab Islam, when the new faith was eminently receptive to thought as alien as that of Aristotle."[28]

Insufficiently equipped to hold their own among Muslim intellectuals, the Brethren could not hope to attain a position of intellectual leadership in their own country. A typical criticism in this vein was leveled by Gen. Muhammad Naguib, a devout Muslim himself, in his book *Egypt's Destiny*: "What most of the Muslim Brethren wanted," he wrote, "was to go back to the days of the Sultan Salah al-Din [Saladin] when Egypt was a theocratic state. The rest of us, while sympathizing with the desire to apply the teachings of Muhammad to modern life, were convinced that to do so blindly was to spell disaster. The rebirth of Egypt . . . depended on the continued modernization of its social, political and economic institutions. . . . This does not mean that I and my colleagues have decided to turn our backs on the Islamic faith. . . . The injunctions of the Koran have as much meaning in application today as they ever did, provided they are interpreted with due regard for the great changes that have occurred in human society since the Prophet preached his message."[29]

The dilemma that faced the Muslim Brethren—and that will always face any fundamentalist Islamic movement—is essentially this: Can a Muslim regime be secularized without jeopardizing the basic religious structure of its Islamic culture and civilization? No answer to this question can be final. It is obvious, however—as one Western student of the Muslim Brethren has put it—that no fruitful compromise can be assured between two so essentially divergent points of view. "A religious group which takes its stand on a crystallized and sacrosanct law cannot logically tolerate any breach in its ramparts."[30]

The deadlock seems complete and the circle unbreakable. While the Muslim Brethren have failed to enlist the allegiance of educated Egyptian Muslims, no Egyptian Muslim has succeeded in establishing a viable contemporary movement to carry forward the reforms and implement the vision of Sheikh Muhammad 'Abduh and his band of Islamic revivalists.

4 | The Secularist Response

Islam and Arab Nationalism: Two Approaches

The Muslim Brethren, under their various guides and throughout their checkered history, consistently maintained a non-nationalist, if not an anti-nationalist, stance that included a distinct distaste for the Pan-Arab school of modern European-style nationalism. If the term "nation" is to mean—as the original ideologues of the nationalist creed in Central Europe understood it—a natural division of the human race endowed by God with its own character, which its members must, as a duty, preserve as pure and inviolable, then Islam as a whole stands in opposition to nationalism. Johann Gottfried Herder, one of secular nationalism's leading and earliest exponents, maintained that secular nationalism as a doctrine teaches that, because nations are separate natural entities ordained by God, the best political arrangement is obtained when each nation forms a state of its own. States in which there are more than one nation, he argued, are unnatural, oppressive, and, finally, doomed to decay. Herder's argument here, as a leading political scientist has pointed out, "is not so much that in such states one element may dominate the others; rather, that they sin against the principle of diversity, for in them the different nations always run the risk of losing their identity, and are not able fully to cultivate their originality."[1]

As noted in the previous chapter, Hasan al-Banna made a clear-cut distinction between the concepts of patriotism and nationalism, maintaining that the European interpretation of these two terms was not acceptable to the Brethren. Another leading exponent of the ideology of the Muslim Brethren, Muhammad al-Ghazzali, describes nationalism as "a return to the first *jahiliyya* (pre-Islamic tribalism)." He holds the doctrine responsible for the loss of Muslim unity—just as he makes the separation of state and religion responsible for the loss of the Ottoman Empire. He writes, "The nationalist approach was our most crucial borrowing from the West and it formed the cornerstone in building the modern state." He goes on to vent his dismay by posing the question: "How could we abandon the Islamic for the nationalist government?" After all, he asserts, the bond of Islam is stronger than kinship based on common blood. Elsewhere, debating the issue with Khalid Muhammad Khalid, al-Ghazzali asserts that nationalism spells ruin for Islam. He explains: "Inasmuch as Islam is a general nationality among its followers throughout the five continents, it has grown weaker in proportion to the growing strength of the particular nationalism."[2]

It is in Hasan al-Banna's writings that we find the most authoritative and forceful expression of the ideology not only of the Muslim Brethren but of Islam as a whole in what is considered its true and pristine form. Al-Banna's approach to the subject of nationalism, while in no way less hostile than that of al-Ghazzali's, is somewhat more involved and sophisticated. He never comes out openly against Pan-Arab nationalism; rather, he seeks to make it seem a mere satellite of Islam and the Islamic "fatherland" as he understands them. His attitude to nationalism has been described as an attempt to neutralize it by declaring the whole Islamic world to be one "fatherland," transcending geographical and ethnic boundaries and dedicated to high principles and pure and correct beliefs "and the truth which God has made the source of light and guidance for the whole world."

According to al-Banna, while Muslims are duty bound to assist in the struggle for emancipation from foreign dominance and oppression, they owe allegiance both to what he calls *al-qawmiyya al-khassa* (the particular nationality—in this case Egyptian) and *al-jinsiyya al-'amma* (the general nationality—Islamic). "The Brethren," he writes, "respect their particular nationality on the consideration that it is the first foundation of their cherished [Islamic] renaissance. . . . After this, they support Arab unity as the next step toward this renaissance. Then they strive for Pan-Islamism as a fence of protection for the general Islamic fatherland."[3] In their program, the Muslim Brethren speak of *wataniyya* (patriotism or territorial nationality) and *qawmiyya* (ethnic nationalism), referring to the Egyptian fatherland in the former and to the Muslim nation (*umma*) in the latter sense. It will be noted that in this scheme of things there appears to be no place for *'uruba* (Arabism) or for *qawmiyya 'Arabiyya* (Arab nationalism).

It is generally understood, however, by Muslim Arabs as well as outsiders, that Arabism is virtually inseparable from Islam, and that the doctrines of Pan-Arabism and Pan-Islamism are thus closely related aspirations. This approach is based mainly on the argument that it was the Arabs who gave their language to Islam—and to its holy book—and also carried its mission victoriously over a large part of the globe. One of the first Muslim-Arab thinkers and activists of modern times made an earnest attempt to place Pan-Arabism before Pan-Islamism. In fact, he sought to replace the latter by the former by concentrating on the *umma* as founded by the Arabs themselves. This was 'Abd al-Rahman al-Kawakibi (1849–1903), who might rightly be considered the first orthodox Muslim reformist to introduce the modern European creed of nationalism to the Arab world. Against all received Islamic doctrine and practice, he defined the umma as "the sum of individuals with a common ancestry or *watan* (homeland, fatherland), language and religion"—thus for the first time applying the Western concept of nation to the Arabs and linking the foundation and expansion of Islam with the Arabs to such an extent that he arrived at a complete identification of the Arab Islamic state with Islam.[4]

Al-Kawakibi was born to a family of Aleppo, Syria, and was of Kurdish origin. He had a traditional Arabic and Turkish education in his native city, then worked there as official and journalist until he fell foul of the Turkish authorities and decided to move to Cairo in 1898. There he frequented the circle of Muhammad 'Abduh and Rashid Rida and wrote for *Al-Manar* and other periodicals. He produced two books, one on the characteristics of tyranny and the other incorporating his program for the reform of Islam and the attainment of Muslim-Arab unity. Some of his circumstances combined "to lead him to draw out with great clarity certain implications of the teachings of the [Islamic] reformers, and develop them in the direction of Arab nationalism." In their essence, al-Kawakibi's ideas spring from the same starting point as those propagated by Afghani, 'Abduh, and their disciples—mainly the decay of Islam and the urgent need to reform it and free the Muslims from foreign dominance. But al-Kawakibi chose to lay emphasis only on certain teachings of his predecessors and peers, especially where Arabs and Arabism were concerned. Both to get rid of Turkish despotism and to liberate the Arabs, he maintained that a shift in the balance of power inside the umma was imperative—a shift from the Turks back to the Arabs, because only the Arabs can save Islam from decay. "Because of the central position of the Arabian Peninsula in the *umma* and the Arabic language in Islamic thought—but also because of other reasons—Arabian Islam is comparatively free from modern corruption, and the Beduin are free from the moral decay and passivity of despotism."[5] The center of gravity must therefore move back to Arabia, and there should be an Arabian caliph of the line of Quraysh, elected by representatives of the umma. This caliph should have religious authority throughout the Muslim world and be assisted in the exercise of this authority by a consultative council nominated by the Muslim rulers. The caliph should also have temporal authority in the Hijaz, assisted by a local council.[6]

Al-Kawakibi was obviously the precursor of those Arab nationalist thinkers who now insist that religion is an essential component of Arab nationalism—the others being language, land, a common history, and a shared cultural heritage. Among scholars, and historians, too, the idea is fairly widespread that Arabism is inseparable from Islam. Hamilton Gibb once formulated the following definition of Arab: "All those are Arabs for whom the central fact of history is the mission of Muhammad and the memory of the Arab empire, and who in addition cherish the Arabic tongue as their common possession."[7] Zeine N. Zeine, an Arabic-speaking scholar and historian, asserts that "Islam and Arab nationalism could not be divorced from each other. . . . Arab nationalism is both a political movement and a religious revival; it is both secular and theocratic; both a positive, constructive force aiming at the ideal of uniting all the Arab countries and a negative, uncompromising attitude towards the West." According to Zeine, the true birth of Arab nationalism took place with the rise of Islam:

> Even as a generalization, there is no support for the contention that Arab nationalism was born as an "intellectual movement" in literary circles and secret societies and especially through the fiery poems of Arab poets. Islam was revealed by an Arabian prophet, in the Arabic language, in Arabia. . . . It was the Muslim Arabs of Arabia that the Prophet glorified in these words: "Ye are the best people (*umma* or nation) that has been raised up unto mankind." One of the basic aims of Islam was to replace the narrow blood and tribal ties existing among the Arabs in pagan days . . . by a broader and wider "religious patriotism" found in Islam itself. The Arabs were to be united into one great community, the Community of the Faithful—the *Umma* or the nation of Islam. . . . The Arab nation, *al-umma al-'Arabiyya* was, thus, a nation originally born out of Islam. Islam was the prime creator of the national life and political unity of

Muslim Arabs. This "religious nationalism" remains an indelible part of the hearts and minds of the Arabs.[8]

One leading Arab nationalist thinker of our own day, 'Abd al-Rahman al-Bazzaz, bases his analysis on a premise identical to that of al-Kawakibi. For him, "the fact that the Prophet Muhammad was an Arab was not a matter of chance; a genius, he belonged to a nation of great abilities and qualities." In a booklet printed in Baghdad in 1952 titled *Islam and Arab Nationalism,* al-Bazzaz accuses the *shu'ubiyya* (non-Arab Muslim detractors of Arabs) of the desire to separate Muhammad from the Arab nation. The Arabs, he argues, were the backbone of Islam. "They were the first to be addressed in the verses of Revelation; they were the *Muhajirin* and the *Ansar;* their swords conquered countries and lands, and on the whole they are as Umar described them in a saying of his: 'Do not attack the Arabs and humiliate them for they are the essence of Islam.'"[9]

According to al-Bazzaz, after this "clear exposition of the intellectual problems and the factors that contribute to the mistaken belief that there is a contradiction between the principles of Islam and Arab nationalism, the factors and assumptions of nationalism are varied, and we do not intend to analyze them in this lecture. But we can assert that modern nationalism is based on language, history, literature, customs and qualities."

Language, then, "is the primary tenet of our nationalist creed; it is the soul of our nation and the primary aspect of its life. The nation that loses its language is destined to disappear and perish. It is the good fortune of the Arabs that their language is not only a national duty but also a religious one and the influence of Islam on its propagation and preservation is very great." Moreover, al-Bazzaz adds, "the Arabs had a glorious history before Islam, and their history is even more glorious and of great moment after Islam. The Muslim Arab, when he exalts his heroes, partakes of two emotions, that of the pious Muslim and that of the proud nationalist."

In fact, says al-Bazzaz, "the most glorious pages of Muslim history are the pages of Muslim Arab history, as the Western historians themselves admit." As for Arabic literature, "which is the result of Arab feeling and emotion all through the ages, its greatest and most venerable parts came from Islam, and indeed the Koran itself, in addition to being a book of direction, is the most awesome example of the elevated prose which the Arab . . . exalts." As for the pre-Islamic poetry, and especially descriptive and wisdom verse, there is in most of it nothing that contradicts the spirit of Islam.

So much for the first three foundations of Arab nationalism—language, history, and literature. The fourth, which consists of "the good Arab customs and qualities," again poses no problem. Here, too, there obtains "similarity, not to say complete identity, between the ethical ideal of Arab nationalism and that prescribed by Islam."

Turning from the cultural aspects of Arab nationalism to an examination of it "as a political movement striving to unite the Arabs and to give them self-government," al-Bazzaz again finds no discrepancy between Arabism and Islam. The Arab national movement, he writes, is democratic, socialist, popular, and cooperative. Islam, "although it did not lay down in detail the organization of government, requires consultation, and does, without any doubt, accept completely democratic organization." Its financial legislation and juristic principles are, in essence, socialist. It is enough to recall something of the life of the Prophet and the caliphs to realize the extent of the cooperative and popular spirit of Islam. This being the case, "the national movement for which we call does not in any way contradict Islam."

To say this, however, is not to imply a call for Pan-Islamism. "To say that Islam does not contradict the Arab national spirit is one thing. . . . It is not natural to expect the union of Iraq with Iran or Afghanistan, for instance, before Syria and Jordan are united."

It follows, al-Bazzaz concludes, that the call to unite the Arabs—and this is the clearest and most important objective of Arab nationalism—is the practical step that must precede the call for Pan-Islamism. "It is strange, therefore, to find that some of those who call themselves supporters of Pan-Islamism in the Arab countries are the most violent opponents of Pan-Arabism. . . . No fundamental contradiction or clear opposition exists between Arab nationalism and Islam."

In various versions and formulations this approach to the subject of Islam in relation to the Arab nationalist doctrine has also been advanced by conservative Muslim Arabs and even by some of the 'ulema in the Arab world. But only up to a point, and only rather equivocally and halfheartedly. Gustav von Grunebaum furnishes a concise summary of the creed of Pan-Arab nationalism:

> The community of the Arabs, i.e., the Arabic-speaking peoples, stretching from the Persian Gulf to the Atlantic inhabits regions that present considerable geographical similarities and that possess great economic potentialities. Their population represents "a young race that has its origin in the harmonious fusion of various human strains which Islam has brought together in one crucible." Within this community there is no distinction of color or race. The blood mixture has resulted in a great similarity of intellectual and moral aptitudes even

though the variety of physical types has been maintained. This Arab "race" is extremely "prolific, courageous, enthusiastic, enduring, patient, and guided by the spirit of fairness." The absolute superiority of Arabic over all other languages allows it a great civilizational role. The influence of Islam confers on "Arabism" a sense of spiritual values which sets it off against the materialism of the West.[10]

This last claim made by Arab nationalists for Islam, as well as innumerable other examples, some of which have been referred to above, seems to justify von Grunebaum's contention that "from its very inception the theory of Arab nationalism was molded by the necessity to establish its compatibility with an Islamic outlook."[11] This is, in fact, the key to the whole subject; it certainly furnishes one explanation for the seeming indecisiveness and lack of finality we encounter in the pronouncements made on the subject by many Arab nationalist thinkers and ideologues. Some of these pronouncements indeed give the impression that they are often made on the spur of the moment rather than being measured and well-thought-out ideological statements. This is especially the case where earlier pronouncements are concerned.

An articulate and fairly consistent formulation of the problem has come relatively recently. Sati' al-Husri (1880–1968) was generally recognized as the leading exponent of secular Pan-Arab nationalism. A thoroughgoing nationalist of the school of Fichte and Herder, al-Husri—unlike many Arab nationalists of his generation—was uncompromising in the separation he advocated between religion and nationalist affiliation. He coined the Pan-Arab slogan *"al-din lillah wal-watan lil-jami'"* (religion is a matter between the individual and God, while the fatherland is the concern of all).

Addressing himself to the subject of religion and its role in the creation of nations, al-Husri points out that universal religions—like Christianity and Islam, for example—that are open to all and proselytize and embrace many regions and peoples, are opposed to nationalism. However, these religions can create ties equivalent in strength to ties of nationalism only to the degree that they are successful in spreading a language. Contemplating the situation in Europe in the nineteenth century, al-Husri perceived that national unity does not necessarily follow religious unity, and religious differences do not prevent the realization of national unity. The lesson for the Arabs is clear: "Arabism was not in the past nor is it in the present restricted to any sect or religion. The cooperation between Arab compatriots, in spite of the differences in their religions, was a strength in the past just as it was in the modern Arab awakening. . . . Therefore, we should be concerned with the spread of the spirit of cooperation among different sects and showing them that they are brothers, and that it is their duty to place nationalist goals above sectarian considerations."[12]

Even al-Husri tends to be wary on the subject of religion. A nationalist, he asserts, is not irreligious. To argue that nationalism is irreligious and demands the abolition of religion is to misunderstand the true nature of the nationalist doctrine. Moreover, Pan-Arabism does not stand in opposition to Pan-Islamism. "The idea of Islamic unity," he argues, "is broader and more inclusive than the concept of Arab unity. We are therefore correct in asserting that he who opposes Arab unity opposes Islamic unity as well."[13]

While al-Husri was trying, somewhat ingeniously, to channel the beliefs of the Pan-Islamists into support for Arab unity, another contemporary Arab thinker, 'Abd al-Rahman 'Azzam, the first secretary-general of the League of Arab States and a noted Muslim scholar, makes a very clear distinction between Islam and Arabism. In a lecture delivered in May 1960, 'Azzam made it quite clear that the main object of the Islamic mission was "the creation of an Islamic nation and not of an Arab nation." He further argued that the coming into being of an Arab nation "was never planned or intended by the Arab Prophet or his followers."[14] Those peoples whom Islam Arabized "were only a by-product of Arab influence," and this "by-product nation, curiously enough, was never seriously conscious of its ethnic or cultural existence until it was aroused to the new doctrine of nationalism by its European conquerors." It was only after this arousal that it became "convenient for the Arabs, and in certain cases even necessary, to use [the doctrine of nationalism] as an instrument of defense against those conquerors."

'Azzam almost gives the impression that for him the fact that the last great prophet was an Arab was a mere accident. Muhammad belonged to a great Arab tribe, to be sure; yet "nothing was more distasteful to him than to glorify his tribe or race, because in Islam there was no room for discrimination whatsoever, on account of either color, language or race." According to the prophet's creed, his followers should live in the service of the one "God of the Universe." "You are one nation and I am your God to worship," says the Koran. Thus, 'Azzam concludes, "what the Prophet and his followers planned was not an Arab nation, but one Muslim nation living under one God and one law." It was this nation that endured for thirteen centuries after the rise of Islam. "From the seventh to the twentieth century, Arabs, Turks, Iranians, Afghans, Indians, Indonesians, Berbers, Chinese, Europeans, and Africans had one citizenship. They were all considered Muslim citizens, irrespective of their origin or the form of local government under which they lived. They had one loyalty and one permanent devotion to the Muslim nation since, in spite of the breakup of the Caliphate into several states, Muslims continued to live under the *shari'a* from which all citizens derived equal rights and duties applicable wherever they happened to be."

The process of Arabization, however, followed the progress of Islam and finally embraced the whole of what is now the Arab world. "The Arabic language became the language of the new empire and, being also the language of the Koran, it was viewed by all Muslims as the eternal language on earth and may even be that of paradise. Even those Christians and Jews who do not themselves speak Arabic realized the importance of the language of the Islamic Empire. Thus they encouraged their children to use it, and in time they too were Arabized." This process—which for 'Azzam was only a by-product of the Islamic mission—continued for several centuries. "Even when the Arab Empire was broken up, the tempo of Arabization gathered momentum in a manner unrelated to the state. It was during the tenth and eleventh centuries, as a consequence of the rise of the Qaramita in Eastern and Northern Arabia and their conquest of Mecca, that mass emigration from Arabia was set in motion and later headed towards Africa. The Qaramita movement, with its communistic and revolutionary tendencies, developed into a malignant growth in the body of the Islamic Empire. . . . Big tribes were involved in its rise and fall, and some had to move in tens of thousands to the North and West." Again, when things did not go well in Tunisia and the rest of their North African domain for the Fatimid caliphs of Egypt, they sought to suppress this insurrection not by troops alone but by encouraging mass emigration of Arab tribes recently settled in Egypt. Under the banners of the famous tribes of Bani Hilal and Bani Sulayn, the Arabs moved westward in very large numbers. In the course of time they, to a large extent, brought about the Arabization of North Africa.

While Arabism has had a largely accidental relation to Islam, it has nothing to do with race either. All nations are a mixture of races and cultures. The Arabs are no exception, 'Azzam asserts. "In order to help clarify this," he relates, "I proposed to a select few of Arab thinkers, meeting in Baghdad some twenty five years ago, at the time when Nazi racialist theories were attracting increasing attention, a certain definition of Arabism, as opposed to racialism. This definition ran as follows: 'Those who live in Arab lands, speak the Arabic language, live an Arab way of life and feel proud of being Arab, are Arabs.' This definition was later accepted by the Conference that laid the Pact of the League of Arab States in 1945."

Having disposed of this problem of definition, 'Azzam turns to the subject of modern Arab nationalism, "a concept of relatively recent origin." Before the turn of the present century, he writes, the old Arab nation was not conscious of the modern idea of nationalism. "These Western ideas flourished in Europe itself and never had much appeal to the rich, humane and universal culture of Islam." In Europe itself, the ideas of nationalism have only developed in modern times. "The Germans and Russians, for instance, did not develop nationalistic patriotism until late in the nineteenth century. Peoples were concerned with loyalty only to kings, emperors, or leaders. Patriotism was tribal and not national." Amongst the Arabs, the Egyptians were perhaps the first people to adopt the new creed of nationalism and to think and behave as patriotic Egyptians. "The Napoleonic invasion of Egypt in 1798 was an aftermath of the French Revolution. While, militarily, the invasion failed, yet the ideas for which the French Revolution stood remained."

Elsewhere in the Arab world things were different. There the old order prevailed. Of course, signs of patriotism were noticeable here and there. "The Arab national revolt of 1916 directed by the late King Husain, the Sharif of Mecca, was only one of these symptoms in a changing Arab world. Arabism as such was not yet a popular creed, even in Arabia itself. The loyalty of the Arabs to the Muslim nation was superior to every other loyalty. It was not the revolt in Mecca against the Ottoman Turk that gave birth to Arabism. On the contrary, it was the defeat that befell the Turks in World War I that awakened the Arabs and stimulated Arab nationalism, which henceforth became an instrument of resistance. The frustration encountered by the Muslims in Arab and other lands as a result of the collapse of the last Islamic Empire was another important factor which stimulated Arab nationalism and, indeed, other national movements in other Islamic lands."

To the Muslims this defeat was calamitous. All Muslim countries fell under colonial control in one way or another. "Muslims, dedicated to their freedom and their dignity as they have always been, were unwilling to accept the humiliation of foreign rule. Thus in nationalism they saw a means of salvation."

It was only in the 1920s that Arab nationalism, together with other Muslim national movements, was born. In the meantime, Egyptian nationalism was making victorious strides—and the British were ultimately forced to recognize Egyptian independence. "Of all Arab lands, however, only Syria and Iraq supported the idea of Arab unity. . . . In Egypt, local nationalism was deeply rooted, especially as it had already won some notable victories. That is why it took many years of preaching before Egypt became convinced in the broader new faith of Arab nationalism and Arab unity." As for the Arabian Peninsula itself, and the Arabs of Africa, the old Muslim loyalties remained. "It was only shortly before World War II that victory for Arab unity loomed on the horizon. Egypt was then undergoing a vital change in thinking and attitude. This trend was given further impetus as a result of Zionist designs against Arab Palestine. During the war, for propaganda purposes, both the Allies and the Axis Powers felt it necessary and useful to flirt with Arab national unity. By radio, press and private approaches both expressed their sympathy and support for Arab unity. This explains Anthony Eden's declaration which initiated the conferences that culminated in the Pact of the League of Arab States in 1945." With this event, "Arabism became an article of faith for all Arabs from the Atlantic on the West to the Persian Gulf in the East, and the League has become since its instrument of expression."[15]

'Azzam's views have been surveyed at some length because they present a coherent and comprehensive summary of a stand which, while not unrepresentative of the ordinary Muslim thinker's attitudes and predilections, is propounded by a man who is neither a rigid Muslim traditionalist nor a radical Pan-Arab nationalist. His position as to the relation between Islam and Arabism is worth contemplating as a middle-of-the-road viewpoint that tries to give each side its due.

As a current commentary on this whole controversy, and as a fitting footnote to the discussion summarized above, it is worthwhile citing here the opinion of one of the leaders of the Palestinian national movement—an opinion aired almost in passing and under the pressure of events. The Iranian Revolution of 1979, whose strong Islamic undertones were clear from the very beginning, gave rise to high hopes in many Arab nationalist circles. This obviously was due more to the "anti-imperialist" and anti-Zionist nature of the movement than to its fundamentalist Islamic character. Nevertheless, some Arab nationalist quarters appeared to be favorably impressed and pleased by the Islamic revivalism that the revolution was said to inaugurate. However, in the midst of these jubilations and cries of approval, Salah Khalaf, one of the leaders of the Palestine Liberation Organization (who was also known by his clandestine name, Abu Iyad) declared in a newspaper interview that the Iranian revolution augured no good tidings for the Arab world if this latter were to be swept by the kind of Islamic fundamentalism that was sweeping Iran.

The reason Khalaf gave for his premonitions was both interesting and instructive. The Arab world, he said, was the home of at least sixteen million Christians. "What has brought Christians and Muslims together within the Arab domain," he explained, "were Arabism and Arab nationalism, not Islam."[16]

Arab Nationalism: The Search for an Ideology

In the mid-1950s Gustav von Grunebaum remarked on the fact that the Arabic-speaking world had not, up till then, been able to develop an adequate self-image — "adequate in the sense that it could reconcile emotional purposiveness and a reasonable respect for facts."[17] This was no doubt largely true at the time it was written — and it continues to be fairly valid today. Up to the late 1950s, it is true, no Arab writer has successfully analyzed the meaning and fundamentals of Arab culture and Arab history to the Arabs themselves, and a balance between what von Grunebaum has called emotional purposiveness and a sufficient respect for facts is yet to be struck in the Arabic literature of self-interpretation and self-appraisal.

From the Arabs' point of view, however, two sets of reasons can be advanced in explaining this phenomenon. The first has to do with the fact that the Arabs are by no means alone in this lack of a literary culture of a marked tendency to develop "an adequate self-image." After all, what people or culture has developed a self-image that would be considered adequate or acceptable collectively by its own members, let alone by outsiders? The other set of reasons has to do with the fact that Arabs have not been too prone to giving much thought to the task of defining the meaning or analyzing the content of their culture or their history, because Arab thinkers and intellectuals see no necessity, or good enough reason, for doing so. The meaning of Arab culture, its content, its fundamentals, and its unity are things that have always been taken for granted by the Arabs themselves.

Be that as it may, it is evident that by the second half of the 1950s a new phase in Arab thinking began. By that time, Arab culture and the Arab identity became epitomized for the Arab intellectual in one comprehensive concept — Arab nationalism. The controversies that had raged briefly in the 1930s and 1940s about what constitutes Arab culture, whether the Arabs have a uniform and comprehensive cultural heritage, or what constitutes an Arab nation, virtually dropped out of fashion and became somewhat irrelevant. Few Arab intellectuals, if any, now found it necessary to write about the Arabs' shared history, their race consciousness, their common language, folklore, traditions, or their common cause. All that became something to be taken for granted. Even such a cardinal question as the compatibility of Arab nationalism with Islam, and the mutual relation between the two, was put aside. Arab nationalism in the 1950s became a living force, not to be justified theoretically by marshaling historical and sociological data, but to be embodied in an all-embracing creed. This creed did not have to be based on any empirical findings or analyses, nor did it depend on a precise definition of Arabism or Arab nationality. It was presented as a philosophy of life as well as an ideal of government, a credo as well as a manifesto. It set out, in fact, to be a complete ideology to match the rival world ideologies of Communism and democratic capitalism. Arab though it was, in the sense that it was formulated by Arabs for their own nation, this new ideology professed to be open to all and to offer a way of life for humanity as a whole after the two world giants had finished their fight and canceled each other out.

Discussion of Arab nationalism as a coherent, all-embracing ideology is thus a relatively recent development, especially stimulated following the events of the 1956 Suez War and its aftermath. Previously, in the late 1930s and early 1940s, the whole controversy over Arab nationalism and whether there could be a theory of it at all was contained in three fairly slim volumes published between 1938 and 1941. This discussion was ably summarized by Hazem Zaki Nuseibeh and now seems quite out of date. [18]

The bulk of the discussions summarized in this section is taken from the pages of the periodical *Al-adab*, a monthly that started publication in Beirut in 1953 but has been all-Arab in its contents and outspokenly Pan-Arab in orientation. It was in this periodical, as far as can be ascertained, that the demand for an "Arab ideology" was first raised by the Syrian educator and Arab nationalist thinker Abdullah 'Abd al-Dayim. His call was published in the September 1955 issue of the periodical, and it was followed by a series of articles in which an effort was made by the various respondents to formulate such an ideology. The controversy that followed continued for some years, but none of the participants questioned the validity of the idea itself.

The first and most systematic effort at a formulation of an all-embracing Arab ideology was made by Sa'dun Hammadi, then of Wisconsin University and later to become Iraqi foreign minister for many years. His paper, published in two lengthy parts, was entitled "The Question of Arab Nationalism: Problem, Solution and Method."[19] His point of departure was that, despite all that had been said and written on the subject during the previous fifty years, "Arab nationalism is still in need of a comprehensive theory of life."

It is true, Hammadi admits, that the spirit of Arab nationalism opened up new vistas of life and thought and aroused "a tangible aspiration to a better life"; but this has not expressed itself in an inclusive and well-knit theory that could illuminate the road to a national renaissance. Direct positive action alone, it is true, can overcome present evils and pave the way to a healthy and progressive future. It also demands "an effort of thought, to discover the principle and the involved logic of the present Arab way of life, if blind aspiration is ever to become organized action under conscious guidance." The "rotten present" of the Arabs has a logic of its own, Hammadi asserts, determined not only by the material bases of their social existence. The problem, therefore, is a definable one and has a definite solution.

A society, Hammadi explains, whether healthy or ailing, is of a certain structure or system. It has a unique nature to which any reform of it must be appropriate. The function of thought is to find a solution suitable to its problem; otherwise, the national spirit will continue probing in a blind alley from which no devotion or sacrifice can extricate it. Hammadi's essay is "an initial attempt to discuss some of the theoretical premises of nationalist action." The differences of opinion between active nationalists as to the means and even the ends of their actions point to the need for a new understanding of the problem.

Hammadi first summarizes what he considers a common misunderstanding on the part of those Arabs who see their own national future too simply in terms borrowed from Western democracy, or from German and Italian totalitarianism and Marxism. He then proceeds to present his own diagnosis of what is wrong with Arab society—namely a deeply retarded development, which he says dates from the disintegration of Arab culture in the later stages of the Abbasid dynasty. In his view, this disintegration followed the Arab conquests and the expansion of the Arab domain. The extension of this domain over so many different peoples and nationalities ultimately led to the Arabs' loss of their own cohesion, harmony, and, finally, their independence. Foreign intellectual trends infiltrated and diluted the Arab spirit, inspired and led by Islam. The Abbasid era was thus one of weakness and decay underneath all the flowering of Arab civilization for which that era became famous. A downward trend then began that, since the original cause was external, affected society as a whole rather than its members. Great individuals still emerged, but deterioration finally overtook the individual's life as well.

The disintegration is now ubiquitous and deep; it is not confined to one aspect of Arab life, nor limited to its systems and laws. It is a malady whose symptoms can be traced to a weakness in the soul of the individual Arab. Of these symptoms, says Hammadi, the first and worst are egotism and rapacity—a kind of self-seeking wholly undeterred by ethical considerations or the public spirit. This selfishness has pervaded every walk of life in Arab society, however small and unimportant. Hammadi sees it everywhere—in the very language of official pronouncements, in "what is called etiquette," in the lack of dissent or criticism; it is also all-pervasive, to be found in the home, in the office, at school, in the clubs, and in the professions. The danger inherent in such a state of mind is all the more apparent since the national salvation of the Arabs calls for a generation of Arabs willing to sacrifice personal interests for the public good. National revival needs men willing to give to it, not men who expect to benefit from it, Hammadi observes.

The second weakness of the Arab individual today is his lack of practical initiative, his inability to try to realize his aspirations by his own efforts. Instead, he sometimes projects a purely imaginary world of pretenses unsubstantiated by any positive action—so much so that talking has become very largely the art of evading realities and of self-delusion. That is why most Arab political parties present programs so nearly identical in their professions of independence, equality, and justice—though, in fact, they differ widely in the amount of sincerity, consistency, and industry with which they work for them.

This personal weakness appears also in the Arab's submission to what is accepted and traditional in many walks of life, even when it is harmful. School is the only place where the individual is to be found in revolt against the status quo. After leaving school he accepts the existing order and fits himself into it instead of breaking with it and joining a nucleus of the new order. Imitative, averse to change, and with a distaste for adventure, he prefers security in a bad and poor livelihood to a good and plentiful life which entails any risk.

Another weakness is the inclination to superstition and the dislike of anything scientific. Together, these enable him to escape from productive exertions into an unreal world, where grandiose hopes are supposed to be realized by boasting and believing in supernatural signs and portents. Thus, we find the average Arab individual a confused and undecided personality at a moment when the supreme need is for decision and resolution. Hence the instability of his opinions throughout the last half-century and the successive waves of conflicting doctrines that have swept the Arab lands one after another, in whichever direction the international situation seemed to point at the time. This was especially the case in and around the period of the Second World War.

From this diagnosis of the individual Arab's problem, Hammadi turns his attention to Arab society as a whole. First, he says, "the problem of Arab society is a national one, because it arises from this society's own experience. The world consists of nations, not individuals, and the Arab nation has its own unique experience; its present condition is the product of the peculiar circumstances of its entire history up to the present moment."

Secondly, the national problem lies in the will of the people, not in laws or systems. Some nationalist groups concentrate all their attention upon the systems that succeed in Arab society and regard their defects as the root of the trouble. Some, for instance, think that the division of the Arab world into small, weak nations is the first evil to be remedied, others believe foreign influence must first be eradicated; still others locate the root of all evil in the political system, the constitution, electoral laws, press laws, or party regulations. A fourth group traces every evil to the economic systems. But Hammadi says they are all putting the effects before the causes. A system is only the apparatus for the organization of society. The nature and efficiency of a system are determined by the character and condition of the people it governs. Systems do not create the backward or the advanced state of a society so much as reflect it.

Not that Hammadi thinks systems unimportant. He does not ignore the parts played by feudalism and imperialism in complicating the Arab problem, nor deny the need for combating these. The prevalent system maintains the present deplorable state of affairs; but the cause of both lies in a deeper social malady. What must be done, then, to start this society on the road to health and progress? Granting that revolution is the only way to a solution of the Arab problem, how, he asks, should it be planned? Could it be achieved by an external factor such as the intervention of a foreign power and the progress of world thought? Could it be brought about by changing the existing political and social systems, liberating them from foreign influence and liquidating feudalism? His answer is that the national character of the problem, as well as its depth, imposes the necessity of an internal movement toward revolution. This can be effected only by a patriotic, nationalist struggle, not by foreign political factors.

The basic character of this struggle for Arab nationalism is that it is voluntary. Its motive force is that of free will, not that of an external force or natural law. Whereas Marxism explains progress by the movement of matter, and Capitalism explains it by the laws of human nature, the Arab nationalist holds that man's free will is the central force in society. Man is the master: He created society out of his own free will. The story of human civilization is but the record of man's increasing control over nature and over the forces of evil.

The second characteristic of the struggle is its comprehensive aim. It is directed against everything that is rotten in the present, not against selected evils. Its aim is to create a new life for the Arabs and not to introduce a partial reform. It cannot be confined to the political sphere, for instance, because literature and the arts also play a vital part in any national renaissance.

Thirdly, the struggle must not only be voluntary and comprehensive, but also practical. A movement to transform Arab society, in which ignorance, poverty, and disease reign supreme, cannot indoctrinate the masses with its principles by theorizing; nor can it succeed wholly by sacrifice and effort on the part of the just and the good. It must also take the form of popular campaigns in support of direct, material demands that exemplify the spirit and purpose of the revolution.

The fourth and final question to which Hammadi offers an answer is— What is the final aim of Arab nationalism? Is it the liberation of Arab lands from occupation by foreign imperialism? Or is it the raising of the standard of living? Neither, by itself, he answers. Not even both together constitute the complete objective of Arab nationalism, although both are indubitably just and must be attained. These are incidental goals that will fade away when they have been realized; they are relative aims imposed by transient conditions.

The ultimate aim of Arab nationalism is Right (*al-haq*). There is in man an inborn, original tendency toward Right, which manifests itself in the civilizing work done by nations in the service of humanity. This tension toward Right has been eminently manifest in the civilizations the Arab nation has given to the world. The mission of Arabs today is the creation of a new Arab civilization whose highest principle shall be Right. The practice of this principle is respect for man. The new Arab civilization, if it is true to its aim, will revere man as the most precious being in the universe, for whose sake all else will be sacrificed and to whose service all nature will be enslaved. Man's happiness should be the criterion of the laws, his welfare the source of all legislation.

The organization of society upon this basis would imply three things. First, that the people are the source of all power. It follows that the political apparatus must be democratic, designed solely to reflect, in an organized manner, the will of the people. Secondly, in order to maintain the dignity of the individual and realize all his potentialities, the economic system must be one that is healthy, that excludes the exploitation of man and frees him from want; it must ensure the good life for each person, for no other reason but that he is a man. The third requisite is tolerance. National and religious tolerance is deeply embedded in the Arab tradition under Islam. Arab society, inheriting that principle of tolerance, is capable of raising Arab nationalism to a sublimity unknown to the intolerant nationalities of the West.

In foreign relations, this principle leads to respect for other nations, to cooperation with them to eliminate imperialism and exploitation, and to the establishment of peace. "Thus," Hammadi concludes, "the objection that democratic socialist nationalism is only a mixture of alien and independent doctrines is baseless. For socialism and freedom themselves are but the overflow from the well of a nationalism infused with this ethical principle—that is, one whose final aim is Right."

Hammadi's second essay, "Realism and Contemporary Arab Thought," is an attempt to "establish in outline one particular aspect of Arab nationalism—its Realism."[20] As a historical movement, Arab nationalism has passed the stage of "knowledge through feeling," which is that of the awakening of consciousness and the resurgence of soul. It has now to enter upon the phase of reason. In the march of history the dominant tendency is toward Right; the divided nations struggle to become united, subject nations to free themselves, societies to enlarge and consolidate civil liberties, and economic systems, also, to develop in the direction of justice.

When we say that Arab nationalism is humanist (*insaniyya*), we mean, implicitly, that it is a manifestation of abstract, absolute Right in one of its forms. The framework in which this form of absolute Right is transmuted into social principles and aims, such as justice, equality, and liberty, is fixed and formulated by the intellect. The intellect works upon material from three sources—the national-historical experience, which may be called the national heritage; existing conditions and requirements; and the experiences of other nations. The soundness of the aims formulated by the intellect depends upon its ability to make a correct evaluation of all these factors.

Hammadi's two essays, published at an interval of fifteen months, were to prove decisive in the history of Arab nationalism. They represent the most comprehensive and systematic attempt to formulate the creed of that movement—to define it as an ideology, a faith, a way of life and thought. His formulation was disputed by critics who objected not so much to its content as to the idea that Arab nationalism was in need of any comprehensive theory.

But while this was being debated, another equally fierce controversy raged about the problem of priorities. Given Arab nationalism—and in these writings it is invariably a "given"—against what or whom should the struggle first be concentrated? Against imperialism, or foreign influence, or Israel, or against deviationists and traitors in the Arabs' own ranks? Or, alternatively, should war be waged upon everything that is opposed to the movement, including all the above-mentioned foes *and* all the social evils which enfeeble Arab society, all at the same time? Two schools of thought emerged. One, commonly known as the "ideological," called for a combined action to sweep away every antagonist and impediment; the other, which included most of those who deprecated any formulated ideology, proclaimed that so long as foreigners remained in any part of the Arab homelands, so long as Israel was there, and while Arab rulers were not uniformly arrayed against imperialism, no elaborate programs of social and economic reform were of any use.

To this latter group belong the anonymous writers of *With Arab Nationalism,* a book published in Cairo in 1957 by the Federation of Kuwaiti [Student] Missions.[21] This book set out to prove three leading theses: Firstly, nationalism is as old as human association and is not a product of the eighteenth and nineteenth centuries. It is the socio-historic being produced by the deep, inner workings-out of relations between the members of one same society. Secondly, nationalism is not, therefore, an emotional propaganda put out by the bourgeois classes in order to maintain their own misrule and exploitation of the people, as historical materialists assume. And, finally, that in its authentic form, nationalism is *humanist,* not racialist or isolationist. A nonhumanist nationalism treats other nations inhumanely. Such was the nationalism of the West, which was not humanist either internally or externally, because the exploiting classes were able to use it for their own ends of domination, at and after the industrial revolution.

The remaining seven chapters of the book deal with various aspects of Arab nationalism. "Thousands of years ago, successive waves of Arabs moved from the Peninsula to the Fertile Crescent and the Nile Valley." They were succeeded by the Islamic Arab wave, which was to give the Arab nation its present territorial domain extending from the Persian Gulf to the Atlantic. Arab nationality is not identical with the Islamic religion, though in no way opposed to it. Nationalism differs from religion because nationality is a being, while religion is a mission directed to the reform of

certain aspects of that being. "There is no contradiction between nationalism and religion, but there would be if and when religion ceased to devote
itself wholly to the virtues by which man realizes union with the ideal, and
became a political movement that denied the socio-historic being of nationality."

Since nationalism is a being, it is above philosophies and doctrines. "We
can say that we are Socialists or non-Socialists, democrats or non-demo-
crats, but we cannot say we are non-nationalists, because the nation is a
being to which we belong by nature." As against the Marxist interpretation of history, which is a partial view based upon only one aspect of it, the
nationalist interpretation of history is comprehensive, combining all the
aspects of human life. It takes account all of the factors that inform human
existence and influence it. Arab nationalism, therefore, is not a matter of
feeling, or ideas or doctrine, nor is it a philosophy; it is the total expression
of a being.

From this theoretical preamble, the authors proceed to practical issues,
arguing that the Arab nation is suffering from a "crisis of being," faced
with the need for the renewal of its being. The starting point for this re-
creation of being can be nowhere but in the heart of the Arab reality, from
which alone the new being can develop and come to birth, and can be no
other thing than the Arab nation's consciousness of itself, as a being extending from the Persian Gulf to the shores of the Atlantic. From that
consciousness follows the vision of the re-creation of the Arab nation as a
society freed from imperialism and its agents. With its plundered lands
restored, with its fear, poverty, ignorance, and disease abolished, the Arab
nation will at last be liberated to fulfill its mission in the community of
nations for the good and enrichment of mankind as a whole.

These authors propose a program of action divided into two phases.
The first of these will "put an end to division by unity, to imperialism by
liberation, to Israel by vengeance." The second phase will be that of the
"building of a Socialist democratic system for the Arab nation."

On the question of priorities, the authors of *With Arab Nationalism*
maintain that "our political, social, and economic problems are inseparable from each other, yet the political problem is the gravest, the most
urgent, and the most acute; it is the problem that first stands in our way
and prevents us from dealing with those of economics and social order."[22]
And "in order to rid ourselves of poverty, of economic and social injustices
in general, we have to eliminate exploitation and make our way to Socialism. . . . Yet imperialism on the one hand, Israel on the other, and the
present ruling, deviating, and self-seeking groups among us are certain to

put up an obstinate and violent resistance. We must therefore get rid of these before we can turn to the economic and social struggle."[23]

Like everything written on the subject in the 1950s and 1960s, *With Arab Nationalism* provoked sharp reactions. It did not appease the prevalent craving for an Arab ideology that could challenge those which now divide the world. The book was accordingly attacked for its lack of a clear theory of Arab nationalism and for various other omissions. Farid Abu 'Atiyya of Kuwait, writing in the July 1957 *Al-Adab*, deplored the authors' division of the struggle into two separate phases. He would allow for "only one liberation, internal and external, both at the same time." Abu 'Atiyya agrees with most of what the authors say in definition of the problem and formulation of aims, but he refuses, sharply and significantly, to having the struggle divided into distinct phases. This crisis of the national being, he says, is also a distortion of the personality of the Arab individual. Authentic personality can be restored to this individual only by a reconstruction extending into every sphere of his life. "To ignore his own struggle in the economic and social spheres would be to fall into sheer contradiction. Where is the type of Arab personality that is capable of doing battle for political liberation? Is it the distorted, sterile personality we now encounter in every corner of the homeland? Can such a struggle be waged by haphazard numbers of individuals without an economic or social existence—as it was, so disastrously, in Palestine? The contradiction is obvious. If we seek political liberation without having the fighting forces to bring it about, we shall never get out of the vicious circle in which we have been turning round and about for the last century or more."

The truth of the matter, according to 'Atiyya, is that the Arab individual, on whom success depends, cannot be expected to defeat his enemies— imperialism, Israel, and the selfish ruling cliques within the Arab ranks— until he is provided with the essentials of economic and social existence. The authors of *With Arab Nationalism* seek the end without preparing the means to attain it. They claim that other societies have first emancipated themselves from external oppression and then built up social systems of their own. It is true that the peoples of Russia, China, India, Yugoslavia, Egypt, and Algeria have gained control over their internal affairs since they emancipated themselves from foreign domination. Nevertheless, it remains true that there is only one struggle, political and economic, being waged at one and the same time.[24]

Neither the authors of *With Arab Nationalism* nor Farid Abu 'Atiyya seem to insist on what one Arab intellectual has called the "philosophizing of the Arab experience." The controversies of the fifties and sixties were quite different from those that raged during the late thirties, an outline of which is given by Hazem Zaki Nuseibeh. Then, the question was whether "the life and thought of a nation can or should be embodied in what is known as a national philosophy." Nuseibeh's own comment is that "national philosophy is, in a sense, a contradiction in terms . . . for the term 'philosophy' denotes a search for universal truths, and a philosophy which deserts the universal for the particular, except insofar as the universal pulsates in the particular, is anything but genuine. In this limited sense . . . we might venture to speak of national philosophies—of British empiricism, American pragmatism, French nationalism, German idealism, Soviet materialism, Indian quietism, and so on."[25]

The old controversy was renewed by Costi Zureiq with his *National Consciousness,* in which he argued that a systematic, forceful, and clear-cut national philosophy was a necessity for a real national revival. "Indeed, there is no hope for an Arab national renaissance unless it is inspired by a national philosophy which reflects its spirit, delimits its orientation, portrays its objectives, and prescribes its methods."

Abdullah al-'Alayli, another advocate of an Arab national renaissance though he deplores the lack of any systematic Arab ideology, draws a sharp distinction between nationalism as ideology and as a program of action. A national ideology, he writes, should satisfy three conditions: "It should have its cornerstone in the heart rather than in the mind, for faith is a securer bond of union than is the intellect; it should be flexible enough to accommodate the continual growth of knowledge and to prevent any hardening of its emotional basis around certain assumed truths; and it should have profundity as a system of thought, in order to attract and satisfy the intellectual aspirations of its nationalist adherents."[26]

It is a far cry from this to the kind of ideology that the younger generation of Arab intellectuals are trying to formulate. Abdullah 'Abd al-Dayim, who, as far as can be ascertained, was the originator of the new controversy, formulates his demand for an ideology in the following terms: "Arab nationalism has to draw up its program and define its characteristics in a clear-cut manner; it is called upon to formulate itself in an ideology which will hold its own against the other ideologies of the modern age."[27] He bases this on the assumption that "Arab nationalism has long ago passed beyond the phase of emotion, when it was mere resentment against an Ottoman or a Western imperialism." This remark provoked reactions and rejoinders, and echoes long reverberated in the pages of *Al-Adab.*

Broadly speaking, these reactions were of two kinds. One came chiefly from the doctrinaire Marxists, who denied the existence of the problem and said that Arab thought was not called upon to frame a distinct ideology "because the final end of humanity is one." Some even denied that there was such a thing as an Arab nation and said that talk of this kind savored of Nazism and Fascism. We need not consider these objections in detail, however, since our present concern is only to find out what Arab nationalists themselves thought about their doctrine and how they proposed to present it.

Of the other nationalists who opposed the call to an independent ideology, the most persistent—who also have something to say—are 'Abd al-Latif Sharara and 'Ali Baddour, both literary critics and men of letters. Sharara's reaction to 'Abd al-Dayim's call was prompt and final. It is not logical, he protested, to demand from the Arab nation of today an ideology comparable to, say, Communism or existentialism. The construction of an ideology must by its nature and necessity be left to the genius of the nation freely unified on its own conditions. It is unreasonable to ask anyone for what they do not have and therefore cannot give. "The only thing the Arab nation can be asked for today is to fight for the independence of its lands, to give what it can for the sake of uniting its sons and resisting its enemies both at home and abroad. When it has achieved freedom and union, it will spontaneously, without being asked, create a new literature, a new philosophy, and an ideology—all of which will be expressions of the Arab mind and the Arab genius."[28]

History has shown, Sharara went on to say, that there are two kinds of nationalism. One is sheer intolerance, a narrow emotionalism, the desire for domination, superiority, and exploitation. In this category we find all European nationalisms ever since the European nations were formed and until this day. The other is "humanist nationalism," which respects the concepts of right and of justice, which believes in man and in the good, and is charged with a mission to other nations. History records, for instance, no aggressions by the Indian nation against other nations, nor do we find in its philosophies any cruelty, intolerance, praise of evil, or distortion of facts. It has never tried to prevent other nations from leading their own lives.

And so it is with the Arab nation, inspired by clearly humanist ideals. The rise of Christianity and Islam within it shows that it is humanist in tendency. Zionism, however, is nothing but a reversion to heathenism and the worship of idols. In its moral and political aspects, it is an experiment in the methods of primitive barbarism—which is why it has found favor with Europeans, who support it and endorse its aggressions.

Hammadi's analysis provoked another sharp reply from Sharara, who asserts that the existence in the Arab world of foreign influence, feudalism, and illiteracy prohibits the "philosophizing of the revolutionary experience of the Arab nation." He goes so far as to accuse the advocates of a cut-and-dried Arab ideology of playing into the hands of the West. Westerners want to see the Arabs formulate an ideology because they think it would show the way to an ultimate compromise between the Arabs and the West. "Arab thought is compelled, by existing political realities, to concentrate upon political independence, even if this retards its progress in other departments of study . . . a drawback which is a direct result of the pressure that Westerners still put upon us." Sharara concludes that since the Arab and Muslim nations agree with both the rival world camps about the best things to have, and disagree with them about the worst, it follows that the distinct Arab ideology demanded by some nationalists "could not, on the one hand, be politically hostile to Communism nor, on the other hand, be hostile to Western democracy."[29]

In two separate and lengthy essays, published in *Al-Adab* in June and September of 1957, 'Ali Baddour sets out to refute the advocates of an Arab ideology. They ignore, he says, the special circumstances of the Arab nation living under the special conditions of the modern world. Contemporary ideologies arose not from the formulation of clear-cut philosophies, but out of the evolution and development of material conditions.

Citing the examples of Italy and Germany, Baddour maintains that the Arabs can find guidance in them. Those two nations possessed all the characteristics required of unified states; the distinctive method by which each achieved its unity was not inspired by a philosophical doctrine that it adopted. The justification for unifying a nation does not reside in its creation or adoption of a doctrine, nor does the absence of one nullify its claim to unification. Now, an ideology exclusively appropriate to the Arabs in their present situation would be impossible to formulate. The attempt to formulate it and at the same time maintain contact with reality would bring it within the framework of one of the two leading world ideologies. It would not produce a third, purely Arab ideology to compete with the other two. That, indeed, would be a highly difficult task.

The truth of the matter, Baddour writes, is that the Arab world as a whole is suffering from three different ailments. First, from the inordinate number of groups competing for leadership, their differences and rivalries; secondly, from the widely different levels of social progress attained in the various Arab countries and the disparity between their political systems;

and thirdly, from the continued existence in some Arab lands of strongholds retained by certain imperialist powers. Those powers would unite for mutual defense if once the flame of Arab nationalism grew hot enough to endanger their interests. And naturally, they are all in favor of Israel and want to strengthen its foothold in Palestine.[30]

The Egyptian Revolution of 1952 presents an excellent illustration both of the effects of these ailments and of their cure. That revolution could not produce a planned economy until it had first cured the "leadership disease" by abolishing the political parties. It could not join battle with the imperialists until it had managed to cut the "supply lines," which they had established through the parties' splits and differences and with the active help of some of them. As for the country's backwardness in social and economic development, the Egyptian Revolution did not permit elections to be held until it had, to some extent, freed the workers, peasants, salaried employees, and small traders from the tyranny of employers, landowners, and capitalists. A revolution does not abolish political parties because it is impatient of opposition—that is a superficial opinion as far as the Egyptian Revolution is concerned. It abolishes them because they are part of the leadership disease, and because they stand in the way of extending the revolution beyond its borders—and this is a revolution informed by Arab unity and Arab nationalism. Why, then, asks Baddour, are some of the advocates of liberation, unity, and Socialism so frightened of what he calls "planned dictatorship?" True, there are members of political parties in some Arab countries with ugly memories of life under dictatorships—of prison and exile, torture, and the violation of human dignity. "Yet this does not affect our respect for such a 'planned dictatorship' as will lead to unity in home affairs, to non-alignment in the world conflict, to Arab nationalism, Arab unity, and a wide front against any aggressor." It is because this has come to pass in Egypt that all Arabs can now hold up their heads; it is this which has given them the hope of unity and confidence in their own thoughts and aspirations.

Democracy is the enemy of continuity. The Arabs' struggle for unity will be long. It cannot be won without perseverance and stability—and a sincere dictatorship is the system which lasts longest. "Our belief in the value of dictatorship is not theoretical. . . . It springs from our need for unity . . . for a system which can under no circumstances be a fluid, democratic one. . . . Liberty is not necessarily identical with democracy. . . . Liberty is synonymous with sufficiency of food, clothes, housing, hygiene—of cultural consciousness and emotional participation in the nation's problems. I do not know whether the Egyptian citizen of today is not getting a greater measure of freedom than he had in the days of monarchy, political parties, of the Constitution, and freedom of the Press, when everything was permitted; but everything had its price!"

As for those who want to formulate an Arab Socialist ideology, they may try, but they will fail because the attempt is premature.

We cannot feel like a unified nation before we attain unity. All that we can do towards such an ideology is to list a few preliminary theses. Indispensable, for instance, are the following:

1. The Arab nation will not achieve unity unless it remains neutral between the two world camps. The world may divide itself into as many camps as it likes; but the Arab nation remains the Arab camp.
2. This Arab neutrality is not negative; it is positive, in the sense that the Arab nation will cooperate with either of the two world camps, within such limits that this cooperation will not appear, in the eyes of the other camp, to entail hostility against it. Those limits will be set by the Arab nation itself, not by either or both of the two camps.
3. Since human civilization is the sum-total of Man's endeavors towards a better and higher life, the Arab nation should emulate the progress of science in both camps; for when the two dominant Powers have ended their bitter struggle in total war, the Arab nation will be the secure refuge of what remains indestructible in human achievement.
4. Faithfulness to the Arab nationalist idea is the duty of every Arab country which does not want to fall into the orbit of one of the two world systems. Since any deviation from such fidelity affects the personality of the Arab nation as a whole, the other Arab countries should consider it their duty to bring the deviating country back into the fold, even if it involved the use of force.
5. The wealth of the Arab homeland is the property of the whole nation, to be applied to the improvement of the lot of all the Arab peoples. Those Arab states which can afford it must aid the needier ones until the time when all will be pooled in one great Arab economy.
6. Western democracy, based on the plurality of political parties and divided responsibility between parliament and government, paralyses the forces of the nation—forces of growth for which ways and means must be found.
7. For the federation of the liberated Arab states which are not tied to either of the world camps, action is needed without delay.
8. Egypt [under Nasser] is the most active and energetic of the Arab states, and is therefore the best suited to the leadership of the Arab

nation. This must be acknowledged by all the Arab states. Furthermore, Israel, and the imperialism which supports it, is the cancer which retards unification, in both the wider and the narrower senses, of the Arab states. There can be no union so long as Israel exists; and Israel will not disappear as long as Egypt's leading role in the union of all Arabs is not acknowledged.

9. The ironing-out of contrasts in the social life, and the strengthening of the armed forces, are both incumbent upon every Arab country striving towards union.[31]

These, then, are some of the concepts prevalent in the post-Suez era among Arab nationalist intellectuals. Even if seen in the perspective of the time in which they were articulated, it is difficult to draw any clear conclusions from them with regard to the general political-intellectual climate of the Arab world in the late 1950s. As for Arab society and government, the picture emerging from these ideological efforts is one of a polity developing toward a kind of benevolent dictatorship that is not Communist in character nor has it anything in common with the democratic capitalism of the West. An illuminating comment was made on this by Albert Hourani, who observed that the regimes then prevailing in Egypt and Syria seemed to be reverting to patterns that existed in Mamluk and Ottoman days, before the incursion of the modern West. Such democratic regimes as Arab governments that have copied from Western nations have indeed shown little capability for efficient or responsible government. And now, Hourani argued, in Egypt and Syria political life seemed to be going back to the old patterns of Mamluk and Ottoman times. These consisted of the following:

1. A military oligarchy in whose hands lay the final authority, with a rapidly changing personnel but also with a certain continuity owing to its military structure.

2. The permanent officials who carried on the daily business of government undisturbed by political changes going on above them.

3. The learned class, who provided the principles of social morality by which government was guided.[32]

It is to this "learned class" that 'Abd al-Dayim, Hammadi, Abu 'Atiyya, Baddour, and the anonymous Kuwaiti students rightfully belong. It is not without interest to note that Baddour writes of the undesirability of government "based on a multiplicity of parties," dividing responsibility and "rendering the head of state without authority." Nor is it a coincidence that he writes in such exalted terms of 'Abd al-Nasser as the leader of Egypt and of

Egypt as leader of the Arab nation. Baddour, and the writers whose work is surveyed above, wrote on the eve of the most daring experiment in the history of the modern Pan-Arab nationalist movement—namely, the Egypt-Syria merger of February 1958, and only shortly before the Iraqi revolution of July 14 of the same year.

It is to be noted, too, that during the few decades following these searching ideological debates nothing appeared in the Arab nationalist corpus that was to add materially to what Hammadi, Baddour, and others achieved in the 1950s. This was fairly to be expected. The Arab nationalist intellectuals whose work is summarized here were engaging in a hard-core ideological quest, whereas Nasser and his men were occupied by more concrete objectives and day-to-day issues. The brief and rather unhappy marriage between Nasserism and the Pan-Arab Ba'th Socialist Party in Syria ended in September 1961 in dismal failure, with the ideologically oriented Ba'th nationalists deploring what they perceived as the misguided pragmatism of Nasser's whole approach, which they considered to be lacking in a hard-core Pan-Arab and socialist ideology.

Indeed, it is the case that in the almost two decades of its existence and progress, Nasserism produced not a single major work of exposition regarding its own ideological notions of Pan-Arabism and Arab nationalism. To be sure, during the early 1960s the education authorities in Egypt, spurred by remarks made by Nasser about the universities and their function in society, sought help from professors and faculty members. In 1961, the Egyptian minister of higher learning made certain "national subjects" compulsory in university training. One of these was called "Arab Society." Despite the vagueness and the generalized nature of this title, the textbooks produced all had to touch upon the subject of Arab nationalism and the Arab nation. From the ideological point of view, at least, the enterprise proved to be an utter failure, with the learned professors and lecturers failing to agree even on such matters as a workable definition of the "Arab nation," the components of the Arab nationalist doctrine, the goals of Pan-Arabism, and other lesser issues that, on the popular and propaganda levels, Nasserism had made to appear so simple and elementary.[33]

This confusion on the ideological plane, coming as it did from a movement professing undying loyalty to the idea of Arab unity, was to continue throughout the 1960s. In the summer of 1967, especially, something happened in the Middle East that was to shake the Arabs as a whole and lead the Arab intellectual to quests of another kind and intent.

5 | The Shock of 1967

Self-Criticism after the Defeat: Calls for Radical Change

When Jamal 'Abd al-Nasser died in September 1970, certain observers and supporters asserted that his ghost would continue to dominate Arab actions and behavior for many years to come. In the event, this proved not to be the case. Indeed, Nasserism as the dominant radical ideology in the Arab world had been on the wane since the mid-1960s, especially among Arab intellectuals living outside Egypt. The defeat of the Egyptian army in the Six-Day War in 1967 accentuated this downward trend; attacks on Nasserism—both open and disguised—started to come from various circles of the Arab intelligentsia.

To evaluate this trend correctly it must be placed in the context of the overall Arab reaction to the 1967 debacle—and also of a number of responses to that reaction. A few weeks after the Six-Day War Nizar Qabbani, a leading light in modern Arabic poetry, published an angry elegy that opened with these lines:

> My friend, I mourn for the language of the past and the old books,
> The discourse punctured like battered shoes,
> The verse of profanity, slander, aspersion . . .
> I mourn, I mourn
> The thought that finally brought defeat.[1]

In the course of this somber poem, which attracted a great deal of criticism and disapproval, Qabbani wrote: "No wonder we lost the war / We entered it / With the oratorial art of the Orient / And the innocuous sonnets of 'Antar / We entered it with the logic of the drum and the lute."

It is characteristic of a certain strain in Arab writing and thinking that the same poet, who expressed these angry sentiments in July 1967, should in October 1969 prove capable of producing the same sort of verse which he himself had condemned as "the oratorial art of the Orient" and the "innocuous sonnets of 'Antar." In a long poem in praise of the Palestinian guerrillas, Qabbani all but wrote Israel off as dead and finished as a result of *fedayeen* activities—and this at a time in which guerrilla action against Israel was already being seen as the ineffectual factor it was.[2] Indeed, even though it was not entirely typical of intellectual and literary reaction to the Six-Day War, Qabbani's record is indicative of a difficulty inherent in any serious attempt to gauge Arab attitudes and reactions. To be sure, balanced, cool-headed, and intelligible self-appraisals are rare in any literature; in Arabic literature and culture they are all but nonexistent. Even so crushing and incomprehensible a defeat as that of June 1967, which many Arabs considered the greatest debacle suffered by their people in all its history, failed to shake the generality of Arab thinkers and publicists into another, fresher and more open-eyed look at reality.

Not only were the lessons of the defeat mostly lost or overlooked; the truth is that in the first months, at least, no effort was spared to blame the debacle on largely irrelevant, outside factors. The very terminology used by these writers was instructive in this respect. The words *nakba* (disaster, calamity) and *karitha* (catastrophe), widely used to describe the outcome of the Six-Day War, indicate an attempt to shirk responsibility and explain the event away—since those whom calamities befall are not normally held responsible for them. A *nakba*, in Arabic, is something that is usually attributed to nature, time, and fortune—things of which man has no control and for whose workings he cannot be held responsible.

There were those, too, who sought to put the blame for the defeat on such imponderables as the contemporary Arab's lack of belief in God. Salah al-Din al-Munajjid, a well-known Lebanese writer and publicist, writes in a book entitled *The Pillars of the Disaster*: "The Arabs have abandoned their belief in God, and God has accordingly abandoned them."[3] The Grand Mufti of the Hashemite Kingdom of Jordan put it this way: "They [the Israelis] possess neither the power, nor the fortitude, nor the courage to make them capable of doing such a deed. . . . But God chose to let this band dominate us because we strayed away far from Him."[4]

A still more novel explanation came from Dr. Kamal Yusuf al-Haj, head of the Department of Philosophy at the Lebanese University, who argued that the real reason why the Jews decided to come to Palestine was that "they want to refute Jesus Christ." Thus, "the war now raging under our skies does not, as Zionist diplomacy claims, involve the Jews and the Arabs; it rages between the Jews and Jesus Christ first and foremost." The fact is, Professor al-Haj continued, that after failing to desecrate Jesus of Nazareth in his own lifetime, "World Jewry has now concentrated all its wiles to desecrate His representative on earth—i.e. his Holiness the Pope as head of the Church." Needless to say, in such an age-old, gigantic struggle between world Jewry and Jesus of Nazareth, the Arabs of today can hardly count.[5]

Finally, some writers tried to exonerate what they called "the real Arabs" from blame. Wondering why some Arab intellectuals were now so prone to downgrade "the Arab man," the critic Husain Muruwwa described the events of June 1967 as "a military defeat that has befallen [the Arab man] owing to reasons for which are to blame only a few individuals whose only link with the Arab *suis generis* is that of descent."[6]

In this welter of intellectual confusion and pervasive emotional stress, few Arab writers proved equal to the task of consistent and fearless reappraisal of their people's present situation. Among those, a young lecturer in philosophy from the University of Amman, Sadiq Jalal al-'Azm, was both prolific and audacious. His book, *Self-Criticism after the Defeat,* must indeed be regarded as a considerable achievement.[7] A Syrian by birth and son-in-law of a Jordanian cabinet minister, al-'Azm has managed to slaughter a surprisingly large number of sacred cows—and has taken in his stride not only so-called reactionary Arab thinkers and regimes, but has included nearly everyone, not sparing even President Nasser and his Arab Socialist regime. Indeed, there is a sense in which his book can be described as a work of post-Nasserist radical Arab socialism and nationalism, although it was published two years before Nasser's death.

At that time, it was certainly premature to speak of a post-Nasserist phase in radical Arab thinking; but in the Arab world of the late 1960s, there were unmistakable signs of a far-reaching reappraisal of the Nasserist experiment. In a very real sense, indeed, the growth in influence and popularity of the Palestinian guerrilla movement was itself not only a standing rebuke to Nasser and other Arab rulers for their continued failure to "solve" the Palestine problem but also constituted a partial, yet clear, refutation of the Egyptian president's hard-core Pan-Arab doctrine. After the Six-Day War, certain Arab intellectuals, especially in Egypt, found themselves engaged in a fierce "dialogue" with the Palestinians, implying in no uncertain terms that the guerrilla organizations were "provincial" in the sense that they were particularists calling for "Palestine for the Palestinians," rather than for joining forces with Pan-Arab nationalists who believe that a united Arab world is the answer not only to the Zionist aggressors but also to the Arabs' socioeconomic plight.

This is only one of the ways in which Nasser's whole style was then being challenged. The free officers' revolt in Cairo on July 23, 1952—until the mid-1960s sacrosanct except with certain Arab Marxist circles and with thinkers of the ultra Right—was itself coming under fire and being undergraded in favor of "the Palestinian Revolution." A whole issue of Beirut's leading theoretical organ of the Arab radical Left, *Mawaqif*, was devoted to a rather novel enterprise—a reexamination of Nasserism—and it had the striking title of "The July 23 Revolution on Trial." Of the six major contributions to the subject, only one—written by Munir al-Razzaz—came out in defense of the Nasserist experiment and called for identification with the July 23 revolution. Among the five "prosecutors" of this revolution, the most outspoken is al-'Azm himself, author of the book mentioned above. His indictment of Nasserism rests upon three major premises:

1. The Egyptian revolution was responsible for two Arab defeats (1956 and 1967) and thus proved impotent.
2. Because this is so, Arab revolutionaries as a whole—and Nasserists first and foremost—must revise their stand vis-à-vis the July 23 revolution.
3. There is an ultimate opposition between the Nasserist revolution and the Palestinian revolution. The latter must in the end supersede the former. Nasserism has thus become an obstacle in the New Arab Path.[8]

In his *Self-Criticism after the Defeat*, al-'Azm furnishes a more "ideological," though less outspoken, case against the Egyptian revolution. He bluntly charges Nasserism with equivocation and "middle-of-the-roadism." The Arab Socialist revolution, he writes, "was neither revolutionary enough nor socialist enough"—especially when judged by the stern standards imposed by the June defeat. He takes strong exception to President Nasser's plea that, when speaking of Arab nationalism or patriotism, "we must, in this particular juncture, forget about many other concepts: The patriot of the Right is just like the patriot of the Left. When Israel occupied the West Bank she made no distinction between a Right-wing patriot and a Left-wing one, so long as both of them were patriots."

The author considers such sentiments—in addition to the evidence he marshals to prove the "middlist" nature of Nasser's regime—as indicative of a lack of sufficient socialist and revolutionary content in the current Arab nationalist doctrine. Nay, he views these manifestations as a sign that "there does not exist any real socialist Arab Left capable of leading the Arab nation in its present predicament."

Al-'Azm's critique of contemporary Arab society and politics, however, is far more basic and incisive. Despite the fact that he purports to confine himself to the Arabs' behavior before and during the Six-Day War, he attempts an appraisal of many of their basic shortcomings. For instance, the chapter that deals with the ways in which the Arabs tried to explain their crushing defeat in 1967—and that takes up a quarter of the text—contains some surprisingly candid observations. Israel's massive air and land strikes on the fifth of June, for example, were described by the Arabs variously as "aggression" or "treachery." Yet the Arabs had always asserted that they were in a state of war with Israel, that Israel's very establishment constituted an act of aggression! In such a state of affairs, the author observes, the Arabs could not behave as though they "always expected generosity and good neighborliness" from Israel. Talk about "treachery" is equally irrelevant, he further writes, since it can be meaningful only in relation to the rules of gallantry and knightly duels, according to which the two sides must be given equal opportunity to display their ability, so that victory will be the lot of the braver and the stronger. In the second half of the twentieth century, he points out, they call it "surprise attack," not "treachery!"

Among the other fallacies the Arabs used to explain their defeat, and which al-'Azm exposes mercilessly, are the following:

1. The argument that Israel had mobilized more than the sum total of her resources and potentials can ever muster—and that were the Arabs to face Israel alone with her limited human and material resources they would have been the victors. To this, the author replies that Israel's power is the sum total of *all* the resources and potential she is able to mobilize at any particular moment, whether these are her own or drawn from outside sources.
2. The Israeli army had used repressive measures, violated accepted norms of behavior—hence the loud Arab outcry against Israel and her "oppressive methods." Al-'Azm points out, however, that the Israeli army "is an army of occupation and, as such, it is its duty to suppress any resistance with the most effective and violent methods available to it."

3. The fallacy of "international Zionism," according to which the Zionist movement dominates the world and determines the course of modern history. This is used by some Arabs mainly to explain the United States' continuing support of Israel. Al-'Azm, however, tries to refute the belief that the Jews control the American economy or that the Zionist movement is a mere satellite and extension of the United States. Both the Zionists and the U.S. neo-colonialists have their sets of vital interests, and these interests happen to converge in this particular period of time.[9]

Al-'Azm does not stop at enumerating these fallacies. Such manifestations of the urge to evade responsibility and to try to blame failure on external factors, he argues, must and can be related both to the structure of traditional Arab society and to the personality type that this society breeds in today's Arab. Among the features of this personality type (which the author, citing Hamid 'Ammar's research in personality and social change in Egypt, calls the "Fahlawi personality") is a constant search for the shortest possible way to attain a particular goal, so that the hard work and maximum effort usually needed to reach that goal may be avoided. Quickly rising enthusiasm, foolhardiness, and underestimation of obstacles are other features of the Fahlawi personality—as well as their natural corollaries of suddenly receding interest, disheartedness in the face of difficulties, and lack of consistent and organized effort.

A crucial problem confronting the committed young revolutionary in the Arab world is that recent Arab revolutions "remain, in the majority of cases, revolutions on the political plane alone." These revolutions, according to al-'Azm, usually go no deeper than the mere surface of the body politic, failing to reach the more decisive sphere of socioeconomic relations and their traditional patterns. This, too, the author attributes to the Fahlawi personality, one of whose leading characteristics is a burning preoccupation with surface impressions. The Fahlawi, he writes, worries more about getting things done than about the way they are done; he is interested not in true, workmanlike accomplishment that comes only through hard and systematic work, but rather in avoiding the impression that he is incapable of accomplishing things. This has a clear bearing on the Arabs' political and military performances. The student who manages, through all sorts of Fahlawi tricks and devices, to pass his examinations successfully, eventually climbs his way to the upper echelons of government and army. In these capacities, too, he remains driven by the urges of the Fahlawi personality. He would not admit failure; he would ever want to masquerade as a success; and finally he would always look for some scapegoat and excuse to cover up for his lack of accomplishment, whether in politics or in the field of battle. Al-'Azm cites many examples of this behavior as it was manifested before and during the Six-Day War.

Another characteristic of the Fahlawi personality cited by al-'Azm is exaggerated self-assertion and a tendency to scorn and belittle others—a quality which often conceals a feeling of inferiority whose victim refuses to admit. The Arabs' resounding threats against Israel, and their repeated allegation on the eve of the Six-Day War that they could subdue Israel in practically no time, is an illustration of this quality in their personality. Even after the debacle, Nasser (who himself had lamented his men's re-fusal to admit their shortcomings) indulged in this kind of Fahlawi ratio-nalization. Al-'Azm is candid enough to quote from Nasser's address of April 29, 1968, in which he first enumerated the reasons for the defeat and then went on to "explain" it. The Israelis, Nasser said briefly, had mas-tered and used four principles of warfare: surprise attack, lightness of move-ment, brisk maneuvering, and amassment of troops. In the course of the same address, however, Nasser went on to point out that—as a matter of fact—the Egyptian army never lost the war, since it never confronted the Israelis in open combat! The same argument was used by the Jordanian prime minister in his book on the Six-Day War: "The Israelis know full well, as they have always known, how the Jordanian soldier fights in a confrontation between men and men—not one between men and fire pour-ing on them from heaven."[10]

Al-'Azm's stern critique of the Arab personality and of Arab society as a whole does not end here. Deep inside, he writes, the Fahlawi personality is torn by a shearing sense of inferiority vis-à-vis others, but considerations of shame and fear of exposure prevent the Arab from openly admitting his shortcomings—and thus he is rendered unable to treat his inferiority and overcome it. This mortal fear of exposure to new situations and new fail-ures also account for the general lack of esprit de corps: collective volun-tary work is always liable to expose one to delicate situations in which one's weak points become known to others—and this the Fahlawi person-ality seeks to avoid at all costs. The striking lack of initiative, the total inability Arab officers displayed during the Six-Day War in face of new, unexpected situations is also attributable to this personality trait. This is the fault not of the individual officers concerned but of the very fabric of Arab society—a society that is rigid, stagnant, and too hopelessly tradi-tional to withstand new situations and new challenges.[11]

A section of al-'Azm's book is devoted to what he terms "the negative features at work in what we are used to calling the Arab Socialist revolutionary line." Many Arab Socialists speak of "an Arab Vietnam," make endless comparisons between the Arab revolution and the great Socialist revolutions, such as the Russian and the Chinese, and their respective attitudes to the United States and to neo-colonialism. All these comparisons and analogies, al-'Azm asserts, are unfair to these revolutions, since there can be no comparing between them and the superficial, improvised, and Fahlawi-type revolutions of the Arab world.

One basic difference the author cites is that, unlike other Socialist revolutions, the Arab revolution failed to proclaim its socialism as both scientific and secular. A host of questions touching upon the very essence of Socialist revolutions are left unanswered by the Arab revolutionaries: Does the Arab revolution seek more agrarian reforms or a radical revolution in the field of agriculture, ownership of the land, and the industrialization of farming? Does it seek merely to transfer the ownership of the means of production from private to public hands, or does it intend to introduce a true revolution in industry, class relations, and the distribution of the national income? Does it plan to radically change the present legal apparatus and revise age-old religious laws? Does it seek mere reforms or true revolutions in such fields as education, social relations, scientific research, and similar others? The Arab revolution during its various stages offered no answer to any of these questions, especially on the level of actual practice.

From this al-'Azm turns to his open critique of Nasser. One of the consequences of this lack of ideological clarity, he writes, is "middle-of-the-roadism," which characterizes the Arab revolution in general and Nasser's Arab Socialism in particular. The avoidance of any serious confrontation with the problem of classes in Egyptian society, the halfhearted nationalization measures, the still inadequate representation granted to workers and peasants in the country's political institutions—all these are regarded by the author as manifestations of "middlism" (*wasatiyya*), which has always been a feature of Nasser's regime. What the Arabs need now, al-'Azm concludes, is the emergence of "new revolutionary forces whose leadership is totally committed to [solving] the problems of the great majority of the Arab people—i.e. the toiling masses and the working class." Only such leaderships can bring out the social content of the Arab revolution; only they can transform the present guerrilla warfare into a real, popular war of liberation in which the mobilized masses can play an effective role.[12]

These are radical and highly unorthodox sentiments. Were they mere sectarian squabbles or were they indicative of a new phase in Arab radical thinking and a revolt against the existing revolutionary (Nasserist) establishment? Was an extensive revision afoot in the Arab world of all theses and concepts prevalent before the Six-Day War? If we are to believe some spokesmen of the new revolutionary Arab elite, we have to conclude that this is so. Al-'Azm himself was in the lead in this field. Toward the end of 1969, he caused a tremendous stir when he published in Beirut a new book called *A Critique of Religious Reason*.[13] Immediately after the book came out, the Lebanese authorities issued an order asking al-'Azm to leave the country, where he was apparently either spending a sabbatical year or had decided to make his temporary home.

It would probably be no exaggeration to say that few books in contemporary Arab history have given rise to so great a commotion as al-'Azm's critique of current religious thinking. Not since the 1920s, when 'Ali 'Abd al-Raziq and Taha Husain published their studies in Cairo on the principles of Islamic government and the origins of pre-Islamic Arabic poetry, respectively, was the author of an ostensibly nonpolitical book so widely criticized, attacked, and maligned—and finally prosecuted in open court. The phenomenon becomes all the more intriguing when one remembers that the book contained nothing that was so shocking or new. As a matter of fact, it was a critique more of currently accepted "progressive" Arab regimes and ideologies than of the religious hierarchy or religious thought itself.

Briefly stated, al-'Azm's main thesis is that religion, along with the other intellectual superstructures of Arab society and its whole "traditional cultural structure," must be subjected to "stern rational criticism" if it was to cease being an impediment to social and economic growth. As things stood, despite the fact that everyone admitted that such criticism was necessary, the Arab world was witnessing what amounted to no more than mere generalities and a repetition of worn-out clichés about fatalism, the mystical mentality, and superstition. There were, to be sure, innumerable calls for adopting the scientific method and the rationalist system of thought; there were also appeals for building the modern secular state. Yet not one of these critics and advocates actually produced a critique of the things he rejected—a critique based on rational, scholarly research. "In these studies," al-'Azm wrote, "I have tried to practice this kind of tangible criticism vis-à-vis prevalent religious thinking."[14]

The implication is clear and, as far as the dominant "progressive" Arab movement is concerned, rather unflattering. So far, al-'Azm wrote, Arab progressive and revolutionary thinkers have failed to subject to this kind of criticism those mental superstructures, including religion, which Arab reaction was using as ideological armory. Moreover, these allegedly revolutionary forces have so far adopted a negative, conservative attitude to any movement seeking to reappraise and criticize the Arab sociocultural heritage and to revise it in accordance with the considerable changes that have occurred in the actual structure of society. Finally, he accuses these progressive Arab forces of actually *adopting* the existing cultural superstructure with all its backward mental habits: "It considered all that worthy of respect and veneration, and surrounded it with a halo of sanctity which placed it outside the scope of scholarly criticism and historical analysis."[15]

Al-'Azm makes the following additional points:

1. The intellectual and cultural efforts of the Arab revolutionary movement have fallen far behind its economic and social efforts, thus creating a yawning gap between revolutionary thinking and revolutionary interest.

2. Even worse, the Arab revolutionary forces have placed obstacles in the way of any harmonization between idea and reality, and its effort in the cultural sphere has served only to maintain the prevalent ideology with its superstitions, its backward institutions, and its medieval culture—all this under the disguise of protecting the people's traditions, values, folklore, religion, morality, and so on.

3. The Arab revolutionary forces have also been guilty of rendering the colonial relationship into a mere abstraction. This has resulted in such a degree of oversimplification of otherwise complex historical realities that "imperialism" (or "international Zionism") now appears to be the only force dominating, directly or indirectly, the movement of Arab society.

4. Whereas religious ideology constitutes Arab reaction's main theoretical weapon in its war against Arab revolutionary forces, "progressive Arab regimes have found in religion a convenient way of pacifying the Arab masses and covering up for failure and ineptitude . . . as well as an effective demagogic device for drugging the masses and quieting them down."[16]

It is this open and merciless attack on "progressive Arab regimes" (led, needless to say, by Nasser's Egypt), rather than his criticism of certain aspects of religious thought, that seem to have been responsible for the violent reaction that greeted al-'Azm's book and led to his expulsion, arrest, and trial. A good deal of typical Beirut intrigue and political muckraking, too, added considerably to the commotion. The facts of the case are mostly well known. On December 7, 1969, before the book reached the bookstores of Beirut, the newspaper *Al-Nahar* came out with the following banner headline: "The Heretic from Damascus—A Rebel Against His Aristocratic Muslim Family and a Genuine Satanic Insurgent: Sadiq al-'Azm: Does a Muslim of the Second Half of the Twentieth Century Have to Believe in Jinnis, Angels, Harut and Yajoj and Majoj?" This improbable headline was then followed by an opening paragraph describing al-'Azm's book as a "Marxist attack on the religion of Islam."[17]

Pro-Cairo Beirut newspapers, too, aware of al-'Azm's unorthodox views on Nasserism, were similarly quick to react. "Freedom of Heresy, not Freedom of Thought," screamed *Saut al-'Uruba,* adding: "Instead of liberating religious feeling in the Muslim, let the Communists liberate Marxist thought suffocating under the dead weight of fossilized beliefs!"[18] A week later, the same paper proposed new legislation against the spread of atheism. Specifically, it suggested the following penalties: "The author should get five years in prison, then ten years if he commits the same crime again—and if he does it a third time then he should be imprisoned for fifteen years." Moreover, anyone caught advocating atheism in a school or a university must be dismissed from his university or school forthwith and committed to trial.[19] Around this time the Lebanese Ministry of Interior ordered al-'Azm to leave the country within twenty-four hours and the book was confiscated. Subsequently, the author was arrested and tried for failing to comply with the ministry's order.

Concurrently with these attacks from certain sections of the press there was a good deal of sympathy for the author. Several intellectual circles, including the pro-Nasser monthly *Al-Adab,* protested against the banning of the book as a flagrant violation of freedom of expression, and said that though they did not share the author's political sympathies, they recognized his right to have a hearing.[20] Others, like the editors of *Al-Hawadith,* warned that a controversy between Marxists and orthodox Muslims at this juncture could only serve the enemies of the Arabs and help those who seek to exploit religious sentiment such as the Muslim Brethren.[21] Finally, what tended to complicate matters even further was al-'Azm's much-publicized support of the Palestinian guerrilla organizations and his advocacy of the "Palestinian Revolution" as the antithesis, alternative, and successor to the so-called "Arab Revolution," by which he meant Nasser's regime and his ideology.

Not one of al-'Azm's many critics, however, thought it fit to go to the trouble of criticizing and/or refuting his arguments against prevalent religious beliefs and his sharp criticisms of the ruling religious hierarchy, both Muslim and Christian. Instead, attacks against him fell into two categories: empty polemics by apologists of the religious establishment and gentle admonitions by spokesmen of the Arab "revolutionary" regimes, mainly pro-Cairo. The former displayed almost total ignorance of the philosophical-theological points made by al-'Azm and contented themselves with generally accusing him of ignorance of "true Islam," basing his arguments as he allegedly did on what he learned from the works of Orientalists and other foreigners.

More serious, however, was the second category of critics, the Socialists. These attacked al-'Azm as fellow Socialists and leftists who, though clearly in agreement with him on his main themes about religion, were afraid lest a wedge be driven between the forces of progress and revolution and the great mass of Muslim Arabs who continue to observe the precepts of their faith. The author equates the attitudes of reactionary Arab regimes to religion with those of progressive, liberated governments. This meant, according to one Egyptian critic, that al-'Azm fails to distinguish between those regimes seeking to use religion as a cover-up for their hostility to the revolution and those who try to discover those aspects of religion that can play a positive role in achieving progress, combating exploitation, and doing away with private ownership.[22]

The burden of this criticism by "fellow revolutionaries" is that, in ignoring the prevailing historical circumstances and insisting on what he considers absolute principles, al-'Azm has displayed all the symptoms of that ailment Lenin had long ago termed "infantile Leftism"; sufferers from it tend to undermine their influence among the masses, help their enemies, and betray their own mission. None of these critics, however, managed actually to refute the author's argument that prevalent religious beliefs and superstitions act as impediments to socioeconomic change in contemporary Arab society.

The Literary Front

In the writing and thinking of contemporary Arabs, the phrase *al-khamis min haziran* (the fifth of June) was to become something in the nature of a transcendental concept, marking a veritable dividing line in history and a decisive sociocultural breakthrough. Open any post-June book or magazine article in Arabic dealing with any aspect of Arab life, society, or literature and the chances are that the author would open with some such sentence as: "Before the fifth of June" or "Following the debacle of the fifth of June." The Israeli-Arab poet Samih al-Kassem, whose sympathies go openly to fellow Arabs everywhere, gave poignant expression to the prevalent Arab mood in the line, "On the fifth of June we were all born anew."

As the Arab country most thoroughly embroiled in the conflict with Israel—and consequently the one that suffered most from the defeat of the Six-Day War—it was in Egypt that the overwhelming body of post-June soul-searching and self-flagellation was done. In literature, the mood was one that could best be described as being "beyond anger." In the course of the Seventh Congress of Arab Writers convened in Baghdad in April 1969, an Egyptian professor of literature and leading literary critic, Shukri Muhammad 'Ayyad, enumerated three kinds of literary reactions to the June defeat. The first was one of "sorrow and disbelief"; the second, following the first though not superseding it, was one of "anger"; and the third—which 'Ayyad said was a maturer and more genuine development of the angry reaction—was one of "defiance."[23]

While this chronological division seems arbitrary, it still fits the facts in a fair way. The phase of "sorrow and disbelief" was, however, one of silence, too—of speechlessness, so to speak. Yet it had its own crop of literary work, though rather scanty and possibly merely coincidental. For in the midst of the sorrow, the disbelief, and the silence, a celebrated Egyptian thinker ventured to publish a book that, under the circumstances, was to prove fairly representative of the general mood. The book was entitled *Al-wadi al-muqaddas* (The sacred valley), and its author was Muhammad Kamal Husain, one of the most respected of Egypt's older writers and intellectuals.[24]

Husain's philosophy turns out to be one of complete withdrawal. His "sacred valley" is the refuge he offers his compatriots from the oppression, the exploitation, and the alienation that he sees so besetting our world. In this proposed haven, the reader is told, "you see yourself as being superior in character to and higher in esteem than those who have oppressed you— and this superiority is guarantee against the rise in you of any futile and objectionable sentiments such as revenge and retaliation against the oppression—for oppression and retaliation make for a closed, vicious circle from which there is no escape. . . . Should despair take hold of you and you start wondering about the meaning of life; should the crushing force inherent in regimes that you are powerless to change overwhelm you . . . you have only one way of escape: to fall back on your sacred valley, where you can obtain salvation from despair and anxiety."

Even in the general mood of sorrow, disbelief, and silence that followed the Six-Day War in Egypt, Husain's counsel proved completely unacceptable. It was also fairly untypical of the author's known opinions and attitudes. For close to half a century, Husain advocated the adoption of the scientific method and called for industrialization and the introduction of more courses in the applied sciences in Egypt's universities. He was also known for his scathing attacks against the "feudal mentality," used to deplore the "medieval approach" of withdrawal and resignation, its lack of inventiveness and originality, and its refusal to criticize and to argue.

Husain's new philosophy of withdrawal into the self, his advocacy of an extreme form of individualism, and his renunciation of all violence and activism of every kind came as a shock to Egypt's literary circles. But the veneration in which he was held, his age, and the general mood of near despair then prevalent in these circles tended to make them largely ignore Husain's work. When his philosophy did get a hearing, however, this was invariably accompanied by firm rejection. At least one younger critic, 'Abd al-Jalil Hasan, wondered whether Husain's call for withdrawal into his "sacred valley" —coming at that particular time—was not "a kind of reaction [to Egypt's defeat in the war]—a quest for internal peace, an attempt to vanquish the self in times of crisis."

The critic continued:

It is this call to vanquish the self, instead of vanquishing oppression, exploitation and the crushing force inherent in state systems that we reject. We reject it because we believe firmly . . . that there can be no salvation from despair and anxiety until we have vanquished the oppression and the exploitation themselves. We also believe that we shall never rise above those who oppress us by deluding ourselves that we are superior to them in spirit. . . . We can be superior in spirit and higher in worth only when we resist the oppression; and it is not enough merely to retaliate against the oppressors: only their complete destruction can give the soul a respite, only that can lead the soul to a state of all-embracing peace and to enjoy living in its sacred valley really and truly.[25]

In these militant words, sorrow was already giving way to anger and defiance. Clearly, the author of *The Sacred Valley* was either way behind the times or a little ahead of them; his onslaught on war, revenge, and strife of every kind was only partially—and temporarily—representative of the general mood in post-June Egypt.

Both Husain's book and the reaction to it were remarkably in keeping with the chronological account of current Egyptian literary moods offered by 'Ayyad. After the corrosive, self-destructive phase of sorrow and anger, he maintained, came the phase of self-criticism and self-purification. The era of complacency and self-congratulation, of exaggerated self-confidence, and of gross underestimation of the adversary's strength had gone forever. Citing numerous works of poetry, fiction, and drama, 'Ayyad sought to show that sorrow and anger in the literary reaction to the defeat in Egypt were subsequently coupled with—and in cases gave way to—a mood of defiance, of a determination to change things while clinging to one's identity, and of an urge to ponder the defeat and try to discover its roots while at the same time firmly believing in ultimate victory.[26]

'Ayyad's account may have been accurate as far as the general post–Six-Day War literary mood was concerned. However, when one turns to examining the actual material—the body of literature produced in Egypt after the Six-Day War—one is liable to encounter considerable difficulties. For one thing, so little of this literature was produced; for another, what had actually been produced was not easy to distinguish from the pre-June literary production. As a matter of fact, at least one Egyptian student of Arabic literature, Ghali Shukri, in 1969 altogether rejected the proposition that there had indeed been such a thing as a "post-June" Egyptian literature. Propounding his view on the subject in the course of a lengthy paper published in the Egyptian Marxist monthly *Al-Tali'ah* and entitled "Egyptian Letters after the Fifth of June," Shukri wonders whether it would be altogether correct to speak of the June war as marking a dividing line between two phases of Egyptian literature. With a good deal of sophistication and not a little shrewdness, he asserts that "the literature of the fifth of June emerged before that date—and the literature which followed the fifth of June is in its essentials no more than a continuation of what was written before that date." The reason for this, according to Shukri, is that "great events in the life of nations are not usually reflected in literary and artistic works on the morrow of their occurrence"; they take long years to be pondered upon and digested.[27]

In support of his view that "the literature of the fifth of June" in Egypt was produced before that date, Shukri cites works by Tawfiq al-Hakim, Alfred Faraj, and Yusuf Idris, all written between 1959 and 1966. Al-Hakim's play, *The Bewildered Monarch,* was among the first works of literature to tackle the problem of legitimacy and democratic government, stressing the primacy of law over force in running the affairs of the kingdom even when this affected the highest seats of power. In a later work of drama, *The Anxiety Bank,* al-Hakim was even closer to current reality and dealt directly with the vexed problem of Egypt's security apparatus—an apparatus whose downfall was to follow hard on the heels of the June defeat.

Alfred Faraj's work was no less relevant to the defeat. His 1964 play, *The Barber of Baghdad,* presented a clear and well-defined case for free-dom—not as an abstract concept but as something closely linked with the broad interests of the masses. Even more far-reaching was Yusuf Idris's *The Servants,* in which he dealt with the theme of freedom. Both here and in his later work, *The Earthly Comedy,* Idris all but rejected every description of government. Although it seemed to verge on the anarchist thesis, Idris's work was in fact an energetic assault on all forms of restric-tion of democratic freedoms—thus serving as a timely warning of the dan-gers threatening these freedoms in Egypt. That these dangers were of the very essence of the defeat was amply illustrated by the fact that immedi-ately after the June war a great outcry was made demanding "the primacy of law"—so much so that this became an official government slogan.

Freedom was only one of three themes directly connected with the de-feat and which Egyptian writers took up before the June war. Another was the problem of social justice, so ably and openly adopted by 'Abd al-Rahman al-Sharqawi, author of *Earth* and *Young Man Mahran;* S'ad al-Din Wahbi in his plays *Bir al-salm* and *The Train of Safety;* and the poet Salah 'Abd al-Sabour in his play *Al-Hallaj's Tragedy.* All three writers agreed that the problem of democracy was first and foremost one of social justice, that there could be no separating of the political and economic aspects of jus-tice since any deviation in the one led inevitably to deviation in the other. Al-Sharqawi, especially, was very daring. In his play, *The Fellah,* most of which was written before the Six-Day War, he revisits the scene of his classic novel *Earth* to find out what had happened in the intervening fif-teen years. With singular courage he does not hesitate to put his finger on the social ills he finds still plaguing the Egyptian peasant's life despite fif-teen years of "socialist laws." (In a television interview broadcast from Cairo at the time, al-Sharqawi, when referring to this period, first described it as "the era of socialism" but immediately corrected himself, saying, "or rather the era of socialist laws").

The third and last significant theme Egyptian writers tackled before the June war had to do with the relationship between the committed intellec-tual and the revolution. Many things were written about what was called "the crisis of the intellectuals," but very few of those who wrote about the problem dared look it in the face. Ghali Shukri in his study gives his own version of the gap which yawned between the revolution and the intellec-tuals. He considers the issue acute precisely because the rift was not with counterrevolutionary intellectuals but with those who had openly taken the side of the revolution. Again, the conflict did not concern the ends of the revolution but the means which the regime was using to attain those ends. No one dealt with this theme better or more effectively than Naguib Mahfuz, Egypt's leading contemporary novelist.

All those brave works, which preceded the war but dealt directly with the factors that were to lead to the defeat, attain a measure of true prophecy, Shukri argues, and are thus part and parcel of "the literature of the fifth of June." That they had fallen on deaf ears—including those of men in high places—is truly unfortunate; but they remain a testimony to the fact that some penetrating and clear-sighted minds saw the disaster before it was to take place. "These writers were indeed the prophets of the defeat; they did not take up arms against the revolution and its regime, but they chose to combat its negative aspects from within its own ranks."[28]

So far for the Egyptian "Literature of the Fifth of June" that preceded the Six-Day War. The works written after the war give credence to Shukri's claim that the literature following the defeat was in essence no more than a continuation of that which preceded it. The same themes of freedom, social justice, and the relationship between the committed intellectual and the revolution continued to occupy the minds of Egyptian writers, the only difference being one of degree. They were now more bitter and more outspoken. Work produced in Egypt in the field of literature—poetry, the novel, literary criticism—no doubt reflected a more general mood by no means confined to intellectuals and men of letters. One illustration taken from outside these circles will suffice: In an Order of the Day issued on October 11, 1973—the seventh day of fighting in the Yom Kippur War—the Egyptian chief of staff asserted that, "even should we be defeated this time as well, no one will ever be able to say again that the Egyptian soldier is not a good fighter."

The depth of the feeling of frustration, humiliation, and anger expressed in this highly untypical statement is hardly surprising. Students of Arab thought and literature have noticed its pervasive presence in Arab and Egyptian writing after the Six-Day War. To give some examples: One talented Egyptian critic and short-story writer, Salah 'Isa, went so far as to coin an adjective derived from the name of the month in 1967 that witnessed what was perceived as the worst setback the Arabs had suffered throughout their history. 'Isa wrote that since June 1967 the Arabs lived in a "Junist" atmosphere and described Arab writers and poets as "les Juinists," apparently in the same way as those politically confused Russian army officers who staged the poorly planned and abortive "December Revolt" against Tsar Nicholas I in December 1825, and who came to be known as "Les Decembrists."

Altogether, 'Isa argued, "all facets of our life are being lived under the shadow of June, formed by its climate—and born of it insofar as these facets themselves had given birth to it." This thesis, he added, may be more valid where literature, the arts, and the various intellectual pursuits were concerned. But the generalization is neither arbitrary nor unfair. "Contemplate the Arab street with a keen eye; try to fathom the real meaning of what people say; glance at the statistics if you like! We are now reaping—years after the event—the crop of what took place in June, when we fell from the immense heights of national boasting and political-propagandistic inflation down to the realm of reality. I almost said 'bitter reality'—but what word is capable of describing what happened?"[29]

'Isa offered no solution to this acute dilemma in which the Arabs lived. Other writers, more politically minded and more eager, volunteered their own solutions—and the dominant thesis was that war was the only "great healer." Muhammad al-Naqqash, a well-known Lebanese writer and journalist, summed up the contemporary Arab's dilemma in an article in the Beirut daily Al-Sha'b: "We have always been of the opinion that the war against Israel should be waged according to one principle: either victory or extinction. This is not only because no political settlement, however just, could ever be in the Arabs' interests. It is because we believe in the nation's need to wage war—to fight a real battle—as a fundamental premise of our modern renaissance." To lend credence to his thesis, al-Naqqash quoted the late Gen. Charles de Gaulle as saying that "wars elevate the meanest of souls." He went on to explicate: "In our ranks today there are innumerable mean souls. The fault is not theirs so much as it is the historical circumstances through which we have lived. These circumstances have resulted in stagnation, sloth and servitude—and have almost succeeded in stamping out Arabism's inherent traits of courage and self-sacrifice."[30]

Al-Naqqash was not the only Arab intellectual who saw in war the great healer. Suheil Idris, editor of Al-Adab, asserted in a leading article that the only way open to the Arab nation was "to wage a major battle which will also be the ultimate purification—purging the Arab land of imperialism and occupation and at the same time purging the Arab soul of corruption and degeneration." The truth, Idris went on to write, is that corruption was cutting into the Arab body on every possible plane—the political, the economic, the social, and the cultural. "It is corruption that has led to degeneration in all walks of our life, so that we find ourselves leading a trivial life devoid of high hopes and guided by no inspiring torch. It may therefore be only natural that defeatism and despair have succeeded in conquering the spiritually weak in our ranks—and sometimes attack even the strong-spirited amongst us."

Idris continues: "It has now become quite obvious that the defeat of June 1967 was nothing but the harvest of a number of fearful collapses in the very structure of the Arab human being. These collapses were caused by several factors, chief among them is the loss of the will to fight, a will that must be present in any nation seeking life in a world torn by struggles, conflicts and ambitions." Idris's conclusion: The will to fight and the martial spirit have disappeared among contemporary Arabs. The only way open to them now is to wage a great, prolonged battle that will at once purge the Arab homeland of foreign occupation and the Arab soul of its present ailments. The battlefield is the only spiritual and moral purgatory for living Arabs.[31]

Reverting to reactions in Egyptian literary works, it is safe to say that the impact of the 1967 war on Egyptian literature is nowhere more manifest and more outspoken than in the works of Naguib Mahfuz. In the period from October to December of 1967, this prolific writer produced six long short stories and five short plays, which were to appear in book form only in 1968–69. In an interview with the literary editor of the Cairo weekly Al-Iza'ah, Mahfuz explained this blandly by owning that he had "waited for an opportunity" to publish those works in which he deals with a state of "frightening chaos," of bewilderment, of a searing sense of defeat, bad conscience, and a surging desire to do something.[32] In this interview, Mahfuz sounds apologetic about the fact that for the first time in his literary career he has chosen to deal with current and burning issues, thus depriving himself of the historical perspective necessary for the creative writer. He knows that his works are affected by his own state of mind after the defeat and are thus lacking in objectivity and clear-sightedness. This is why, he said, he chose the allegorical method in his stories and plays, which he said was always useful for the creative writer when he has to grope his way in the dark.

Three of Mahfuz's post-June stories are worth citing here. *Under the Awning* is the story of a group of people who appear to have lost their faculties of movement and action, and are content only to talk and to dream. All around them things keep happening, terrible events take place, people are born and die, rain falls and storms blow—and our heroes are content to sit under their awning, waiting and chattering away. Waiting for "the happy end," but who would know that the end would be a happy one? Mahfuz's play seemed to have been misunderstood, and many of its spectators wondered to whom he was referring. To this, Salah Jawdat replied in *Al-Musawwar* of March 21, 1969: "The story's heroes depict us, all of us without exception. We all stood in Mahfuz's street looking on while murder, dancing, love, death, storms and rain took place; we all waited with indifference under the awning while the thief turned into a murderer, the policeman looked on without lifting a finger, and so on and on."

The Sleep, Mahfuz's other tale, is remarkably similar to the first. It tells the story of an intellectual whose sweetheart is murdered in his bed while he continues in his deep slumber following a night of preoccupation with calling up spirits and stargazing. Mahfuz declined to reply to the question: "Who was that sweetheart who called for help while all of us gave no heed and continued in our deep sleep?" He told the *Al-Iza'ah* interviewer that his vision was not yet so clear for lack of historical perspective!

Mahfuz's third short tale is called *The Assignment*. In it, two persons, Number One and Number Two, are depicted as whipping a young man crying of pain. The young man is being whipped because he evaded his duty and forgot all about the assignment given to him. What makes things worse is that he cannot even remember the nature of his assignment. The young man is a history teacher, yet all the history lessons about ancient man, his discovery of agriculture, his invention of the calendar, and his building of the pyramids fail to make him remember or even give him a hint about the nature of the assignment. Adding poignancy to the allegory is the fact that the two whips constantly exercised upon the bewildered young man have names—Remorse and Bad Conscience. The *Al-Iza'ah* contributor tells his readers that the play serves "to remind us that each of us has an assignment to fulfil. The play does not give a coherent idea as to the kind of assignment you have to carry out; you only realize that your life passes and that something is lacking—something which you yourself have to find out about. So long as you don't remember the assignment, your life remains devoid of content."[33]

Mahfuz's central theme in these and other stories, novels, and one-act plays he wrote on the subject was the mood of the ordinary Egyptian in the aftermath of the Six-Day War. With one exception, however, he resorts in these works to various allegorical devices in order to avoid the censor's strictures. But in one single novel published in July 1973 he took daring liberties he was to allow himself only in works he published after the Yom Kippur War. This was the novel *Love Under the Rain*, in which Mahfuz depicts moods and attitudes prevalent on the home front at a time of war and war preparations.[34] In his work, these range from the extremes of helplessness and near-despair to those of indifference and cynicism. Ibrahim, a soldier on short leave from the front, complains that "no one seems to think of us except our close relatives." The girl to whom he is proposing tries to account for this in a spiritual way, but she also offers a friend's opinion that this apparent public indifference stems from a deliberate government policy:

"What does he mean?" asks Ibrahim.
"He means they would mobilize the people for war only shortly before starting the actual fighting."
"Frankly, I don't understand."
"Neither do I. No one pretends to understand. Is war going to break out again?"
"On the front we are quite convinced it will," Ibrahim asserts.
"Here we can hardly believe it!"
"How *do* you see things?"
"You find all possible contradictory opinions."
"You," Ibrahim laughed. "You would like to see victory as a news item in the papers one of these days!"

In another episode in the same novel, 'Ali and Muna, brother and sister—both white-collar professionals—discuss plans for emigration. "The defeat has shaken us," Muna says with no apparent reason. "And enlightened us," replies her brother. Earlier, when they discuss their plans with their parents, 'Ali retorts to their argument that there is no wisdom in the decision since both have a bright future in Egypt itself.

"It is the state of the country," 'Ali explains.
"And it's quite unbearable," confirms his sister Muna.
The father, an old-style patriot, then tries to rouse his children's national sentiments.
"A homeland," 'Ali replies, "is no longer a specific [piece of] land and geographical boundaries. It's the homeland of the mind and the spirit."

In another scene, Muna discusses the subject with a disgruntled, dissenting but prominent lawyer who is courting her:

"Graveyards will continue to be crowded, and so will hospitals," the lawyer says. "But that will not prevent us from eating, drinking and marrying."
"We were on the verge of emigrating!" Muna exclaims.
"Ah, how badly I wanted to emigrate myself! But there is no hope. However, it would be better to find another subject for discussion."

"We were told," Muna persists, "that we were running away when the homeland is facing difficulties."

"Well," says the lawyer, "I confess I was brought up a patriot, but I no longer care about anything. Please help me change the subject."

"Don't you care about the homeland being victorious?"

"What I care about," the lawyer retorts, "is that we live in peace and happiness. If this comes through victory then victory is welcome; if it is realized through defeat then this too is quite welcome!"

"I don't understand!" Muna says, shocked.

"I don't blame you. But I brought you here because I love you."

The truth is, he wants to say more than that, and precisely on the subject he was trying to avoid. He tells himself that there was no avoiding politics; it's like the air we breathe.

"Had they," he says almost inaudibly, "had they emerged victorious in the June war, what would people like us have done? Defeat, you see, is not devoid of a blessing for citizens who are powerless in the face of authority!"

Muna is silent. She feels she couldn't understand his utterances....

"A homeland," he says in a different tone, "is where one is happy and valued."

"And would we be happy and valued if Israel defeated us?"

He could not utter a word in reply, and Muna says with a sigh: "Be that as it may, I am not going to throw a stone at you since I myself once decided to emigrate."

Even more striking than Mahfuz's novel is a play by Sa'd al-Din Wahbi entitled *Seven Waterwheels*. In it, Wahbi resurrects five Egyptian soldiers who perished in Sinai in the Six-Day War. He makes them come to Cairo to look for a more fitting burial ground. Their souls are troubled by a long stay in the desert that had not yet been recaptured by their compatriots. After one and a half years of useless waiting they decide to make it on their own to Cairo, where they may be buried side by side with other Egyptian victims of wars past and present. Here a debate rages between them and the victims of the 1948 war with Israel, the latter arguing that the burial ground is destined to those who actually fought in the field of battle, while the five wandering souls from Sinai, though they too met their deaths in the battlefield, did not fight and thus have no right to be buried alongside them.

Eventually a tribunal is set up to decide between the two sides. The head of the tribunal is none other than Ahmad 'Urabi Pasha of the 'Urabi Revolt fame. In the course of the hearings one of 'Urabi's soldiers addresses his commander in these words: "Your Honor! I fought under you in Al-Dawwar village, but your army was defeated as a result of treachery; the army of 1948 was also defeated as a result of treachery; but in 1967 the army was defeated because of its staff command which failed to stand up to its responsibility."

Severe criticism of the media is made in another scene. A radio reporter interviews the mother of one of the five dead soldiers—a simple peasant woman who works twelve hours a day in the field to eke out a living. To the reporter's query as to how she felt, the old woman replies simply: "Thanks be to Allah, my daughter!" Content with this cryptic reply, the reporter turns to her listeners with these words: "Abd al-Ghaffar's mother, who works twelve hours in the field, is happy—happy about her part in the campaign to raise production. As you see for yourselves, this simple peasant woman lauds the aid which the authorities extend to her. O listeners, here is an example of the progress which has been made in the life of the *fellah* in our land. In the past the authorities fought the *fellah,* but now they serve him."[35]

Not surprisingly, the Egyptian censor tried to ban *Seven Waterwheels,* but the outcry which followed succeeded in making the censors desist. Muhammad 'Afifi, a literary critic, wrote in *Al-Musawwar* of April 4, 1972: "If current rumors are true, and the censors decide to ban the play, the only conclusion will be that there is no more place for freedom of writing in Egypt."

Mahfuz's novel and Wahbi's play vividly reflect the mood of discontent and resentment that prevailed in Egypt between June 1967 and October 1973. Egyptian writers, intellectuals, and journalists during this period found themselves unable to express their views or give vent to their feelings of frustration at the no-war, no-peace stalemate. However, the world of *Love Under the Rain* and *Seven Waterwheels* seemed to come to life early in 1973, in a kind of "cultural manifesto" signed by more than five hundred Egyptian writers, artists, and intellectuals and circulated privately in those circles. The statement, which protested against what the signatories described as "the stagnation and corruption pervading the country's cultural life," spoke of the danger of Egyptian culture "dying a slow, painful death under the stranglehold of innumerable constrictions—censorship; religious, social and political bigotry; graft and corruption." The signatories complained, too, that "the suffocating official policy prevents writers and intellectuals from shouldering their responsibilities as part of the conscience of the Egyptian people."[36]

New Lessons for Old: Costi Zureiq and the Revival of Arab Culture

Shortly after the Six-Day War, as soon as the dimensions of the Arabs' military debacle became known, *Al-Adab* put together a double issue devoted to the results of the war and the lessons to be drawn from them. Among the men whom *Al-Adab*'s editor approached was Constantine Zureiq, professor emeritus of history at the American University of Beirut and one of the most prolific writers on Arab nationalism and Arab culture.

Zureiq was a natural choice for the task. An Orthodox Christian born in Damascus during the first decade of this century, he taught history at its university and later became president of that university. He also served as councillor plenipotentiary at the Syrian embassy in Washington. Since the late 1930s, Zureiq—who in the meantime had decided to make Beirut his permanent home—wrote several books dealing specifically with the Arabs' present condition and furnishing advice as to how they can deal with their situation and improve their chances of survival in the modern world. One of these books was his well-known *Ma'na al-nakba* (The meaning of the disaster), a small volume he wrote immediately after the Palestine war of 1948, which was published in Beirut the same year. It was thus rather natural that *Al-Adab*'s editor should have expected Zureiq to have something new and significant to say about the new, even more humiliating "disaster."

In this he must have been disappointed. It is a reflection on the apparent lack of any real change in the general condition of the Arabs that Zureiq should have chosen to respond rather briefly with a few paragraphs that were later incorporated as an introduction to what amounts to a mere reprint of his 1948 booklet, which he was to give the evocative title *Ma'na an-nakba mujaddadan* (The meaning of the disaster—Once again). In this short article, the man who might have been said to be the leading veteran Arab nationalist thinker could say only that the lessons he had drawn from the 1948 defeat continued to be valid after the 1967 debacle. Ultimately, in fact, Zureiq admitted that he had nothing to add to what he had said almost two decades earlier.[37]

There is, therefore, a sense in which the Arabs' bitter experience in 1967 could have been taken by Zureiq as a sort of personal affront and a slight to his public status. He had warned his fellow Arabs; he had diagnosed their present ailments many times and in many ways; he had shown them the way things were done and blueprints were drawn in the modern world; and he had gently and persuasively shown them the way to cope with this world and face its many challenges. But his voice was unheard and his counsels were unheeded—and look what the consequences are!

At one stage in his *Meaning of the Disaster* Zureiq speaks of the Arab-Israeli conflict as being between two "systems," two civilizations. Yet surprisingly few Arab thinkers even attempted to define their civilization or explain its characteristic features and its nature. Among these was Zureiq—in "The Essence of Arab Civilization," a paper he read at the UNESCO Conference in Beirut in November 1948.[38] Though in this work he promises "to analyze the features of Arab civilization" as an undertaking "necessary for a true understanding of the present problems of the Arab world," he proceeds to offer what is mainly a historical account of the rise, blooming, and partial decline of that civilization.

Zureiq sets out to do this by enumerating what he calls the "attitudes" of Arab civilization. These are "the spiritual urge, the universal outlook, and the deep-seated belief in the unity of truth." He points out, however, that these attitudes "had far-reaching effects in practice." One of the most remarkable of these effects, he asserts, is "the cooperative nature of Arab culture."

> When the Arabs came out of the Arabian Peninsula into lands that had been saturated with the achievements of successive civilizations going back to the dawn of history, they did not—as did other conquerors, ancient and modern—destroy or eradicate the marks of those civilizations. On the contrary, with an open mind and a tolerant spirit, they encouraged the continued growth of the cultures of the various peoples that participated in the Empire, and provided the conditions for the unification of those cultures into one goal. Thus Arab civilization is not the achievement of one people; it is rather a cooperative enterprise undertaken by many peoples of various racial origins, cultural backgrounds, and religious affiliations. Muslims, Christians, and Jews; Arabs, Aramaeans, Persians, Turks, Berbers, and others—all shared together in this common effort.[39]

Zureiq then takes up some of the criticisms he says are leveled at Arab civilization and tries to refute them. One such criticism is that Arab civilization has been claimed to be a hodgepodge of many heterogeneous elements, thrown side by side without organization or order. "Had this been the case, Arab civilization would not have been creative. Its contributions in science, philosophy and art, which are being increasingly recognized by Western scholars, could not have been possible except on the basis of a unity of outlook, of endeavor, and of final accomplishment."

A second criticism is directed at the Arabs themselves. What, it is asked, did the Arabs contribute to this process?

> Leaving aside the distinctive contributions of the Arabs—the original spiritual revival, the genius of the language, the faculty of expressing condensed experience in sharp clear-cut verse or prose, the individual achievements of Arabs in the various disciplines—leaving aside all this, I wish to venture the suggestion that even if the Arabs had themselves offered no single element to this whole, it is sufficient to their undying credit that they provided the original spirit and the necessary conditions for the bringing together and the cooperation of all these various peoples in one common effort. It was they who started the empire on a policy of tolerance, who opened their gates in Damascus, Baghdad, Cordova, and elsewhere to scholars and books from the ends of the earth, who gloried in the patronage of the arts and the sciences.[40]

Like all other civilizations in history, Arab civilization had its period of growth, creativity, and glory, and then—like the others—it broke up and disintegrated. After two centuries of unity and expansion, the Arab Empire became divided into various states and principalities—and individual, racial, and regional interests tore up the common loyalty. Then, one after another, waves of wild invaders broke upon it from the East—Genghis Khan, Hulagu, Tamerlane—each cutting deeper into its body and doing its part in damaging Arab life and character. In the meantime, the West was undergoing a renaissance and a reformation through the liberation of reason and the rediscovery of the positive tradition of the past—an achievement toward which, Zureiq asserts, the Arabs themselves had contributed so much.

As a leading exponent of the ideology of Arab nationalism, Zureiq's religious status as an Orthodox Christian manifestly gives him a certain feeling of unease. In an address he gave in the late forties on the anniversary of the birth of the prophet Muhammad, which was entitled "Arab Nationalism and Religion," Zureiq points out that "there has lately been much noise and talk" concerning the relation between nationality and religion.[41] This is not in the least surprising, he asserts, since religion is "one of the most important forces which we have inherited from the past—a past which many factors have worked together to anchor in our lives, to such an extent that most of its aspects have been stamped with the peculiar stamp of religion."

However, while the influence of religion lasted for long centuries, new factors emerged in recent times—"since our contact with the West—to weaken it or to confine it to a particular side of our individual and social life." These new factors "encouraged the Arabs to seek a new kind of life which guarantees for them freedom, happiness and civilization." As the national spirit increases its influence daily and gathers new strength, it is no wonder that there should ensue "attraction and revulsion, union and disjunction," between this national spirit and religion—"sometimes one influencing the other and at other times engaging in a struggle which shakes the very roots of Arab life."

It is also no wonder that the Arabs should today adopt toward these titanic forces varying attitudes. This is "partly because our souls are troubled concerning their significance and partly because of the friction and the clash between the two forces." Some Arabs link their nationality to a particular revealed religion; for them, communal feeling has the better of the national idea. Others make nationalism and religion radically contradictory and therefore advocate that religion and men of religion should be combated in order that the structure of nationalism be erected over their ruins. Between these two extremes, Zureiq points out, there are shades of thinking and varieties of feeling that can be neither delineated nor enumerated. All this is due to a lack of distinction between the religious spirit and communal fanaticism. "True nationalism cannot in any way contradict true religion, for in its essence it is a spiritual movement which aims at resurrecting the inner forces of the nation and at realizing its intellectual and spiritual potentialities."

Eventually, Zureiq comes round to the question, "What is the connection between the Prophet Muhammad and Arab nationalism, and what is his message for it?" Zureiq's answer to this question is clear enough. Muhammad, he asserts, is first and foremost the prophet of Islam; to him was revealed this religion and through him it was spread to the four corners of the world. "This religion has influenced every aspect of our Arab culture, for we cannot today understand our ancient Arab heritage, be it in philosophy or science or art, except after a deep study of the tenets and laws of the Muslim religion, and after reaching a correct understanding of its spirit and organization. This Arab heritage is part of our present culture; it is rather the foundation on which it stands. What is preached by some, namely that we should throw away this ancient heritage and adopt the new Western culture, is indeed mistaken. The Arab heritage is part of us, whether we like it or not."

Moreover, it was the prophet Muhammad who unified the Arabs and brought them together. "He was sent to them when their divisions and quarrels were at the extreme: They were envious of one another; there was no strong tie to bind them together and no banner to unify them and create unity among them." Muhammad inspired them with his spirit, and suddenly these quarreling tribes became friends and drew nearer, formed one single whole, melted and refined in the crucible of faith.

Finally, Muhammad is an example of the man of conviction. He appeared in Mecca and remained unhonored there a long time, putting up with all kinds of humiliation and persecution for the sake of his convictions. "This strong and burning conviction is the foundation of the great Prophet's personality, and it is he who gave his companions the inspiration and transformed them from simple people with narrow horizons and limited powers into leaders and commanders who destroyed the thrones of despotic nations and laid down the foundations of a new civilization." Whatever his sect or his religious community, therefore, it is the duty of every Arab to interest himself in his past culture. "This interest is the first duty enjoined on him by his nationality. He must come forward to study Islam and understand its true nature and thus sanctify the memory of the great Prophet to whom Islam was revealed."[42]

Both in its 1948 and 1967 versions, Zureiq's "meaning of the disaster" teaches that a united, progressive Arab national being is the only thing that is capable of averting "the Zionist danger" — or any other danger for that matter. This, however, will never be achieved "unless there is a fundamental transformation in Arab life." The external struggle whose aim it is to repel the forces of aggression is thus linked with the internal struggle to establish a sound Arab being. "In fact the latter is the pivot of the former and is essential to its success."[43]

What, then, is to be done? Zureiq's prescriptions are as clear as his diagnoses. If they are to face the Zionist danger effectively, he writes, the Arabs must follow in the steps of their adversaries. The reason for this is that the will to struggle and to survive "can be effectively opposed only by another will of equal or greater strength." A unified loyalty, likewise, "can be subdued only by a more complete unity and a stronger loyalty." Again, a system steadily pursuing modern civilization can be conquered only by a system that is more thorough in its pursuit of it and which is more completely armed with it. Finally, a progressive, dynamic mentality "will never be stopped by a primitive, static mentality."

To sum up: "Only a united Arab being possessing these characteristics will repel the Zionist danger — and the Arabs will attain a being of this type only through a fundamental transformation in their way of life. The minds of the intellectuals and of those in the Arab countries who earnestly work for an effective and fundamental solution of the Zionist problem—or, better, of the whole Arab problem—must be so directed as to understand the reality of this being and to seek ways of bringing it about."

What does this whole transformation—on which Zureiq makes the Arabs' very survival conditional—amount to? What are the characteristics of the new "Arab being" whom Zureiq wants to bring into existence? The more one reads into Zureiq's proposals the clearer it becomes that this eminent Arab intellectual advocates nothing short of complete Westernization—a thorough and wholehearted cultural reorientation toward the West, its methods, its techniques, its sociopolitical structure, and its mentality.

This becomes clear right from the outset. The first of the characteristics of the new Arab being Zureiq calls for is "unity." The Arabs, he writes, "should organize themselves into a unified state in which their foreign and economic policies and their defense forces are united." Five, six, or seven states, each completely independent of the other—not counting the weak tie the Arab League represents—each concerned with its own affairs and internal interests, each subjected to various foreign influences and to internal forces with conflicting interests—"states in this condition cannot repel the harrowing blows of our times."[44]

This union, however, is not enough by itself. In fact, it cannot even be achieved if another fundamental condition is not met. This is "economic, social, and intellectual development." The reason why a socioeconomic and intellectual transformation is a prerequisite to building a united Arab nation is adduced by Zureiq from the history of Europe. In the Arab world, he writes, nationalism "has become a catchword bandied about on every tongue." What does not seem to be noticed, however, is that "the formation of nationalism did not occur in the West, and will never occur anywhere, until specific economic, social and intellectual conditions have been met." Nationalism was formed only when there was a breaking down of feudalism (not to mention tribalism), sectarianism, fatalism, and occultism. "It prevailed only when the machine appeared and a primitive, static and disunited system of economics and of living was transformed into a dynamic, specialized and interdependent system, when the powerful barriers between different classes of people were lowered, and when organized, logical knowledge spread and controlled the yearnings of the imagination and the course of thought, thus changing a simple, naive mentality into one that is wide-awake, open-minded and complex."

The attributes Zureiq ascribes to the new Arab being are thus three in number—nationalism, union, and progressivism. In his opinion, each of these attributes is tied to the two others by strong bonds; none of them can stand without the others. But what precisely is meant by progressivism? Zureiq speaks of a number of elements that make up this attribute. Briefly, he states that the aims of the revolution he advocates "merge into a single, clear goal: It is that we become in fact and in spirit, as well as in name and in body, a part of the world in which we live—that we harmonize with it in life and thought, that we speak its language, that we tie ourselves to its roots, and that we rally our fortunes to its fortunes." In order to attain this goal, the Arabs must take numerous steps to turn their life from the mode of ancient and medieval times to the mode of modern times. The most important of these steps are the following:

1. The machine must be acquired and used on the widest possible scale.
2. "The State must be absolutely separated from the religious establishment, since nationalism is not consistent with theocracy. The states of the West have only realized national strength to the extent that they have uprooted sectarianism and organized their lives on the basis of the latest achievements of open-minded, cumulative thought."
3. "The mind must be systematized and organized by training in the positive and empirical sciences, and the nation's cultural efforts must be directed towards the realization of the greatest possible degree of scientific organization."
4. "Generally speaking, heart and mind must be opened to the acquisition of the highest mental and spiritual values which human civilizations have achieved—values whose validity for building a civilization has been confirmed both intellectually and practically."

In the course of Ma'na al-nakba, Zureiq draws a distinction between the immediate and the underlying causes of the disaster—admitting however that the distinction is not absolute, since "in many cases the former are but symptoms of the latter." Thus, the path of the immediate solution and the path of the underlying fundamental solution are not independent of each other. "The thinker or reformer must undertake the two duties together and view them as one." However, it is when he treats the underlying causes—and with their corollary, the fundamental solution—that Zureiq is at his most revealing. The war the Arabs are waging "to uproot Zionism and to conquer it completely," he writes, "will not be finished in a single battle, but will entail a long and protracted conflict."

To put it briefly—and in all frankness and sincerity—this conflict will not lead to the victory of the Arabs as long as they remain in their present condition. The most that they will be able to accomplish under the circumstances is to guard against the immediate Zionist evil and to protect as much of the Arab being as possible. The road to final and complete victory over this evil is different. The road to this victory lies in a fundamental change in the Arabs' condition, and in a complete transformation in their modes of thought, action and life.

The explanation of the victory the Zionists achieved—and only a person who deceives and blinds himself can deny that victory—lies not in the superiority of one people over another but rather in the superiority of one system over another. "The reason for this victory is that the roots of Zionism are grounded in modern Western life while we for the most part are still distant from this life and hostile to it. They live in the present and for the future while we continue to dream the dreams of the past and stupefy ourselves with its fading glory."

At this point, as if remembering something he had somehow forgotten, Zureiq poses a number of searching and relevant questions. He wonders "whether it is right for us to say that there is an Arab homeland." His reply to his own question is understandably involved but ultimately fairly clear. "If by homeland we mean simply the mountains and the rivers, the plains and the shores, there is no doubt that an Arab homeland existed ever since the Arabs settled in their present abode." However, if—as is clearly the case—we mean the permeation of the meaning of the concept into the Arab mind and mentality, the birth of the will to defend and exalt this homeland, then "the answer is in the negative."

Another question posed by Zureiq concerns a rather more fundamental problem. "Is there an Arab nation?" His answer is again clear, if somewhat wary. "If we mean by a nation a people who speak the Arabic language and who possess the potentialities for becoming a nation, then the answer is in the affirmative." However, if—as is meet and right—we mean by this word a nation "which is united in its aims, which has actualized its potentialities, which looks forward to the future and which opens its eyes to the light, then the answer is no!"

In a book published in 1964, Zureiq returns to the subject of civilization (*hadara*) though he does not deal specifically with Palestine.[45] Instead, he attempts an overall appraisal of the current phase of Arab culture and civilization and offers guidance as to the direction in which the Arabs ought to fight on their crucial, cultural front. Over half of the book is devoted to general observations on civilization. Explaining the aim of the study as "the formulation of a sound view of civilization among the Arab peoples in order to make them understand their past, present and future more accurately and soundly," Zureiq proceeds to define the concept of civilization and its components, the disparity between and the unity of civilizations, cultural change, the diffusion of cultures, and the present state of civilization. Here, however, he comes up against a vexing difficulty in terminology; he uses the Arabic *hadara* to denote both "civilization" and "culture." For on the one hand he defines it as that complex of mores, ways of life, religious beliefs, and forms of government characteristic of a certain nation or group of nations; but on the other hand he uses it to denote urban as against nomadic organization, technology, and the other attributes of modern living. He calls the former the "descriptive" and the latter the "value" definitions of *hadara*.

The distinction is rather important to bear in mind in the present case since Zureiq in fact subsequently tries to define the Arabs' present state of civilization rather than culture, listing a number of what he considers its leading shortcomings, and pleading to the contemporary Arab to try and overcome them. The first and more crucial of the Arabs' civilizational problems, he shows, is that of "backwardness." This manifests itself in many ways: scant mastery of nature and inability to exploit its resources; a shaky economic and social organization; wastage of available human resources; and a crippling lagging behind in science and scientific research.

The second problem facing the Arabs on this front, according to Zureiq, is their refusal to be candid with themselves and their fear of self-criticism. It is easy for an individual or a nation to forget or ignore their weaknesses and shortcomings and resort to boasting and self-satisfaction; but the consequences of such behavior are very grave indeed, since it ultimately leads to confusion and loss. It is equally easy to direct one's criticism to others, blaming them for his various misfortunes and shortcomings. The real difficulty, Zureiq reminds his readers, is for an individual and a nation to confront themselves face to face, to bring themselves to account, and to take responsibility for their own actions and shortcomings. This is essential for progress and success, in addition to the fact that self-criticism is a sign of maturity, ability, and self-confidence. The choice confronting the Arabs is clear: either empty boasting and self-satisfaction and ultimately escape from reality, or candor, self-confrontation, and responsibility.

It is not enough that this should be felt by thinkers and intellectuals only. What Zureiq terms "the longing for civilization" (*al-tawq al-hadari*), he believes ought to be experienced by every Arab, since without it the Arabs cannot hope to attain their goals. These goals are worthy of effort and sacrifice: liberty, sovereignty, solidarity, unity, social justice. But the Arab peoples will not attain these goals unless they reach a corresponding phase in their cultural development. There can be no real liberty, no genuine independence, no solidarity, and no unity unless the Arabs prove themselves to be worthy of them—and this will come about only when they have achieved certain attributes of modern civilization.

First and foremost among these is a belief in reason and a search for truth. The Arab peoples must realize that they have no hope for survival unless they equip themselves with the devices of modern science, which will enable them to exploit and organize their natural and human resources to the full. This, Zureiq is careful to point out, does not mean using the scientific attainments of others. "It means that we become capable of producing, discovering and inventing things ourselves, thereby mastering and controlling science and its devices." This belief in reason and the findings of modern science is dictated to the Arabs by the realities of their present condition, which no longer permits clinging to "fantasies and illusions"— for the criterion of progress today is no longer numbers but quality, no more empty claims but solid achievement.

The other attribute which Zureiq finds essential is "an open mind." Instead of turning round in the restricted circles of themselves and closing their windows to the outside world, he writes, the Arabs must acquire an open mind, let the light come into their world from all over. Cultural isolation and narrowness of mind lead to suffocation and are signs of lack of self-confidence, backwardness, and an inability to take up the challenges of modern life.

6 | Patterns of Disillusionment

Reactions to Westernization: "Mental Invasion" and Self-Assertion

In his book on the contemporary Arab world, *Les Arabes d'hier a demain*, Jacques Berque outlines three distinct phases in the development of the Arab mind. The first of these phases he characterizes as a traditional state of harmony with the world—complete undividedness. The second phase was beset by great confusion, when the Arabs were uprooted by the necessity—at first imposed on them and later deliberately chosen—of controlling nature and taking the initiative in history. The third, and final, phase has been one of an increasingly critical attitude, a strong surge of ideas, and forces hitherto repressed both by internal standards and outside forces.

While the first of these phases of the intellectual-spiritual development of the Arabs was characterized by harmony and internal tranquillity, the second was represented politically by the struggle for independence; socially by the mutation of the group; and aesthetically by a renewal of sensibility. The third, and current, phase is represented by a prodigious impulse of the collective will, what the Arabs call *al-thawra*, the revolution. This, according to Berque, entails a complete rearrangement of rival and united forces that govern the contemporary Arab's life. It affects his actions, his feelings, his situations, and his person.[1] It is this phase of the Muslim Arabs' intellectual history that will be dealt with in this part.

It is difficult to fix even an approximate date for the onset of that process of "rearrangement" that has characterized the general intellectual climate in the Arab world. It would be safe to say, however, that insofar as this phase was one of disillusionment, the reaction has been two-edged. Muhammad Wahbi, whose work is surveyed in the following pages, represented one type of reaction to the impact of the West, one of accommodation and integration, while Hisham Sharabi—who wrote more than two decades later—is an excellent example of the other type of reaction, which is one of emotional rejection. In between these two we encounter a number of Arab thinkers and intellectuals who find themselves vacillating endlessly between the two extreme trends. When the Iraqi poet and literary critic Nazik al-Malayka, for instance, gave a lecture at the Fifth Arab Writers' Congress held in Baghdad in 1965 deploring the West's "mental invasion" of Arab culture and literature, several fellow writers expressed reservations.[2] Not one, however, would commit himself either way. While all of them were critical of certain of her views, they chose to ignore the most controversial points she raised. Significantly, these critics kept complete silence about al-Malayka's main argument, namely that the whole temperament, the personality traits, and the moral fabric of the Arab are different from those of the European—and that any attempt to graft the latter into the former tended to produce harmful results.

But if al-Malayka's thesis failed to provoke a really coherent, relevant, and comprehensive reaction from her own colleagues and fellow intellectuals, what is an outside observer to make of them? In trying to tackle this subject two important features of the situation are to be borne in mind. The first is that Nazik al-Malayka's views as expressed in her lecture actually constitutes a marked departure from her own previous positions. As a leading contemporary Arab poet, she was always identified with the innovators and the "progressives," writing free verse and reading and admiring such European writers as Sartre and Camus, as well as supporting new revolutionary movements in the Arab world. In other words, the views expressed in her address represent the reaction and disillusionment of someone who had experienced and appreciated European culture and values and came out disappointed and disenchanted.

The second point to bear in mind in appraising al-Malayka's views is that her attitude is not wholly unrepresentative of the new Arab mood. Muta' Safadi, a noted Arab intellectual and novelist, admits that al-Malayka's lecture constitutes a document outlining a new literary, intellectual, and national mood that was then being formulated and given shape "in some Arab capitals" following the setbacks and the disappointments experienced by progressive Arab political groups.

Do al-Malayka's views, then, represent the first signs of a general Arab reaction against the impact of the West and of its values? There was a period—a rather long one—in which the Arabs, along with other peoples that found themselves under European dominance, used to have a highly ambivalent attitude toward the West and its ways. This attitude, by no means uncommon, was one of great admiration coupled with a good deal of resentment, frustration, envy, and even hatred. In recent years, however, there have been indications that this attitude is changing—and not only where Muslim Arabs are concerned—into a possibly maturer one which, instead of blindly imitating the West and copying its ways and devices, tends to acknowledge the deep-seated cultural differences between East and West, between Afro-Asia and Europe.

In some cases, this new attitude has emerged as one of total rejection of the West, its culture, and its philosophies. This is the attitude al-Malayka seems to represent. It differs only in degree from the militant, aggressive, and uncompromising views expressed in Africa by intellectuals for whom a writer like Frantz Fanon may be considered the leading spokesman. Fanon's, like al-Malayka's, is an overall rejection of Europe. "Leave this Europe," Fanon demands in his book *The Wretched of the Earth*. "The European game has finally ended; we must find something different. We today can do everything so long as we do not imitate Europe, so long as we are not obsessed by the desire to catch up with Europe [which] is running headlong into the abyss." In this way, what used to be little more than hostility to and fear of innovation becomes rejection based on value judgment. Resentment and hatred become scorn and loathing. "They never stop talking about the dignity of man, yet they shoot him whenever they encounter him," jeers Fanon.[3]

There are, of course, other likely explanations for such a total reaction against the West. The historian Alfred G. Meyer, discussing some ideological aspects of the concept of "culture" in Germany and Russia, found that the stress laid by German and Russian thinkers of the nineteenth century on the unique cultural patterns of their respective nations, as against the political, scientific, or philosophical achievements of Western civilization, "can be regarded as an attempt to compensate for a deep-seated feeling of inferiority on the part of German [and Russian] intellectuals once they had come in contact with the advanced nations." As proof for his thesis, Meyer goes on to point out that Russian cultural nationalism developed in measure as Russian contacts with the West intensified. He concludes: "The *Kultur* theories, then, are a typical ideological expression—though by no means the only one—of the rise of backward societies against the encroachment of the West against their traditional culture. *They consist in asserting the reality of something which is just about to be destroyed.*"[4]

This view of the ideological reaction of developing nations against the dynamics of Westernization and industrialization, convenient though it may appear as an explanation of intellectual attitudes such as the one to which al-Malayka gives expression, is not necessarily as applicable to non-Western countries outside Europe as it is to European ones. It is hardly possible, for instance, to apply Meyer's theory to the trend—also noticeable in Arabic writing of the past three decades—whose exponents make the claim that it is nonsensical to speak of a Western civilization as opposed to an Eastern one, since the Arabs have as great a share in shaping the former as anyone else. One example of this approach is provided by Muhammad Kamal 'Ayyad, a Syrian university lecturer and one of the more critically minded of the Arab intellectuals of the 1950s. In a paper he contributed to a collection of studies published by the cultural department of the Arab League in 1953, 'Ayyad dwells on this thesis—the universality of civilization—at some length. Writing of the familiar controversy concerning the West's alleged "materialism" as contrasted to the East's reputed "spirituality," 'Ayyad dismisses as altogether unfounded the opposition often claimed to exist between Orient and Occident.

What, he asks, do we mean by these terms, and where is the dividing line between East and West? "Are there not obvious differences between Anglo-Saxon culture and Latin culture? Are the Spaniards and the Italians nearer, in temperament, sentiments and ways of thinking, to the Scandinavians and the English than they are to the Egyptians, the Lebanese, or the Syrians? Was Japan prevented by her Oriental character and geographical situation from adopting Western culture and civilization? Lastly, did not the civilization of, e.g., ancient Egypt, when it was in full flower, spread over most of the world, followed by Greek civilization, and then by Arabic-Muslim culture? And did they not benefit all nations by promoting the progress of the human race?"[5]

Why, then, this wish that modern civilization be reserved for the Western nations and that other nations cling to their ancient cultures? Did not Western culture, in its day, borrow most of its components from the Greeks, the Chinese, and the Arabs? At this point in his paper, 'Ayyad writes:

> From these and similar questions we arrive at the inevitable conclusion that our traditions do not forbid our borrowing from contem-

porary Western culture. Indeed, apart from a group of conservatives in certain Arab countries—a group which fortunately has dwindled to a small minority—no one among us disputes the necessity of such borrowing. There is a group of people who call themselves moderates, who urge that our borrowing should be limited to what is good in Western civilization, to the adoption of those elements which can be harmonized with our own traits, traditions and customs. The weakness of this argument, however, lies in the difficulty of defining the characteristics that we ought to preserve, or of clearly distinguishing the bad from the good in Western culture.

In any case it is advisable, 'Ayyad goes on to argue, when the Arabs talk of their culture, traditions, and customs, that they trace these to their roots in history, and that they ponder the circumstances in which they were first formed, then modified and remodeled.

Above all we must ask ourselves whether we ought to preserve everything that we have from the past; whether the persistence of a custom for one or even ten generations entitles it to preservation, even though circumstances have changed—even if, in fact, it was originally the product of a period of decline or of foreign domination. We are all—conservatives, moderates and modernists—proud of our Arabic culture in its days of splendor, of its ability to adapt itself, to widen its horizons and keep abreast of world progress. Indeed, our ancestors were prompt borrowers from all nations, and that on a very large scale. They borrowed the methods of government, administration and finance, as well as the arts of architecture, music, and decoration, from the Persians and the Byzantines; irrigation and agriculture from the Nabateans; mathematics from the Hindus; and the manufacture of paper and ceramics from the Chinese. They also went to the Greeks for medicine, mathematics, physics and philosophy; nor did they fear to study other creeds and religions, such as Judaism, Christianity, Mazdaism and mysticism, all of which they discussed and by some of which they are influenced.

'Ayyad then turns to the contribution made by the Arabs to the molding of Western civilization. "Arab culture," he writes, "has played an important part in the creation of modern civilization. The Renaissance in Europe was a direct result of its impact upon Europeans, when the Arabs were in Spain and Sicily, and during the Crusades. Europeans derived much of their mathematical sciences, algebra, physics, medicine and astronomy from Arabic works. The works of Abu Bakr al-Razi, Avicenna, Ibn Rushd, Ibn al-Haytham and Abu al-Qasim continued to be studied in European universities until the sixteenth and seventeenth centuries." The influence of Arabic literature was not confined to the rise of lyric poetry in the south of France or to Dante, Boccaccio, and Cervantes. It is still evident in the works of Goethe and Rueckert early in the nineteenth century.

In sum, 'Ayyad and like-minded Arab intellectuals hold that the Arabs must rejoin universal, modern history if they wish to regain their rightful place in history. It is to be noted here that 'Ayyad, in his advocacy of the universality of civilizations, was by no means the first Arab intellectual to stress the points at which Western and Middle Eastern civilizations meet and converge with each other. Indeed, the old but now somewhat irrelevant debate concerning the "spirituality" of the East and the "materialism" of the West was settled once and for all by the Egyptian thinker and man of letters Taha Husain, who used to be described as "the doyen of Arabic literature." Pointing out that European civilization possessed great spiritual content though there was a great deal of materialism in it, Husain argued as far back as the late 1930s that the Near East was the cradle of all three revealed religions, those adopted by Europeans as well as those embraced by Easterners. "Can these religions," he asked rhetorically, "be 'spirit' in the East and 'matter' in the West?"

Taha Husain made this point in the course of a plea that Egypt view herself as part of Mediterranean civilization, not of the East, and that his compatriots aim for out-and-out Westernization, having anyway taken Europe as their model both materially and intellectually.[6]

Since this spirited plea was made, Egyptian and Arab attitudes toward the West and Westernization have taken many turns and undergone many changes. Advocates of Westernization—including Taha Husain himself—began to waver, many of them becoming vehement in their rejection of the West. Opponents of Westernization tended to become more confirmed in their convictions. And waverers, for the most part, continued to vacillate. Regardless of what the contemporary Muslim Arab thought about the West, its culture, and its ways, he remained its captive, capable neither of rejecting nor of accepting it.

This ambivalence often takes very pronounced forms. One Egyptian writer, referring to this phenomenon in the mid-1960s, branded the attitude as "adolescent." Indeed, he argued, a certain measure of adolescence in the behavior of the Arab intellectual of today was inevitable. Adolescence, he explained, was the unconscious revolt against parental authority. It is natural that the Arab intellectual should revolt against Western culture, "that teacher from whom he had learned his ideas and concepts of the modern world—the sum total of the attitudes and the norms according to which he conducts his everyday life."[7]

This was written in 1964. The situation in the 1970s and the 1980s differed substantially from what it was then only in the sense that the Arab intellectual, along with Arabs as a whole, now had more self-confidence and felt he could stand up to the constant challenge Western culture and civilization had been posing to him throughout the past hundred years or so. Hisham Sharabi's latest writings, including an autobiographical work published in Beirut in 1978, bears witness to this trend—as we shall see later in this chapter.

The Broken Cup: Muhammad Wahbi and the Modern Arab Predicament

"In the beginning God gave to every people a cup, a cup of clay, and from this cup they drank their life. They all dipped in the water, but their cups were different. Our cup is broken now. It has passed away." Ruth Benedict, to whom these words were said by a chief of the Digger Indians of California, explains that the chief did not mean that there was any question of the extinction of his people. What he had in mind, she writes, was "the loss of something that has value equal to that of life itself, the whole fabric of his people's standards and beliefs." There were other cups of life left, to be sure, and they held perhaps the same water; but the loss was irreparable. "It was no matter of tinkering with an addition here, lopping off something there. The modelling had been fundamental, it was somehow all of a piece. It had been their own."[8]

At some undetermined and indeterminable date toward the end of the eighteenth century or the first decades of the nineteenth, the cup of life of Muslim Arabs began to crack. Since that date, their writers and thinkers, their religious and secular leaders, have been trying to locate the malady and prescribe a cure. Speaking generally and from a broad perspective, modern and contemporary Arab intellectuals and scholars cannot be accused of failing to put their finger on the source of the many ailments that have been plaguing their society and culture these past hundred years or so. One Arab thinker whose work can properly be included in this category is Muhammad Wahbi, a Lebanese Muslim educator and social critic who began writing on the state of contemporary Arab culture and society in the mid-1950s. A radical and rather outspoken critic, Wahbi nevertheless has attracted relatively little attention in Arab intellectual circles, partly perhaps because he has refused to identify himself with any of the fashionable Arab political movements or "isms" of the day. He has written only two books and has confined himself to publishing in modest and soft-spoken monthlies with no definable political or ideological orientation or radical pretensions, *Al-Adib* of Beirut and *Al-'Arabi* of Kuwait.

Wahbi's first book, published in 1956, apparently before the Sinai War of October–November that year, sets out in brief but lucid fashion all the elements of his thinking and his approach that he was to develop and elaborate upon in his later writings. Typically, the title of the book is *The Crisis of Arab Civilization* (Azmat al-tamaddun al-'Arabi).[9] It had a first printing of two thousand copies and, as far as can be ascertained, has never been reprinted.

In his introduction to the book, Wahbi describes the state of the Arabs as "psychological collapse" (*inhiyar ma'nawi*). This collapse, he asserts, brought about largely by the terrible shock of the Arabs' debacle in 1948, now threatens them with even greater and rather deadlier disasters; for one of the consequences of that debacle has been "this daily growing doubt about the Arabs' capacity to survive as a nation." Clearly, the Arabs' very existence poses a problem these days, Wahbi asserts. "Yet the student of the Arabs, of what they say and what they do, cannot get a clear picture of the way they view the reality of this problem." Perhaps the most eloquent proof of the confusion besetting the Arabs' present condition is the perplexing multiplicity of the schools of thought that try to come to grips with that condition. Broadly speaking, Wahbi writes, three widely divergent groups of Arab thinkers grapple with the problem simultaneously. These are the following:

1. The sentimentalists, whose dreamy stare is fixed on memories of a glorious history and whose hearts beat with loyalty and compassion, but whose wills and minds are fossilized in the alleys of a dead past. These naturally fail to grasp the nature of the problem.
2. The "professional nationalists," who see in the problem a convenient political device they use for purely personal gains.
3. An active, dedicated minority whose efforts remain sterile because it has either no defined objective or no valid point of departure. The general approach of this group, moreover, springs from the old mentality and thus turns round and round in a vicious circle.[10]

The best definition of the Arabs' predicament, Wahbi believes, would be to term it "a problem of civilization" (*qadiyyat tamaddun*); for, "appearances to the contrary notwithstanding, Arab life in all its facets and foundations is an ailing one shamefully lagging behind modern civilization." The Arabs, Wahbi adds, "utilize modern concepts and institutions with old mentalities and to serve ancient needs." With them, "democracy is put in the service of feudalism, science is turned into a mask for ignorance . . . and morality remains an assortment of anachronistic commands and precepts that are mystical, frozen and humanly insupportable." The Arabs have failed dismally in digesting and assimilating modern civilization. "It is often argued that unity is a precondition for Arab progress. It would be more correct to say that Arab progress is a prerequisite of Arab unity."[11]

The opening chapter of *The Crisis of Arab Civilization*, rather liberally entitled "Concerning the Arabs' Psychological Make-Up," deals mainly with what Wahbi terms "national character," which he defines as the sum total of "a number of psychological traits which grow and take form with the passage of time, and accompany the nation throughout the ages without undergoing any fundamental changes or mutations." A glance at the national character of the Arabs, he writes, would throw much light on the course of their history and help explain the reasons for many of their problems. Two features of this character are singled out by him as being especially important because of their persistence and the far-reaching effects they have had on the Arabs' fortunes. These are impulsiveness (*al-infi'al*) and what Wahbi terms "the mystical bent" (*al-nuzoo' al-ghaybi*).[12]

Impulsiveness, Wahbi explains, robs men of the ability to plan ahead and base their decisions and actions on cold, concrete calculation. It reduces their deeds to mere improvisation and renders their words meaningless. As soon as failure befalls them, they tend to turn from burning enthusiasm to paralyzing inactivity, resignation, and despair. One characteristic trait of people who suffer from impulsiveness is that, like a baby or a prehistoric creature, they live wholly in the present and thus expose themselves to the whims of outside, unpredictable forces.

"The mystical bent," the second trait of the Arabs' national character Wahbi dwells upon, is "perhaps the dominant feature of their psychological make-up." This is not in the least surprising since the Arab world was the birthplace of the world's three revealed religions, a fact which stamped all the changes and upheavals in Arab history with the imprint of religion—so much so that even the national idea seemed incapable of taking shape in the Arabs' mind in isolation from religion. The mystical frame of mind, however, does not necessarily relate to man's attitude to religion. "What we mean by it here is a pattern of thought, a type of general psychological reaction."

In a chapter entitled "The Crisis of Values," Wahbi turns to the moral aspects of the crisis. In the Arab mind, he writes, the idea of morality is associated with a concept of purely imperative precepts and commands. In this view, morality consists of an assortment of commandments and precepts based largely on irrational foundations and offers no explanation or justification. Honesty, for instance, is not a quality sought and commended for its own sake; it is adhered to solely because God decreed it. And so it is with other moral values: they are observed and praised not because they are good in themselves but because God commands us to observe them and forbids us from committing deeds contrary to their tenets. This phenomenon has proved to be a serious impediment to Arab progress, since it has deprived the Arab of the all-important element of freedom of choice that is the essence of man's humanity.

Wahbi then invites us to look into the state of these values in the contemporary Arab world. True, they are on every tongue and invoked on every conceivable occasion and at all times. But to what purpose? Are these values spoken of as realizable ends and as ideals to be sought after for their own sake? The answer is an emphatic "no!" These values have become meaningless words, "fossilized symbols" lost in an expanse of ignorance and materialism. The Arabs no longer know the importance of these values as pillars of progress and civilization, as things that establish man's humanity and distinguish him from other animals. With them, values have become mere symbols, and this metamorphosis has resulted in a total distortion of concepts and ideals. Such higher values as Truth, Love, Beauty, Art, Knowledge, and Dignity have lost their true meaning, each in its own way, and have become strictly relative concepts. Even the meaning of Honor, probably the most famous of the Arabs' values, has become confined to the field of sexual relations. In the Arab world today it can best be defined as "conformity with inherited customs, traditions and habits pertaining to the relations between man and woman." The fate of such other values as freedom, free expression, and man has not been any better. The national idea itself has suffered a great deal of distortion and deterioration. In addition to its confusion with religion, it often rests upon a deep division and a fundamental difference of feelings and tendencies—so much so that national feeling is now centered on falsehood and deception.[13]

No less falsified and corrupted is the Arabs' conception of politics and political action, Wahbi argues in the course of his book. In Arab society, he writes, politics has become synonymous with the art of lying, plotting, and self-seeking, while the politician is seen as merely engaging in a successful profession or trade. The way in which the idea of democracy is grasped and practiced by the Arabs is a case in point. Freedom is the essence of democracy; if democracy is introduced into a society whose individuals are ignorant of the meaning of freedom, it is not likely to last there any more than a plant can survive in a rocky terrace or a medicine can be effective in a lifeless corpse. In the Arab world, the principle of "government of the people, by the people, and for the people" is no more than an empty phrase, a body devoid of any life.[14]

In the remaining chapters of his book, Wahbi writes about the state of contemporary Arab society and economy. Arab society, he asserts, is closed (*mujtama' munghaliq*), retrograde (*raj'i*), and disintegrating (*mutahallil*). The Arabs lack social cohesiveness, Wahbi concludes; their society is torn by personal and tribal feuds and conflicts, treats its women like virtual slaves, and breeds men who are suspicious of all authority, devoid of a public spirit, and exclusively preoccupied with their selfish interests and private pursuits. This society is also retrograde, witness the notorious trinity—poverty, disease, and illiteracy—which pervades such large sections of it. Obviously, these and other social ills have their deep roots in social injustice, ignorance, and the huge gulf separating the society's various classes. They can, therefore, be cured only by eliminating illiteracy, establishing social justice, raising the general intellectual level, and ensuring freedom in all its forms. Then and only then can the Arabs set out to build an open, progressive, and healthy society for themselves.[15]

Having surveyed and analyzed the ailments of contemporary Arab society and culture, Wahbi turns—two years later—to a critique of the Arabs' attitudes toward Western civilization. In the process, he manages to make a number of new and equally outspoken statements about the current state of the Arabs' mental and intellectual world. This he does in his second and, in a way, more comprehensive book, *Arabism and Humanism,* published in 1958.[16] In many senses, this book is a sequel to his first work.

Following its invasion by Western civilization, Wahbi writes, the Arab East was pervaded by two leading intellectual trends—one characterized by conservatism and the other by a revolutionary stance. The former carried the banner of opposition and resistance to Western civilization; its followers maintained that this civilization was "materialistic and that materialism was all that there was in it, motivating all the actions of people who embrace it. The East, on the other hand, is spiritual, and its spirituality should not be wasted." Western civilization, the conservatives say, abounds in methods and motives of war—a feature that tends to prove it has its deep roots in materialism. They also claim that this civilization has come to the Arabs along with imperialism and thus represents and embodies imperialism and serves its ends. It is also steeped in Zionism, whose actions it endorses and guides.

As for the second trend, admiration for Western civilization makes its followers call for total adoption of its tenets and methods. "This call, however, emanates from that same belief in the materialism of this civilization and the spirituality of the East which informs the conservatives—so much so that this admiration must be viewed as a sign of the 'revolutionaries' bitter disappointment with spirituality and their infatuation with materialism."

Somewhere between these two mutually exclusive trends, there is another current of thought—namely, the one that favors partial adoption of Western civilization. This current "calls for a middle-of-the-road course which demands moderation in everything adopted. The supporters of this trend believe in adopting one facet of Western culture, i.e. the scientific method whose necessity for progress has been proved, while leaving aside its other facets, especially its morals. . . . Basically, this call is also based on the belief in the materialism of the West and the spirituality of the East."

If we now try to consider the views of the followers of these three schools, Wahbi writes, we find that all three of them agree on one point—namely, that Western civilization is materialistic while Eastern culture is spiritual. "Truth to tell, however, I cannot understand how this consensus has come about or by what logic it has struck roots. Is it because Western civilization abounds in products that are embodied in material forms, in spite of the fact that these products have come only as the result of a spiritual driving force? What, after all, is the meaning of spirituality if not the attainment of harmony with values aiming at the subjugation and utilization of matter instead of evading it and taking refuge in the negativism of empty talk about sentiments and fancies? What are the morals of the Orientals and what is their spirituality compared to the honest love of truth, the high respect for beauty and the deep reverence for the freedom of others which the behavior of civilized man actually manifests?"

None of these three currents has anything to recommend it to reason, Wahbi adds, because all of them are based on a fallacy. "There is no spirituality today in the East. Spirituality is to be found in the West, and the essence of progress embodies this very spirituality." If, however, we agree that all these three trends are erroneous and objectionable, one of them—the one that calls for partial adoption of Western ways—contains an element of danger. This trend, though masquerading as a moderate one, is a falsehood itself and has a much more harmful influence than the other two, since its power of persuasion is greater than theirs. This is because of the quality of wisdom attributed to it in spite of the fact that it rests on a fundamental contradiction. Wahbi explains: "Western civilization has no science that had not originated in and flourished on moral foundations. Thus, there is no sense in adopting science and at the same time discarding this foundation. . . . Western civilization is one of a piece, and all its parts draw on the same source, to the extent that division would destroy all its value and benefit." The only meaning of the call for partial adoption of Western civilization is in fact "no more than cowardice and incompetence." Suffering from an incapacity to grasp the facts, this trend has surrendered itself to fear and indecision.

Wahbi goes on to show the inevitability of the process of a total adoption of Western ways. "The truth," he writes, "is that neither our acceptance nor our rejection of any of these three currents would alter the course of events, since the impact of Western civilization actually and automatically exists as a result of the continuous contact imposed by the conditions of modern life and the availability of modern means of communication." However, there is one important and incontrovertible fact: This influence would be worthless if it were to remain accidental and involuntary. Indeed, it would be dangerous to the Arab mind if this continues to have a mistaken view of the spirit of Western civilization. "If we persist in this view, we would not only draw no benefit from this influence, but would derive the opposite of it, and with grave consequences to ourselves. For as long as we remain very far from the spirit of what we are adopting failure would be our lot: We would isolate ourselves and remain within the narrow circle inside which we are revolving today and which inspires us with many false ideas and concepts."[17]

Correcting the Arabs' view of Western civilization is of great significance, Wahbi asserts, since a balanced view of the issue would demonstrate the necessity for total adoption by them of this civilization in an open and voluntary way. "Ours is the age of one civilization for the whole world. There is, indeed, no choice for any people but to go right in the direction of this civilization and wholly absorb it if that people wants to live in the present and not cling to an extinct past."[18]

The universality of Western civilization, the claim that it is a composite rather than a "pure product," the fact that it contains many borrowings from other civilizations, especially Arabic, and that in the Middle Ages the Arabs acted as transmitters and disseminators of the arts and sciences that made up this civilization—all these are themes that modern Arab intellectuals are eager to stress when comparing the present condition of the East with that of the West. Not unnaturally, special emphasis is usually placed on these themes by those Arab writers who advocate borrowing the devices of Western civilization and adopting its methods. Wahbi, indeed, takes considerable pains to point out that the very term *Western civilization* is something of a misnomer—that it "contains some exaggeration and there-fore calls for definition and delineation." For while the term suggests that this civilization belongs to the West alone, "in reality it is the civilization of the whole of human society."[19]

This, then, is how Muhammad Wahbi views the crisis of contemporary Arab society and culture and the relationship between Arab civilization and what he terms modern universal civilization. Elsewhere—writing five years after the publication of *Arabism and Humanism*—Wahbi makes a daring diagnosis of the ills of present-day Arab politics. Under the pro-vocative title "The Arabs' Political Problem Is a Moral One!," he argues that at the core of all the troubles, the unrest, and the instability from which the Arab world suffers today there obviously lies an acute political problem. When one tries to define and delineate this problem, however, one is faced with "a thick veil of obscurity and confusion."[20]

What, then, is the Arabs' political malaise? What do they complain of? What is it that stands in the way of their wishes and aspirations? Accord-ing to Wahbi, the most prominent of the Arabs' political problems—and the one which also happens to be the most talked about and repeated—is that of Arab unity. Now Arab unity is "an age-old aim of the Arab nation-alist movement"; but when one considers the great deal of talk and writing being done on the subject these days, one is shocked to see how they are immersed in "an atmosphere of theoretical thinking and abstract general principles, thus failing to come to terms with contemporary Arab reality."

To illustrate his thesis, Wahbi cites one widespread notion he says has become the great common denominator of all treatises on Arab national-ism and Arab unity. This is the one that stresses the so-called "necessity of concentrating on the popular endeavor" and advocates "more participa-tion by the masses in order to safeguard nationalist gains." Out of this widespread notion sprang other similar slogans, such as the one calling for freedom of political action and the setting up of a party system "springing from the ranks of the conscious masses and reflecting their will."

Is this confidence in the Arab masses justified? "Would it not be more in order, before we grant a people its freedom, for us to verify that people's fitness for shouldering all its responsibilities, and to see to it that this free-dom would not in the end prove a disaster?" Before engaging in theories and general principles, Wahbi believes, we have to realize that the first requisite for action aimed at attaining the goals of Arab nationalism is "to understand the psychological make-up of the Arab people." He further believes that "the conclusion we can draw from studying contemporary

Arab psychology is . . . spiritual void." It is this moral crisis that is at the root of all the Arabs' troubles, Wahbi concludes. "Indeed, all the problems facing the Arabs today are as nothing—and are rendered irrelevant—when compared to this major problem, whose solution would lead to the disappearance of all the others." Thus, it is futile to speak of the Arabs' political problems. It is meaningless and idiotic to search for "political systems best suited to the Arabs," since the foundation of all political action is morality, which Wahbi says the Arabs lack completely.

Wahbi's views, as summarized above, can properly be said to belong to the so-called "literature of the Fifth of June" even though some of them were published some twelve years prior to the Six-Day War. There is, however, a final point which may prove to have a bearing not only on Wahbi's writing but on the whole body of Arabic literature of self-criticism and self-interpretation. In his earlier book, *The Crisis of Arab Civilization,* Wahbi refers to the bout of self-criticism and self-blame that swept the Arab world following the Arabs' defeat in the war of 1948 with Israel. Examining this voluminous body of writing, he observes, might lead one to believe that the Arabs had at last "arrived"—that they had finally reached maturity and acquired the consciousness they had lacked for so many centuries.

Further examination would, however, reveal that "in reality this [bout of self-blame] is nothing but a new ailment that has been added to the assortment of complaints from which the Arab psyche suffers, and that it itself needs treatment and cure." For although there has been a great wave of admonitions and criticisms, all these have been directed against governments and regimes. None of the critics had the stamina to stand up and tell the people, "It is you who are to blame! You are the first culprit!" For what are governments and who are their leaders? "Is it not the people that invest them with power, elevate them, and have the power to remove them if they so wish? . . . A people that has not absorbed the concepts of a healthy national life, that fails to grasp the meaning of politics, democracy, freedom and social solidarity, and which blindly follows any victorious leader, has no right to accuse others."[21]

Under the Spell of the West: The Case of Hisham Sharabi

The question as to how to set themselves and their society free from the fetters of what they variously call the West's "cultural imperialism" or "mental invasion" has exercised the minds of many Arab writers and intellectuals throughout the sixties and seventies. The problem, as most of them formulated it, has been that, now that the Arabs have finally managed to liberate their lands from Western political and economic dominance, the time is ripe for them to try and do away with the cultural, psychological, and intellectual manifestations of that dominance.

There has been no uniformity of views as to how to accomplish this feat. There are those who argue that the break with the West should be total, since there is an intrinsic, unbridgeable basic difference between the culture of the West, its norms and its civilization, and that of Muslim Arabs. Another school of thought has advanced the thesis that since much of what is now taken to be Western culture owes its origin and flowering to heavy borrowing from Arab and Islamic culture back in the Middle Ages, such a break would be unnatural, unreasonable, impractical, and harmful. Finally, there are those who advocate full-scale Westernization as the only way to face the challenge of the West—and of Israel as part thereof.

As we have seen in the course of this section, these issues are debated in the Arab world fairly periodically, and there is considerable literature on the subject. Until comparatively recently, however, the debate was usually conducted largely by traditionalists and by people whose knowledge of the West and its culture was indirect and rather limited. Thoroughly Westernized Arab intellectuals with a sound, firsthand knowledge of the West, and whose academic tools and working language are Western, have generally been reticent and wary of dealing with the subject. One notable exception is Hisham Sharabi, a well-known author and political scientist, who in the mid-seventies published a book in which he sets his views on such issues as Westernization and its consequences, contemporary Arab society, and his own personal experiences and reactions as an Arab who has known the West and fell under its spell.

Sharabi taught political science and the history of civilizations at Georgetown University in Washington beginning in the late fifties. He is a Palestinian of middle-class origin whom the turmoil in his native land during the late forties caught while studying in the United States. Finding himself a niche in the academic world there, he taught and wrote in English and enjoyed the friendship of those around him, usually spending his summer vacations in Beirut. In the mid-seventies, he became editor of the Beirut-based *Journal of Palestine Studies* and a thoroughly committed writer politically. He has also been active in the work done by Arab Americans to promote the Arab cause inside the United States. For the best part of the three decades he spent in the United States, Sharabi relates, his only two concerns were books and friends. "Little had I known, however, that books can become a way of escape and hiding, and that friendships come to an end, leaving only a bitter taste in the mouth."

Sharabi's book, from which the above remark is taken, was published in Beirut in 1975 and is called *Introductions to the Study of Arab Society.*[22] One of the most interesting aspects of the work is that, though its author had written several books in the past, this was the first he was to write in Arabic, his mother tongue. As Sharabi relates in his preface, at one point in the recent past "I vowed not to publish any book in any language other than Arabic—and I still stand by that vow." An important point here is that Sharabi's decision to write only in Arabic seems to have coincided with a certain process of radicalization he says he had gone through since the Six-Day War. The year 1967, he writes, marked the beginning of a new phase in his life. Disasters sometimes lead to despair, he explains, and at other times they lead to a strengthening of the will to fight. "The impact of the shock of the Six-Day War strengthened our consciousness and deepened it day by day. . . . To surrender to despair was tantamount to surrendering to the enemy."

Sharabi's liberation from "the dominant culture"—in this case the Western culture of the United States—came in a somewhat unexpected way. Immediately following the Six-Day War, he relates, he was engaged in preparing his lectures for the coming semester. The subject was the evolution of political and social theories in Europe, in which Marx was to figure merely as "another" European thinker and Marxism was to be subjected to a critique in light of its founder's "failure" when he spoke about the inevitability of the fall of capitalism. "For some reason whose source I cannot fathom I started with Marx. I still remember my reading of Marx that summer! I felt as though I was reading him for the first time. I had not known any experience which was to shake me so since I first read Nietzsche when I was seventeen. Nietzsche's impact, however, was more emotional than intellectual, whereas Marx penetrated the very foundations of my thinking." The result was that Sharabi discovered "the extent to which the dominant culture is capable of forming the mentality of the individual, of subjugating him to its values, and of deceiving him on the deepest of levels. I felt that I began to break the mental fetters which had incapacitated me."

From then on, we are told, "I started taking an independent intellectual course which I derive from an inner force, not from a force that dominates me from the outside; and I realized that the first step to liberation consists of self-liberation, and that the beginning of liberation consists of rescue from enslavement to the dominant mentality."

The way this "enslavement" manifested itself and the damage it has done to the Arabs are dealt with in a chapter of the book entitled "The

Arab and the Cultural Challenge." Arab history during the past hundred years or so, Sharabi asserts, "is in its essence a series of responses to the cultural challenge—and this on all levels, the political, the military, the economic, the social and the cultural." On all these levels, he adds, "it is impossible to comprehend the nature of the changes which our society has undergone unless we understand, on the one hand, the reality of the continuous challenge posed by the West to our society and, on the other hand, our reactions in response to these challenges."

To the extent, then, that what the modern Arab did and the way he behaved were in the main mere "reactions" to the West and its challenges, "our modern history, both in its negative and positive aspects, has been the work of the West, directly or indirectly." It is true that the Arabs, at long last, have succeeded in wresting some of their rights from the West; however, "on the psychological and cultural planes we continue to be under the West's domination—and here, in my view, lies the crucial factor in our confrontation with its challenge."

The nature of this "cultural imperialism" and its sociopsychological repercussions are obvious. "For us, when in our daily speech we use the terms 'civilization' and 'culture' we mean simply European or American civilization, i.e. Western civilization. Since the beginning of our relations with the West we have been suffering from a feeling of inferiority vis-à-vis all that is Western. . . . For us, the West has become the source of everything that is valuable, superior and noble—so much so that we became used to viewing ourselves, our society and our history through the Westerner's perception of us; our paramount worry, consciously or unconsciously, has become to earn the approval of the Westerner and his admiration."

Perhaps the most instructive—and the most sophisticated—of Sharabi's reflections on this subject concerns the controversy between the modernists and the traditionalists in modern Muslim Arab thought. The most important manifestations of the Arabs' "feeling of inferiority" vis-à-vis Europeans and Americans, he asserts, "have been the attempts made by our writers and thinkers since the beginning of this century to stress the greatness of the cultural legacy of Arabic Islam and the extent to which it had affected the civilization of the West and its growth." From the psychological point of view, he adds, "these attempts are but an expression of this feeling of inferiority, aimed at compensating [us] for that feeling by finding an honorable link with the West that would make us a part of it even if only from an abstract historical viewpoint." This same feeling of inferiority, according to Sharabi, "pushes us in the opposite direction as well—i.e.

the rejection of everything the West offers and blind devotion to our heritage and traditions."

What then is to be done? In order for the Arabs to successfully face the Western challenge, they must get rid of the West's cultural domination in the same way they freed themselves from its political dominance — "otherwise we cannot attain healthy interaction with it and we cannot liberate ourselves from it." That this is going to prove a difficult enterprise is due to the fact that, whereas political imperialism aims at the material and tangible, "cultural imperialism" is a psychological phenomenon. In order to successfully face the West's challenge, then, Sharabi advises the Arabs to try to do two things:

1. Attain a correct understanding of the West and of what they want from the West.
2. Transcend both the modernist and the traditionalist stances and take an independent cultural course.

It is not quite clear whether Sharabi himself manages in this study of contemporary Arab society and culture to transcend both the modernist and the traditionalist stances. Indeed, it appears that he freely uses, and with telling effect, all the tools the modern (Western) disciplines of sociology and anthropology offer. This becomes clear from a reading of the relevant chapters, which will be surveyed here. The book, it ought to be stated at this point, can, on the whole, be considered part and parcel of the post-1967 Arab quest for self-knowledge and self-understanding. To be sure, self-criticism and soul-searching are not new phenomena in Arab writing. Since the events of 1948, when five Arab armies failed to prevent the establishment of the state of Israel, Arab writers and intellectuals have been closely scrutinizing their society and culture, and the literature in this field has proliferated. The quest reached a peak after the Six-Day War, when self-scrutiny often took the form of breast-beating and self-flagellation. Very little of this voluminous literature, however, was based on solid, systematic sociopsychological research. In his book, Sharabi goes a long way in rectifying this state of affairs. He makes a valiant attempt to explore the roots of the problem, relegating politics and polemics to a fittingly low order of priority and concentrating, instead, on Arab family structure and behavior patterns as the real sources of his people's condition.

Two characteristics of the Arab family singled out by Sharabi are that it is tribal and patriarchal. The terms *tribe* and *family,* he writes, become interchangeable when we consider the structure and patterns of behavior of extended Arab families of the middle and lower-middle classes. In these families, the child is introduced into the society only through his links with his family, his dependence on it, and his support for it. One of the most significant results of this is that the child grows up feeling his basic loyalty is to his family, not to the society as a whole. As a result of his upbringing and education, a dutiful, loyal son feels it is his duty to work in the interests of his parents and brethren first, and then of his relatives. Society and the public interest come only next.

The dominance of the father and his aloofness and remoteness have results that are no less harmful in their effect. Sharabi quotes from the writing of a young Muslim from Tunisia, Mahomed Karoui: "Who among us Arabs can claim that his family and the environment in which he grew had really wanted, accepted and loved him and acknowledged his identity as a person?" His answer: "No one, assuredly; for how could a person be loved when his very existence is epitomized in his being a useful object brought into the world for the continuation of the family and as security against the parents' old age—or merely to satisfy the father's pride by proving his ability to beget many children. . . . He [the father] begets us not for our sakes but for his own sake. . . . He begets us in order to be one of the supports of his existence, and ultimately deprives us of a life of our own: We do not live but merely allow him to live through us, and this makes our lives distorted right from the beginning."

Though Karoui adds, almost as an afterthought, that this state of affairs is to be found in other societies and other ages, Sharabi proceeds from this description to show how, in its basic features, the Arab family is a microcosm of Arab society as a whole. Regardless of the political ideology and the existing regime, the patterns that prevail in the family remain dominant in the wider society. The result is that the individual remains oppressed and persecuted in both. In the same way as the family allows the child only very little leeway to realize his independence, so does the sociopolitical system, which curbs the individual's tendency to ask questions and bars his independent mental and intellectual maturity.

In Sharabi's own words: "The educational and social system deters the child from nurturing confidence in his own opinions and encourages him to accept the views of others without hesitation or questioning—and this in turn leads to submission to authority, i.e. to his father and teachers, and later to anyone who is stronger than himself or occupies a higher position of power or prestige. When he grows up, moreover, he learns to be wary and refrains from taking a clear-cut position on any specific issue."

There are other features of family and upbringing Sharabi considers detrimental to the growth of a healthy and rounded Arab personality. Education, he points out, places very little emphasis on persuasion and reward, concentrating instead on coercion and corporal punishment. Side by side with this, sex is considered taboo and sexual activities are surrounded by an air of secretiveness and stealth, so that the child's sexual experience is beset by pain, confusion, and chaos. In the end, sex produces a feeling of guilt in him and puts him always on the defensive, in constant fear of "what people will say" and at all times trying to gain the approval of others.

These and other features of upbringing and family life make the Arab individual, when he enters practical life, wary and suspicious of others whom he considers strangers. This in turn results in a feeling of insecurity. He generally feels that in his dealings with others he is being deceived, exploited, or liable to be trodden on if he does not assume an aggressive and domineering stance. Ultimately, the individual's experience of the world outside disappoints him and he returns to the bosom of the family. The hold of the family is thus strengthened, and this prevents him from attaining independence as a person and curbs the growth of his social consciousness and psychological maturity.

Throughout the book, Sharabi describes contemporary Arab society as being "bourgeois-feudalist." Basic to what he calls "bourgeois-feudal behavior," he writes, are dependence, lack of ability, and evasion. These three attributes characterize the conduct of the individual who, in refraining from facing difficulties, in leaving things to others, and in withdrawal and evasion, exemplifies the pattern of behavior of the whole system when confronted with a challenge—a pattern which Sharabi sums up as follows: "evasion of confrontation, refusal to commit oneself, an attempt to avoid conflict, and evading responsibility."

Needless to say, dependence has deep social and cultural roots. A child brought up and educated in a competitive society, for instance, tends to acquire the ethic of competition and hard work. In a society where the place of the individual and his role are defined as a priori, on the other hand, the individual tends to become dependent and submissive. The child in the bourgeois-feudal family, through his dealings with authority, such as the father, the teacher, and the uncle, learns two main lessons. He learns, first, how to curb his aggressiveness when dealing with authority; and he learns, secondly, how to avoid a confrontation with it. This leads to dependence and submissiveness. Dependence, when it reaches these dimensions, leads to evasion and withdrawal, both of which are far easier than confrontation.

The result, according to Sharabi, is that generations of young Arabs consist of mere "onlookers" who entrust their affairs to their elders. This type of upbringing, he writes, produces individuals alienated from their society, feeling no commitment toward it and caring only about what concerns them personally, largely because they feel powerless to influence it in any way. It is the bourgeois-feudal society, Sharabi asserts, which makes submission a substitute for challenge and confrontation, deception and stealth a substitute for a spirit of courage, and retreat and withdrawal prevail instead of endeavor and initiative. He quotes one Arab saying, among others, which he says exemplifies this attitude: "The hand which you cannot break you should kiss—and then pray it will be broken."

One result of this feeling of powerlessness is fatalism, which Sharabi considers a form of failure to perceive and prepare for the future. Bourgeois-feudal society, he writes, pays dearly for this failure. The belief that "the morrow will take care of itself," useful though it might be psychologically, robs society of the ability to plan for and control the future. The prevalent mentality, indeed, perceives time itself in a mystic manner—for it, the past is "glorious," the future offers "the rewards of Heaven."

Summing up his section on "the bourgeois-feudal society"—the description he chooses for contemporary Arab society—Sharabi lists a few of its other "negative" features. He speaks of the prevalence of superstition as a way of "rearranging reality" and thus justifying and covering up for failure to influence events. He also points to a tendency in this society to belittle and downgrade the individual and humiliate him. He claims, too, that even the highly educated of this society remain basically unaffected by their training. He cites as proof their "failure actually to master foreign languages, absence of academic discipline, inability to perceive the fine shades of meaning and express them, and failure to be systematic in facing and tackling given problems."

Other weak points of Arab society, as Sharabi depicts it, are sociopolitical fragmentation, political rivalries, class polarization, and communal and racial divisions. Finally, he laments the fact that this society—apart from the mere national and religious abstractions it professes—does not allot any place to the poorer classes, a state of affairs showing that until this day, irrespective of the prevalent regime and ideology, "the deprived majority does not occupy its rightful place in society."

Throughout his book, Sharabi seems fond of using the word *self*. He speaks of "self-knowledge," of "return to the self," of "liberation of the self," and so on. He admits that it is a rather difficult task, both for the individual and the society, to attain "real" knowledge of the self, not to speak of liberation of and a return to self. The roots of this difficulty, and some of the answers to the many questions he raises in his book, are partly expounded in an essay written in 1961 by Sharabi himself. The subject of that essay was the political and intellectual attitudes of the young Arab generation. Referring to the dilemma facing the young Arab intellectual and pointing out that "so far" this intellectual "has refused to face the needs implicit in the rebuilding of his world," Sharabi wrote:

> The vital task of defining and formulating the fundamental problems inherent in his condition, which he alone can properly perform, he has left to Christian and European scholars whose works are just about all the knowledge the Arab has of himself, of his present, and of his past. Self-knowledge achieved through the eyes of others remains at best external, limited and inadequate; so it is in the intellectual atmosphere of the contemporary Arab world, which lacks real subjectivity and the capacity for self-criticism on any profound level. It is not surprising, therefore, that behind the thin exterior of the Arab intellectual's aggressive self-confidence there exists in reality a solitary void and a lostness that await the remedy provided only by the turning of the mind upon itself. In a way, this is a state of adolescence in which doubt and the simultaneous need to believe set a limit to consistent, logical thought and make the urge to dream and to talk an imperative psychological necessity. Meaning loses its measurable content, and appearance holds precedence.[23]

Are we to conclude, then, that since these lines were written, the intellectual climate in the Arab world has changed as radically as Sharabi seems to indicate in his "introductions"? All that one can say with certainty on this matter is that in the interval between 1960 and 1975 the author himself underwent a substantial change—together, perhaps, with a select few of his fellow Arab intellectuals. However, the challenge of the West is still very much with us, and it may be sobering to reflect that the kind of radicalization of views undergone by Sharabi—just like all-out modernism on the one hand and diehard traditionalism on the other—is simply another way of reacting to that standing challenge. Interestingly enough, Sharabi's approach to the study of contemporary Arab society and culture offers a remarkable illustration of how deep-seated and profound the impact of the West has been even on those who choose openly to rebel against it. Sharabi's own autobiographical work, also written in Arabic, is another testimony to this phenomenon.[24]

7 | October and After

Nasserism: Decline and Fall

The year 1970 marked the end of an era in Arab political and ideological thought. This is not so much because of the demise in that year of the founder and leader of a briefly influential radical Arab nationalist ideology, Jamal 'Abd al-Nasser, as it was because by the end of the 1960s that ideology had all but spent itself. For a short spell of about five years, however, the regime succeeding that of Nasser continued to pay lip service to his ideological heritage. In a speech marking the fourth anniversary of Nasser's death, for instance, President Anwar al-Sadat declared in September 1974 that he took his full share of responsibility, along with his predecessor, where successes had been achieved and blunders had been made.

The background of the evidently apologetic nature of Sadat's remark is to be sought in the rather critical reappraisals some of the best-known Egyptian writers and intellectuals were then publishing about the Nasserist era after a forced silence of more than two decades. These reappraisals came not from interested parties and functionaries of the new regime but from a number of the most valued and respected leaders of opinion whom Nasser's regime had in no way molested or oppressed. Chief among these were Tawfiq al-Hakim, the grand old man of Egyptian letters, and Naguib Mahfuz, Egypt's best and most prolific novelist and short-story writer.

It was about al-Hakim's work that the storm raged at its fiercest. The occasion was the publication, late in June 1974, of a booklet by this author with the evocative title *'Awdat al-wa'y* (The return of consciousness).[1] Not the least annoying part of the affair was the fact that the book's title was drawn from al-Hakim's most celebrated work, *'Awdat al-ruh* (The return of the soul), which first appeared in the 1930s and which many of the spokesmen of the free officers' revolt of July 1952—including Nasser himself—presented as a harbinger of their movement.[2]

The full story of the book's publication is of considerable interest. In its September 1973 issue, the Paris monthly *Esprit* printed a French rendering of parts of the book, already reported to have been making the rounds of Cairo's intellectual circles in a few mimeographed typescripts of the Arabic original. Some four months later, the enterprising Beirut daily *Al-Hayat* printed in two full-page installments what it claimed to be a translation of the extracts published in *Esprit* but which even a passing scrutiny revealed to be the author's own Arabic original. Eventually, a Beirut publisher managed to secure the rights to publish the book in its entirety, paying the author 10,000 Egyptian pounds, an unheard of fee in the Arab publishing world. The book was finally published in August 1974, with an introduction in which al-Hakim indirectly defended himself against criticism published about the book prior to its appearance.

According to al-Hakim, the book had been written in July 1972, on the twentieth anniversary of the revolution, not as a history of that event but as a collection of the author's reflections and reminiscences. It was also an attempt to evaluate the Nasserist era in the perspective of two decades. Above all, he warned, the book must be viewed as the author's "testimony vis-à-vis his own conscience" rather than representing a political stand; it is, he added, "a quest after the truth, [since] it is the duty of the writer to reveal the truth." The truth, as al-Hakim sees it in this book, is that Nasser's regime was characterized by "absolute individual authoritarianism," to be condemned in the same measure as King Faruq's own regime, which he brands as one of "irresponsible chaos." In the course of the book, al-Hakim also asserts that Nasser's 1952 movement was in no way a "revolution," which he defines as "an armed, civilian popular uprising," but only a coup d'état.[3]

'Awdat al-wa'y, in fact, may best be seen as a record of its author's gradual disenchantment with a movement on which he had pinned very high hopes. In perspective, al-Hakim now realizes that his disillusionment had in fact started at a very early stage—when the free officers led by Nasser decided to style themselves the actual rulers of the country rather than the mere instruments for change they had professed to be at the beginning. He recalls that in the first months of the movement a number of

experts in constitutional law consulted by the free officers expressed the opinion that the new revolutionaries had no right to promulgate laws or act as the country's legitimate rulers, while others hastened to lend the new regime an aspect of constitutionalism. The result was that the former were isolated and a "revolutionary command council" was set up which granted itself the right and the freedom to issue new regulations and laws and generally to run the affairs of state. At this point, al-Hakim writes:

> Where were we then? Where were the intellectuals of this land? Where was *I*, who had always been concerned about freedom of expression? Let me speak for myself. I confess that, at the time, I felt no misgivings whatsoever. On the contrary, I was optimistic about the advent of those young men, whose courage captivated me. As to the loss of constitutional political life, no one among us fully grasped the dangers inherent in that loss, since prior to July 23, 1952 we had lived through a period in which the Constitution lost much of its lustre and democracy fell prey to opportunists of all walks and descriptions.[4]

Then come specific criticisms of Nasser's own thought and temperament and the way in which he chose to run the country's affairs. Besides being an absolute dictator with many caprices and whims, Nasser is depicted by al-Hakim as a cheat in that his aides saw to it that his public appearances were always accompanied by outbursts of popular support and mass rallies they themselves organized. Al-Hakim does not seem to make much of Nasser's writings and pronouncements, either. Citing an appraisal printed in a French newspaper of Nasser's first programmatic statement of his thoughts and plans, *The Philosophy of the Revolution*, al-Hakim implicitly accuses its author of aspiring to establish a vast Arab-African empire under his own leadership. He suggested that Nasser was convinced that he himself was the "hero" to whom he had referred in the book and for whom he claimed the Egyptian people were searching in the same way as Pirandello's six characters were said to be searching for a hero! Al-Hakim goes so far as to give credence to what he claims were reports circulating in Cairo at the time to the effect that Egyptian *and* Israeli embassies abroad had distributed free copies of the English translation of *The Philosophy of the Revolution*, with the aim of telling the world that a new Hitler-type leader had appeared in the Arab world.[5]

Perhaps the most damning part of al-Hakim's book is where he records his impressions of the "disasters" Nasser brought on the heads of the Egyptians since assuming power. Accusing him of acting on sheer impulse and engaging mostly in reaction rather than sober action, he cites a passage from a book by Muhammad Hasanein Haykal. In the passage, this leading spokesman of Nasser's relates how, after having prepared a detailed plan setting out his vision of peace in the Middle East, Nasser was irked by a word dropped by the American ambassador. He promptly made changes in the speech that was to contain his plan, with all that those fateful changes were to mean in terms of Egypt's future.

This, we are told, took place in an early stage of Nasser's rule. Subsequently, Nasser was to become responsible for three defeats, one worse than the others. In 1956, he avoided utter defeat by ordering withdrawal from Sinai before his army was to be annihilated—and then duly proceeded to claim a great victory. A few years later came the Yemen adventure, which in addition to the untold millions wasted brought with it defeat and shame for the whole country. Finally, as though two defeats were not enough, came the disaster of June 1967. Even then, Nasser managed to capture the sympathy of the Egyptians, promising them victory. "Victory, however, changed its content: It came to mean merely Israel's withdrawal from the occupied territories and the return back to the state of affairs that prevailed prior to June 5, 1967!"[6]

There is a good deal of apologetics in al-Hakim's version of his own behavior in the face of all this. "What," he asks at one point in his book, "would History's verdict be on this regime? I don't know. I do hope, however, that History will judge with the utmost severity a man like me, whom emotion had blinded to the point of losing his critical faculty. My confidence in Nasser made me find logical explanations for all his actions."[7]

However, al-Hakim's own critics decided not to await history's verdict either on him or on Nasser. Owing to the rare position he holds in both Egyptian and Arab intellectual circles, his book was condemned by hardcore Nasserists as the work variously of a coward, a political opportunist, a misguided liberal, or a senile author in search of material gain and sensation. One of the first to come to Nasser's defense was Haykal himself, who in an interview in the Beirut weekly *Al-Sayyad* said that all those who now criticized Nasser had been well and alive during the leader's lifetime, but apparently lacked the courage of their convictions and thus failed to stand up and say what they thought was right. They were, he asserted, "weak, frightened ghosts."[8]

Haykal was too politic to spell out what he actually thought—namely that Sadat and his men stood behind the campaign against Nasser and his legacy. A more independent journalist, the left-wing writer Muhammad 'Oda, was more specific. Having written a full-length book in defense of

Nasser and his policies, 'Oda complained in an Iraqi newspaper that he could not find a publisher for his book, for which he significantly chose the title *Al-wa'y al-mafqud* (The lost consciousness).[9] 'Oda's main criticism of al-Hakim—and of Naguib Mahfuz as well—was that they had so easily stooped to the shameful level to which he thought they had descended. What he could not understand, he said, was that they should have done so when, in fact, they had been the most respected and spared of all of Egypt's men of letters.

"They have reached the top together with the revolution," 'Oda wrote, referring to al-Hakim and Mahfuz. "No one deleted a line from what they wrote. No one banned a single book they wrote. No one asked them any questions." A writer who finds himself in disagreement with a regime, 'Oda explained, had two alternative courses of action to take: To effect an "internal emigration" and start fighting the system from within, or to leave the country and fight the regime from abroad. "But a thinker who gets all the distinctions and privileges from a particular regime and then proceeds to stand in the first ranks of the forces opposed to that regime cannot be forgiven."[10]

Egypt and the Arab World

The controversy to which the publication of al-Hakim's book gave rise was partly personal, partly political, and only marginally ideological in character. In the few years that followed, the debate tended to intensify and openly became one between Nasser's various critics and denigrators and those members of the Egyptian intelligentsia who were still willing to defend the basic ideological premises of Nasserism. Shortly after Sadat's renewed peace initiative and his visit to Jerusalem in November 1977, a seemingly innocuous exchange of views was launched by a Cairo newspaper which was to develop into a full-scale debate concerning Egypt's identity—national and cultural—and the way the Egyptians should view themselves and the role they have to play in the Arab world. The exchange was in a way only a continuation of what since the 1920s and 1930s had remained a running controversy between those who claim that Egypt is an integral part of the Arab world and the Pan-Arab movement and those who argue that Egypt has its own separate cultural identity while admitting the many links it has with the Arab world as a whole.[11]

The renewed debate was again started by Tawfiq al-Hakim, who in a short article in *Al-Ahram* expressed the opinion that Egypt should proclaim its "neutrality" in the ongoing conflict between the Arabs and Israel.[12] The article caused quite a stir, and al-Hakim's stand was subsequently supported by Husain Fawzi, the well-known author of *Sindbad Masri* (An Egyptian Sindbad) and other books on Egyptian history and culture. Right at the start of the exchange it became clear that in speaking of neutrality al-Hakim and Fawzi were restricting themselves to the political and military spheres. In his single contribution to the debate, Fawzi wrote: "Egypt's neutrality in the present circumstances opens the door before it to help the Arab states as a whole in their predicament and in their international relations."[13] Al-Hakim, in the seventh and last of a series of articles he was to write in defense and explication, wrote as follows: "The neutrality [I advocate] here is purely political and military, and it refers to one specific eventuality. This is whether, should war become the option, Egypt is going to be called upon to fight for the Arabs. Alternatively, should peace become the option, are Egypt's interests to be observed in the framework of this peace—or is Egypt going to be told: 'Let the adversary occupy your territory so long as he refuses to accept our demands in their entirety?' This is the question to which the majority of those who have participated in this controversy avoid giving an answer."[14]

One of the first to take exception to al-Hakim's views was Ahmad Baha al-Din, a leading intellectual of the Nasserist era, who advised "those who seek to destroy Nasser's legacy" to look for some subject other than that of Egypt's Arab affiliation. Those Egyptians, he wrote, who wanted to opt out of Arabism forgot that they were working against a heritage of 1,500 years; they were also playing into the hands of the country's worst enemies.[15]

To this and other charges advanced by Baha al-Din, the answer came from Louis 'Awadh, a former university professor and a prolific translator and literary critic. 'Awadh, a Copt, chose to delve deeper into the subject, which ultimately concerned the basic issue of Egypt's involvement in the Arab world and whether it should be considered part and parcel of the "Arab nation." Attempting to define Arab nationalism, 'Awadh referred to an argument advanced by one of the participants in the debate who asserted, among other things, that Arabism had never included the concept of race as one of its ingredients. If that was the case, 'Awadh asked, why then did the advocates and ideologues of Arabism always start the history of the Arab region from the great Arab conquests? He then went on to say that his library contains dozens of books on Arab history and Arabic literature that reek of a clear racialist tendency when their authors deal with the meaning of Arabism and the components of Arab nationalism. Arabism, he concluded, was to him incomprehensible outside the boundaries of the Arab Peninsula. Any scientific definition of the Arab nation would confine it to the inhabitants of that part of the world and to it alone. Egypt, he advised, should set itself two main goals—namely the containment of Israel and "self-reconstruction."[16]

This kind of plain speaking was bound to create an uproar. Some of 'Awadh's critics were content with merely denying any racialist tendencies in Arabism. One of them, Sa'd al-Din Ibrahim, a lecturer in political science at the American University of Cairo, challenged 'Awadh to produce a single piece of evidence in support of his thesis. Two points in Ibrahim's rejoinder are worth citing. The first is his contention that the Arabs' failure so far to attain national unity does not necessarily mean that they do not constitute one nation; the second is that the Arab nation is admittedly a nation comprising several "peoples" whose geographical and historical separateness inevitably produced in them distinct characteristics of their own. Egypt, Ibrahim argued, was the best example of this distinctiveness; but it is an Arab country nonetheless.[17]

It is characteristic of debates on the nature of the Arab nation that advocates of Arab nationalism and Pan-Arabism almost always make the mistake of listing "religion" among the elements constituting Arabism. Ibrahim speaks of the Arabs' unity of language, history, geography, and religion—seemingly oblivious of the fact that in 'Awadh's person he was addressing a Christian. For if religion—which in this case is obviously a reference to Islam—is a component part and thus a condition of Arabism, where would 'Awadh and his fellow Egyptian Copts fit in an Egypt that is part of a Pan-Arab commonwealth? 'Awadh, however, did not choose to dwell on this sensitive point. Instead, he asserted in his reply to Ibrahim and others that, as long as political boundaries continued to separate the various Arab states, it was not feasible to speak of an Arab nation or an Arab homeland. Besides, he asked, if the Arabs were indeed one nation, why then did they fail to grant the Palestinians living in their midst automatic nationality instead of keeping them forever separate—guests enjoying some measure of hospitality but treated as just another national minority whose members are scattered in various separate Arab states?[18]

The debate about Egypt's "neutrality," having thus grown into one over Egypt's national-cultural identity and the nature and content of Arab nationalism, was not to be left there to rest. Egypt's leading institute of research in political and strategic studies hastened to put together a full-length volume on the subject. The task of editing and selecting was entrusted to Sa'd al-Din Ibrahim, who had taken a fairly clear stand in the debate. In addition to a selection from the articles published in *Al-Ahram, al-Akhbar*

and *Akhbar al-Yaum,* which all participated in the debate, the volume includes an introduction by the editor as well as a number of new contributions and studies by Ahmad Yusuf Ahmad, 'Abd al-'Ati Muhammad, Jihad
'Oda, Hani al-Ma'dawi, and Sayyid Yasin, the last being the director of
the Center for Political and Strategic Studies, which sponsored the volume.[19]

In his introduction, Ibrahim places the debate in context. He writes that
the controversy, considering that it opened at this particular juncture, is to
be viewed within four different contexts. The first is that it is part of a
process of reappraisal of the Nasserist era; the second is that it is conducted in the context of efforts aimed at reaching a peace settlement with
Israel; the third is that it is to be viewed as one of the facets of the war
between the generations; and lastly, it is a reaction to the acts of violence
committed against Egyptian nationals at the time—a reference, no doubt,
to the assassination of the Egyptian writer and journalist Yusuf al-Sina'i in
Nicosia in February 1978. As to the outcome of the debate, Ibrahim is
convinced that, despite everything, this was "in favor of Egypt's Arabism,
of Arab nationalism and of Arab unity." After all, he writes, the Arabism
of Egypt is not a mere garb used whenever a whim arises. It is a truth
backed and witnessed by the facts of history, geography, and culture.

Ahmad Yusuf Ahmad reiterates in his article the view that Arab nationalism has no racial component. He also explains the relationship between
Arab nationalism and Arab unity, two concepts he says were somewhat
confused and used interchangeably by some of the participants in the debate, implying that the absence so far of a united Arab political entity
proved that the Arabs were not one nation. Ahmad, however, draws attention to a distinction between nationalism as a social and cultural phenomenon, which rests mainly on the existence of a nation and of consciousness
of that existence, and the nationalist movement as a political movement
aiming at asserting that national existence and cultivating its political and
economic components. It is self-evident, therefore, that the existence of a
nation or a nationality always predates the rise of a nationalist movement.
The fact that the Arab nationalist movement has not yet managed to attain
its goals—even its failure therein—cannot be considered as proof that the
Arab nation itself does not exist.

'Abd al-'Ati Muhammad writes on the historical and political relations
between Egypt and the Arab nation. He shows how Egypt's links with
Arab nationalism and the Pan-Arab movement were natural. Asserting
that the Arab nationalist orientation had been predominant in Egypt even
before the free officers' revolt of 1952, he argues that the July revolution

served to reinforce this orientation by making Arab unity a strategic aim of the Arabs' struggle.

The one contributor who takes up 'Awadh's unspoken hint at the position of the non-Muslim minorities in a Pan-Arab union is Hani al-Ma'dawi, who wrote on "The Role of the Minorities in the Context of Arab Unity." Ma'dawi argues that the Copts, like the Muslims, display more than one orientation toward Arab nationalism and Arab unity, some supporting and others opposing these movements. It is, therefore, wrong to formulate the question in a way that makes it center on whether the Copts are for or against Arab unity. The correct formulation, according to the writer, ought to be this: What sort of unity, and what kind of entity would emerge from that unity—and, finally, what sort of role can minorities play within the framework of such a unity? In other words, the basic issue for Ma'dawi is how to deepen the democratic content of Arab unity so as to make it possible and desirable for minorities to play a meaningful role in it.

It is interesting to note here that, in its final form as it appears in Ibrahim's compilation, the point of view that links Egypt with the Arab world and the Arab nationalist movement emerges as having, by far, the upper hand. Sadat's regime, to be sure, managed gradually to veer away from the kind of active advocacy and leadership of the Pan-Arab movement adopted by his predecessor Jamal 'Abd al-Nasser, and even concluded a peace treaty with Israel in face of virtually unanimous Arab opposition. Nevertheless, in ways too numerous to list here—and which are not necessarily political or national in character—Egypt's links with the Arab world are solidly based and permanent. In any controversy of the kind summarized above, therefore, the outcome is bound to be—to use Sa'd al-Din Ibrahim's own formulation—ultimately favorable to Egypt's Arabism and to Arab nationalism and Arab unity.

The Literary-Cultural Scene

The debates over Nasser's legacy and concerning Egypt's national affiliation furnish a fairly accurate picture of the political-ideological mood in Egypt, and to some extent in the Arab world as a whole, in the first years of the post-Nasserist era. On the literary and cultural fronts, the situation in Egypt differed only marginally from that obtained in the Arab world generally. That situation, as depicted by the Arabs themselves, was fairly bleak and was to become even less supportable after the Yom Kippur War of 1973, also known as the October War.

Early in 1974, a middle-aged Arab poet, Nizar Qabbani, declared in a newspaper article: "The best book to appear in the Arab world in 1973 was the soldier's boots." This of course was meant to be a tribute to Arab achievements in the October War. That war was a watershed, in the cultural and political sense. Shortly after the breakout of hostilities on October 6, a well-known Egyptian man of letters lamented: "We are all deserters." Tawfiq al-Hakim cabled Sadat begging forgiveness for himself and for fellow skeptics for harboring doubts about the greatness and resourcefulness of their "leader." He appealed to the authorities during the first days of the war to let him do some work, no matter how menial, to contribute to the national effort.[20]

These initial, spontaneous reactions to the October War sounded so pathetic that at least one Arab cultural critic called them "literary masochism," though on the whole he found them rather understandable. What some Arab intellectuals found intolerable, however, was that the new mood of relief and jubilation put an abrupt end to the process of self-criticism and soul-searching the defeat of the Six-Day War had helped start in the Arab world. In the words of one literary critic, Talal Rahma, writing in the Beirut weekly *Al-Hawadith*, Arabic culture after the defeat of June 1967 experienced a real shock, "but the short interval that separates us from June has failed really to help us achieve a breakthrough in our cultural concepts." Certain new ideas and values that began to emerge as a result of that defeat did not have "enough time to crystallize, especially that the post-June process of rejection took place within a framework of mutual invective and of peddling people's sorrows."[21]

This rather novel way of viewing the intellectual consequences of October's politico-military victories calls for some elaboration. Its exponents, few as they were, took the following line of reasoning: The October War brought much-needed psychological relief to those Arab intellectuals and writers who had been consumed by deep sorrow and mental anguish since the humiliating defeat of 1967. At the same time, however, the October War "brought to a cruel halt those birth pangs which had started in June." In the field of creative literature, this development led to "masochistic moods" plaguing writers and poets, and a consequent "artificial literature representing a unique case of the defeat of creativity as well as a rare example of hasty retraction," to quote the writer in *Al-Hawadith*. The results were deplorable. Certain writers and poets effected a complete volte-face in their attitude and style; self-styled nonconformists took to conformism not only in the political but also in the literary sphere; oratory and the oratorical stance enjoyed an unprecedented revival; culture was made synonymous with information and guidance; and commitment became identical with cheap and superficial writing.

This cheapening of literary values and standards—the argument went—resulted in a sort of cultural inflation followed, as monetary inflations often do, by drastic devaluation. Writers produced novels, short stories, plays, and literary criticism in plenty; poets wrote verse as they never had done before; and publishers kept publishing, mostly indiscriminately. Literary and cultural periodicals multiplied—and so did exhibitions, public lectures, symposia, interviews, and newspaper articles. However, the real creative value of all these cultural commodities continued to slump, and Arab cultural life seemed as meager and uninspiring as it had been in the past.

Some Arab observers of the cultural scene went so far as to call this state of affairs "a crisis of creativity in contemporary Arab culture"; some chose to describe it as a state of "cultural devaluation"; but all seemed to agree that something was fundamentally wrong somewhere and were unanimous that the two most vicious manifestations of the crisis were imitation and repetitiveness. As one critic put it, the young imitate the old, the old imitate each other as well as the young, and no creative writer seems able to challenge what the tribe accepts as the prevalent norm. Repetitiveness is best illustrated by the boring frequency with which certain words were used by these writers during the post-June period. A sampling is furnished by the critic: *The Rock, The Wall, The Fall, nausea, chimera, illusion, lostness,* and dozens of other such fashionable literary terms. In the past, Arab poets and literary men used to avoid the phrase "full moon" because classical Arabic verse was replete with it to the point of exhaustion; it is now time for the younger Arab poets, novelists, and literary critics to discard the use of certain "new" words.[22]

A case in point often cited by these Arab critics is post-1967 Palestinian literature, comprising works whose central preoccupations are Palestine and the fate of the Palestinians. It is in this literature, written mostly by Palestinians but including works by non-Palestinian Arab writers as well, that the crisis of creativity was said to be at its worst, especially where imitation and repetitiveness were concerned. The trouble appeared to have been that the overwhelming majority of these literary efforts continued to conform to a pattern their authors had followed religiously ever since Palestinian literature captured the market in the late 1960s. This pattern, whose predictability some have likened to the timetables listing the arrivals and departures of trains, is set on internal divisions and stylistic lines as clear as statistical tabulations, especially in works of fiction. In these works, the hero is invariably depicted in one of the following four situations:

1. Under siege by "the enemy" in a village, a house, or a bush.
2. Being interrogated by an enemy officer or laboring inside a torture den.
3. Sitting at his desk feverishly writing his memoirs, which always have to do with his expulsion from his village or town.
4. Preoccupied with a series of reminiscences and "stream of consciousness" bits having mostly to do with the village, the mother, the grandmother, or the sweetheart at the moment of parting.

Altogether, in the words of the writer in *Al-Hawadith,* the new literary efforts are almost replicas of the old, the difference being that they have a tendency "to inflate the story's events, general exaggeration in depicting the scenes, and a rhetorical and emotional style."[23]

According to some Arab literary critics, there is a certain causal connection between the tendency to repeat and imitate and to exaggerate, which is not uncommon in contemporary Arabic writing. Rahma quotes the German sociologist Georg Simmel to the effect that those who fail to comprehend what goes on around them tend to exaggerate, and that the prevalence of exaggeration in a society decreases people's awareness of the existence of the phenomenon itself. Thus, it strengthens the tendency by making people compete among themselves in the use of this particular device. To Rahma, this means that when imitation prevails, those who lack creativity seek distinction by exaggeration. When a mood of exaggeration becomes all-pervasive and people's awareness of it is thus lowered, the prize tends to go to the highest bidder and cultural life is reduced to a series of miscomprehensions and false visions and concepts. Ultimately, this results in a satellite culture, what anthropologists call "culture lag."[24]

For a number of historical reasons, Arabic culture in certain of its aspects has always lagged behind, Rahma writes. Generally speaking, it has been imitative and backward insofar as the Arab world as a whole has been reduced to the status of a Western satellite. There have, however, been many attempts to break out of this vicious circle, and some of these attempts have even been successful. But the current crisis, "the crisis of creativity," threatens to turn contemporary Arabic culture as a whole into a lagging, satellite culture consisting of a series of illusory and fake ideas and visions. What makes this even more dangerous is that the tendency toward imitation has not always been merely an individual trait in the sense that a person tends to imitate when he finds he is not capable of creativity. The grave aspect of it is that several sociopolitical factors combined have strengthened the tendency and have militated against any serious attempt to break out of the circle.

Rahma mentions two of these factors. One is that the prevailing ideologies in the Arab world have insisted that creative writers follow their own narrow ideas and concepts, and that works of literature faithfully and literally reflect them and their worldviews. In an attempt to gain distinction, moreover, these ideologies vied with each other in imposing discipline on the creative process. The other factor mentioned by Rahma is the totalitarian character of the various Arab regimes. According to Rahma, this totalitarianism was conducive to conformity in literature and, in the long run, resulted in a state of affairs in which literary writing itself became restricted to certain styles of expression and a limited pattern of looking at sociopolitical phenomena. Thus, the absence of democracy and freedom of expression played a crucial role in the recent decline in literary standards; witness the dozens of writers and poets who since the 1950s were subjected to pressure and persecution in various Arab countries.

In this connection, another dilemma tends to confront the creative writer —a dilemma that is both basic and bewildering and something of a cruel paradox. For quite a number of centuries now, the Arab world has been exposed to various kinds of foreign influence and dominance, leading to what some Arab writers have called "the cultural invasion." In reaction to the inroads the West is said to have been trying to make in their cultural life, many prominent Arab thinkers and opinion leaders advocated a revival of their people's cultural heritage, a return to the roots. However, since the Arabs' cultural heritage is inexorably linked with the heritage of Islam, this call perforce took on what tended to be considered a reactionary character. Moreover, certain thinkers and men of letters who were otherwise enlightened and open minded got into the habit of rejecting everything that smacked of modernity, having decided that "modern" was synonymous with Western or European. This attitude was extended to literary patterns and styles, leading some—to cite only one example—to reject free verse in favor of the old, rhymed poetry.

It is true that, side by side with these calls for a return to the past and to its glories, there were those who advocated a diametrically opposite course— namely, a complete break with the past and an all-out drive for Westernization. There were, too, those who advocated a middle way, arguing that the two cultures should be merged and the good and healthy traits of each be preserved. However, as far as literature and literary forms are concerned, what is significant here is that when new forms and new styles were rejected, they were rejected not because of their intrinsic unworthiness or because they were in any way unsuitable, but simply because they denoted the new. Anything new or novel was suggestive of the West and its ways and its suspect long-term aim of invading the Arab world culturally after dominating it politically. The paradox here, of course, is that instead of making Arab culture safe for the Arabs, it led to its partial stagnation and immobility.

Into this sorry state of things, into this circle from which there seemed to be no breaking out, came the cruel shock of the defeat of 1967. To the more radical-minded of the literary and cultural critics writing in Arabic today, however, that shock is seen as a gift from heaven. Exposing all the stagnation, the evils, and what one of these critics has termed the "rottenness" that penetrated right into the deeper roots of the Arab cultural situation, the setback of 1967 put the Arabs, at long last, on the right course of self-examination and intensive soul-searching.

What some radical Arab critics regretted, however, was that because of the October War and its results, the Arabs were simply not given sufficient time for a long enough and searching enough look at their cultural condition to begin effecting the changes needed. The euphoria the war of 1973 brought in its wake put an abrupt and premature end to a process of rethinking and reevaluation that could have proved extremely beneficial to contemporary Arabic culture. Instead, so the argument goes, the Arabs are now right back in the midst of their "crisis of creativity," what Rahma termed "literary inflation," and its corollary, cultural devaluation.

Egypt's Embattled Intelligentsia, 1967–1987

Among the dictionary definitions of the word *culture* are "refined taste or judgment," "high intellectual and aesthetic development," and "state of intellectual, artistic and social development of a group." When, therefore, we hear it said that a certain culture is passing through a crisis, we cannot help feeling at a loss. We want to know whether the trouble lies with the state of the culture itself or with its organs, with its consumers or with its producers.

This is especially the case in those countries where culture, its organs, and its products follow the free-market rules of supply and demand. In countries where culture is run by the state, the confusion is considerably less pronounced. In Egypt, for instance, the ever-current talk about a crisis of culture is often explicable merely by the fact that one group of intellectuals feels unhappy about the way the powers that be are running the cultural show. In the case of post-Nasserist Egypt, the liberal radicals (all those who are variously grouped under the Left) became extremely resentful about the Ministry of Culture under the late Yusuf al-Siba'i, who was said to have given preference to a certain "trend" of culture to the near exclusion of all the others.

Siba'i's own career, which was ended abruptly in 1978 when he was assassinated in Cyprus by a Palestinian terrorist organization, is an excellent case in point. Siba'i, a prolific novelist and writer in the lighter vein, was very much President Anwar al-Sadat's man; he was, in fact, so constituted as to be capable, given half a chance, of being any boss's man. He was, among many other things, secretary general both of the Arab Writers Union and the Conference of Afro-Asian Writers and Men of Letters. However, possessed of an excellent sense of just where the wind was blowing, Siba'i tried to put an end to pronounced left-wing influences in the various organs of culture and place some of them on a more rational basis financially. The result was an outcry from the group aggrieved that Egyptian culture was passing through "a real crisis."

The manifestations of this crisis were said to be many and variegated. In the opening presentation to a symposium organized by the Marxist-oriented Cairo monthly *Al-Tali'ah,* for instance, no less than ten such manifestations were enumerated. These included a dearth in the number of books and periodicals published by the Ministry of Culture; the fact that these periodicals were all edited either by Siba'i himself or by his trusted aides; the growing predominance of the commercial motive in the theater, where even the official Theater Board tended to cater to popular taste rather than concentrate on quality; and a similar, but even more pronounced, trend in the cinema and film industry.

Seven other major sins were attributed to the authorities in charge of culture: (1) negligence of the fine arts and failure to furnish art galleries, offer grants, and make the necessary tools available; (2) the inadequacy of public libraries; (3) a marked decrease in the number of graduates of institutes and academies of art; (4) the low standard of the cultural programs broadcast on radio and television; (5) the placement of obstacles in the way of those trying to set up *democratic* writers and artists unions; (6) the lack of avenues of contact between Egyptian writers and artists and their colleagues in other parts of the world; and (7) the ineptitude and inadequacy of cultural organs connected with the Ministry of Culture, such as the Higher Council for the Promotion of Literature, the Arts, and the Social Sciences, whose activity was said to be confined merely to deciding to whom to grant the various state-donated annual prizes.

After reading his presentation, the moderator of the symposium asked those present—all of whom belonged in various degrees to the cultural

Left—to concentrate on three main topics. The first was to define the nature of the crisis Egyptian culture was passing through and ways and means to ending it. The second related to the kind of culture the participants believed Egypt needed now—the alternatives they would suggest to the prevalent state of affairs. Lastly, the participants were asked what they thought the role of the Egyptian intellectual and writer was in steering the cultural life and gaining some sort of supervision on decisions taken in that respect.

As was to be expected, the most intriguing part of the discussion revolved around the second topic, although most of the participants were either not clear about the subject or unwilling to reveal the full thrust of their thinking thereon. A noted exception was Ahmad 'Abbas Salih, who had just been fired by Siba'i as editor of the radical cultural monthly *Al-Katib,* which he had edited for several years. Salih said that, insofar as one could describe a culture as modern, what Egypt now needed was a modern culture. Our age, he explained, is one of secularism and rationalism, "and merely starting from this point of departure will lead to a socialist content."

Salih explained further that many thinkers of our time, both in the Arab homeland and the outside world, "in one way or other agreed that, as a system of thought and study, socialism is the most important achievement of our age." At any rate, he asserted, the time for mystical and superstitious beliefs is gone forever, finally discarded by nations both socialist and capitalist.

Though he was a self-confessed Marxist, Salih here can be said to continue to represent a far broader spectrum of opinion in contemporary Egyptian society and culture. The issue, in fact, was not and is not one of Marxist versus capitalist, but—in the opinion at least of Salih and his friends—one of progressive versus reactionary, a forward-looking, open, and modern culture as opposed to a backward-looking, conservative, and traditionalist one.

There is a sense in which the crisis of culture Salih and others spoke of started considerably before Nasser's death in 1970 and continues right down to our own day. Here, a brief recapitulation will be in order. The shock of the military defeat of June 1967 was so great, and its aftereffects so lasting, that in the course of time Egyptian and Arab writers and intellectuals engaged in the subsequent wide-ranging probings and self-searchings were at some point called "the Junists." As far as can be ascertained, the first Arab writer to use the term in this sense was the Egyptian critic and short-story writer Salah 'Isa, whose coinage was first referred to in chapter 5.

The novelty of 'Isa's approach was its openness. He was the first to write so candidly on this highly sensitive topic, and he is still active as a commentator in left-oriented opposition newspapers and periodicals. His column in *Al-Katib,* the literary-cultural monthly of the Egyptian left, appears regularly. It is always pointed and often highly provocative.

However, the "Junist" atmosphere is an old one, according to 'Isa. "We knew it before its appointed day dawned in 1967. At times we even used to feel its smell—but our nostrils were full of fake perfumes. The shadow of June is traceable in our national consciousness, our social relations, our political systems and our thought patterns. We commit a fatal and mortal error if we consider it a passing phenomenon and leave it at that—without exhaustingly studying it, trying to fathom its hidden mysteries and intractable essences. We are indeed in danger of doing just that, for we live in the era of 'fallen gods' and feed on their wisdom."

Turning to Arabic writing of the time and its leading themes, 'Isa points out that prior to June 1967, critics used to complain of the prevalence of verbosity in Arab writing; they used to say that articles were being measured by the meter—or the kilometer!—and that the essential thing was not to write articles that say "the right thing" but ones that say new things. After all, what use is it to know about things that were known long ago and read a thousand times? "We have known the printing press and are no longer desert nomads who repeat things a thousand times in order to learn them by heart."

This was in the old days of time-honored rhetorics, ornamented language, and thoughts and sentiments repeated ad nauseam. Now the trouble lies at the other extreme. Quoting one literary critic complaining that he cannot muster enough patience to dig up the facts or probe the depths of this subject, 'Isa wonders: "Have we lost our urge to write? I think something of the sort happened after June. Amidst the noise of the great fall we discovered that we talk too much, dream too much. . . . As far as I know, most of our writers stopped writing for a year or so after the setback. Do we continue to be plagued by the same ailments?" Here 'Isa cites the example of the periodical in which he was writing, the Beirut cultural monthly *Al-Adab,* whose editor had complained he was unable to solicit enough material for a special issue he had planned on Nasser and Nasserism a few months after the leader's death. "This, then, is the Junist's complaint which recurs in us all. It is a healthy phenomenon not devoid of malignant diseases!"

Surveying the contents of previous issues of *Al-Adab* to illustrate his point, 'Isa remarks on the fact that apart from the generous dose of verse offered, poetry and poetic themes predominate in the articles printed. Five out of nine dealt with poets and poetry. For him, this signified an "obsessive preoccupation with the world of dreams." He asks, "How else would the cultivated Arab psyche be able to confront what has happened? The truth of the matter is, simply, that verse is the one means of expression most appropriate to the soul in moments of painful fall and the collapse of dreams."

With the Arabs, especially, this is more so than with other peoples. In his *History of the Arabs,* Philip Hitti asserts that it was only in the field of poetry that the pre-Islamic Arabian excelled. "Herein his finest talent found a field. The Bedouin's love of poetry was his one cultural asset." It was natural, therefore, that poetry should become the main channel of literary expression following the June War. "No one can eulogize lost illusions more eloquently than those who had built the dream."[25]

Historicism versus Traditionalism: Role of the Intellectual

While these and other similar sentiments were being aired by writers and thinkers in various countries of the Arab East, a somewhat more sophisticated and more radical evaluation was formulated in the Maghreb by a Moroccan intellectual and historian living and teaching in Rabat. In 1974, Abdullah Laroui published a paper titled "The Crisis of Intellectuals and the Crisis of Society." In this paper, which was subsequently included in a book on the crisis of the Arab intellectual, Laroui argues that to understand the historical process is to understand both oneself and others in a temporal perspective. So far, he writes, the concept of history has been peripheral to all the ideologies that dominated the Arab world. To the extent, therefore, that Arab intellectuals have a nonevolutionary conception of reality—a conception that places no stress on understanding the historical process—"all collective action in the Arab milieu [will] be deprived of a constant and definite orientation," while politics will be "reduced to the level of short-sighted tactical manoeuvering subservient to egotistical interests."[26]

It is because of this that Laroui calls upon the Arab intellectual to espouse and propagate what he terms a historicist rationale. His analysis of the Arab cultural scene—and the crisis of the intellectual therein—is somewhat involved. He distinguishes between two types of alienation: "The one is visible and openly criticized, the other all the more insidious as it is denied on principle." Westernization indeed signifies an alienation, a way of becoming other, an avenue to self-division—though one's estimation of this transformation may be positive or negative, according to one's ideology. But there is another type of alienation Laroui perceives in Arab society today—one that is "prevalent but veiled." This alienation is characterized by Laroui as "the exaggerated medievalization obtained through quasi-magical identification with the great period of classical Arabian culture."

The cultural policy of all Arab states, Laroui explains, seeks to combat the alienation of Westernization by two means: "the sanctification of Arabic in its archaic form and the vulgarization of classical texts—the revival of the cultural legacy." Now, he asks, "Who can fail to see that the fossilization of language and the promotion of traditional culture as a badge of nationality constitute the most decisive means of keeping medieval thought alive, as well as an effective ruse to obliterate from general consciousness the very experience of historical positivity?" The *salafi* (traditionalist) imagines that his thoughts are free. "He is mistaken: In reality, he is not using language to think within the framework of tradition; rather, it is tradition that lives again through language and is 'reflected' in him."

According to Laroui, Arab intellectuals think in accordance with two rationales: "Most of them profess the traditionalist rationale, the rest profess an eclecticism. Together, these tendencies succeed in abolishing the historical dimension." However, if the intellectual erases history from his thought, can he erase it from reality? Of course not, says Laroui. "History as past and present structure informs the present condition of the Arabs quite as much as it does that of their adversaries. Ahistorical thinking has but one consequence: failure to see the real. If we translate this into political terms, we may say that it has the effect of confirming dependence on all levels."[27]

It is true that while this dependence can be said to beset eclecticism as a matter of course, since it opens itself to every outside influence, the traditionalists continue to pretend that they are in some way immune to this eventuality. But Laroui seeks to show that this is far from being the case. "Indeed," he writes, "how can [traditionalism] oppose modern technology, modern economic and social systems, and modern intellectual schools, when it is incapable of understanding them and has not the slightest possibility of inventing competitive systems? Dependency, visible or concealed, means not only exploitation, loss of liberty, and damage to the pride and material interests of a nation, but also and above all the continuance and exacerbation of historical retardation."[28]

The great majority of Arab intellectuals today, then, lean toward either *salafiyya* (traditionalism) or eclecticism and, what Laroui finds even stranger, they all "believe they enjoy complete freedom to appropriate the best among the cultural products of others: the freedom of a Stoic slave!"[29] Laroui's alternative to these two modes of thought—the only alternative, in his view—lies in strict submission to the discipline of historical thought and acceptance of all its assumptions. These are, as he himself enumerates them, "truth as process, the positivity of the event, the mutual determination of facts, the responsibility of the agent . . . the existence of laws of historical development, the unicity of the meaning of history, the transmissibility of acquired knowledge, and the effectivity of the intellectual's and politician's role."[30]

Laroui, then, advocates an almost total break with both traditionalism and selective Westernization—the former on the ground that it leads to "medievalization," the latter because it leads to alienation, and both because they lead to dependence. He admits, however, that abandoning *salafiyya* and transcending the limitations of what he calls "justificatory nationalism" would prove a rather overly arduous task. It is interesting to note that among the "outside obstacles" said to be detrimental to the attainment of this task, Laroui gives pride of place to what he describes as "the Arab problem *par excellence,* that of Palestine."

The Palestine issue, Laroui explains, has had the effect of reinforcing traditionalism, first ideologically, then politically. How did this come about? First, "by the political utilization of the very existence of the Zionist state as a tangible proof that modern science and religious nationalism can coexist." The traditionalist Arab thinker would say to those—like Laroui—who maintain that modern science is intimately linked to democracy, secularism, historical thinking, etc.: "Look around you. Don't you see that the Zionists have constructed a system in which technology, militarism, and religious and cultural nationalism naturally strengthen one another?"

Laroui rejects this argument on the ground that the traditionalist "often confuses appearance and reality, namely what the Zionists believe themselves to be and what they are." Nevertheless, he concedes that the traditionalists' argument in this case has been extremely effective—and that Israel has thus been "one of the determining causes in the process of continual traditionalization."

Curiously enough, Laroui is convinced that the Palestine problem is not all negative from the Arabs' point of view. Because of its complexities and "objective contradictions," he argues, the problem of Palestine "is allowing the Arabs, while demanding much of them, to become truly conscious of history." "Each one of us," he adds, "must applaud this awakening and see to it that it does not come to naught."[31] Laroui's advice to progressive Arab intellectuals is that they "must accept the Palestinian drama as a fact and the attitudes of others—rational or irrational—as facts." The Arab intellectual, he counsels further, "must define his position with regard to the cardinal problem of the Arabs: their historical retardation. He must not invert the terms by defining his position vis-à-vis historical retardation with an eye to the attitudes of others vis-à-vis the Palestinian question."

Laroui admits that this is a difficult position for the Arab intellectual to take; it is even heroic in the present circumstances. "Without taking it, however, there is little hope that the Arabs will find their place in the modern world."[32]

Laroui's reflections present an interesting combination of philosophical detachment and sociopolitical commitment. But the subject with which he grapples here, namely the attitude of the intellectual toward the concerns of the day, is of course an old one. In the early 1930s, Julien Benda, the French philosopher and essayist who himself was a passionate advocate of "extreme democracy," wrote a book in which he strongly denounced intellectuals who allowed their attitudes to be tainted by political bias and warned against any compromise over what he terms the intellectualist approach to life.

Benda's book was titled, appropriately enough, *La trahison des clercs.* An English translation of the work appeared under the title *The Great Betrayal.* Nearly thirty years later in Egypt of the early 1960s, a new phrase began to gain currency in political and cultural circles—*azmat al-muthaqqafin* (the crisis of the intellectuals). The phrase was coined by Muhammad Hasanein Haykal, the influential editor of *Al-Ahram* who was also Nasser's confidant and adviser. The crisis to which the phrase referred sprang not from the intellectuals' involvement in politics but from their not being involved enough. The crisis, Haykal argued, was not one of political loyalty to the revolutionary regime but one of *participation* in the revolution. What he advocated, in fact, was the very opposite of an intellectualist approach. He asked the Egyptian intellectual virtually to surrender his faculty of thinking and judging for himself in favor of total submersion into the current "revolutionary process."

Haykal's complaint against the intellectuals of the 1960s might have had some justification. After the Six-Day War, as we have seen, even Haykal would not have claimed that Arab intellectuals in general, and Egyptian intellectuals in particular, had not become sufficiently involved in public affairs. A glance at any issue of one of the literary-cultural periodicals published in Cairo, Beirut, Baghdad, or Damascus between the years 1967 and 1973 would suffice to show how completely and inextricably Arab intellectuals and men of letters allowed themselves to be submerged into "the revolutionary process."

The commitment, however, went much deeper. In Nasser's Egypt, particularly, the phenomenon of the intellectual as time-server became rather common. One of the more curious results of the fairly thorough purge Sadat carried out in May 1971 in the ranks of his government and in the leadership of the Arab Socialist Union was the impact of these changes on Egypt's nationalized press, and ultimately on the political intellectuals who usually wrote for that press. No sooner was the purge effected than declarations of support and allegiance started to pour forth in headlines and editorial columns—with the result that very few changes in personnel took place in a press that had been firmly controlled by some of the men ousted by Sadat.

An interesting aspect of these developments was the revelations leaked by the regime and its supporters concerning the dismal state of the Egyptian press during the last ten years of Nasser's life. *Al-Jadid,* a Beirut weekly generally considered to be Cairo-oriented, at the time gave a hair-raising account of what things had been like in Nasser's days—adding that the condition of the press was one of Sadat's "main preoccupations." Sadat knows, the paper revealed, how newspapers in Egypt were run, the kind of stuff they printed, and the sort of climate they lived in. "He knows that *Al-Gomhuriyya,* for instance, is put together at five in the afternoon, printed and distributed at 8 p.m.—and then hurriedly collected from the newsvendors at eight the next morning in order that it might be claimed that it was sold out. He also knows that the situation with regard to the other papers is not much different."

It seems, too, that Sadat knew that some two hundred journalists were employed by the Akhbar al-Yaum Concern, publishers of the daily *Al-Akhbar* and the weeklies *Akhbar al-Yaum* and *Akher Sa'a,* but only about ten of them actually worked while the others took cover behind the broad back of the regime, protected by men in power. "He knows that 'Ali Sabri who now stands trial," the paper also revealed, "used to send the editor of *Al-Gomhuriyya* a list of some 30 or 40 names, asking him to employ them as journalists at salaries ranging from 200 to 300 Egyptian pounds a month, provided he fires a similar number of editors regardless of their abilities or qualifications. If the editor dared object that the men recommended knew nothing about journalism he usually found a letter on his desk the next morning ordering his transference to the job of a clerk in some shoe factory."

Working in such conditions and subjected to such pressures, it is certainly no wonder that Egyptian journalists, columnists, and intellectuals presented such a sorry spectacle of servile conformity. The newspapers and journalists were not the only ones to be adversely affected by this state of affairs. In the late 1960s, Louis 'Awadh, a professor of literature and literary editor of *Al-Ahram*, spoke of the "literary dearth" which he said prevailed in Egypt at the time. To be sure, the number of books published or reprinted in any given year had not diminished; but the general standard of these works was woefully low. Listing the names of some thirty of Egypt's most outstanding writers and artists whose works appeared in 1970, 'Awadh complained that these works were second-rate—and declared himself profoundly shocked at discovering how little these writers seemed to be able to express themselves. As for the others, 'Awadh claimed they had either chosen to take refuge in silence and isolation or emigrated from the country. He was careful to add, too, that the dearth of which he was complaining was not confined to creative literature and other forms of writing but also pervaded the academies, the theater, the cinema, and even music.

There are, of course, several reasons for this literary dearth that 'Awadh suggested amounted to "a culture crisis." It is widely admitted, however, that one of the most crucial of these was the almost total absence of free intellectual discourse caused by the regime's determination to dictate its ideas and policies to its journalists and political intellectuals. So much so that—to quote the Egyptian critic Ghali Shukri—"intellectual creativeness was stamped out and the intellectual's role became one of mere explanation and justification of official attitudes and actions."

This being the case, it was natural, according to Shukri, to find demagogy pervading intellectual discourse, with writers and men of letters vying with each other for the approval and friendship of the regime. In this way, many of these intellectuals became "mere mechanical radio transmitters broadcasting to a public that has itself been reduced to the status of totally passive radio receivers." The result, Shukri added, has been an attitude alternating between all-pervasive confusion and sheer indifference.

An even more damning consequence of this lack of free intellectual discourse is the fact that intellectuals and would-be opinion leaders became mere time-servers. What is variously called moral courage, a public spirit, or just plain "conscience" gave way to self-seeking. Men and women whose fathers had courageously raised their voices against the corrupt rule of the monarchy in the 1930s and 1940s became cowed, their main concerns being personal safety and the good life. The revolution, it would seem, was quite generous to these members of the intelligentsia, compensating them with money and positions in the now wholly nationalized "culture industry."

'Awadh's lament and Shukri's strictures are quite characteristic of the post-Nasserist era of Egyptian culture and literature. Curiously enough, the two choices that 'Awadh thought were the only ones open to the concerned intellectual of the day—taking refuge in silence and isolation or emigrating from the country—happen also to have been the ones chosen by 'Awadh and Shukri, respectively. 'Awadh, who had several pioneering literary studies and translations to his name as well as a brilliant academic career, chose silence and isolation and was hardly heard until his death in the early 1990s. Ghali Shukri, on the other hand, chose to live outside Egypt in self-imposed exile, contributing to various periodicals and publishing books of literary and cultural criticism. Indeed, what with the steadily growing number of Arabic periodicals published outside the Arab world, especially in Paris and London, many Arab writers and intellectuals still find it convenient to contribute to these publications, especially those who have chosen to live abroad.

Not all Egyptian intellectuals of the Left, however, have chosen to take one or the other of 'Awadh's two extreme choices. Some of these have in fact gradually found their way back to semiofficial jobs in journalism and various other branches of the culture industry. This was made possible by the slightly different approach to the subject characterizing Hosni Mubarak's regime. As a matter of fact, there is a sense in which a whole generation of Egyptian intellectuals, who in the heyday of Arab socialism in the 1960s viewed themselves as spokesmen of the Left, are now an endangered species, aging and mellowing and generally too weary to keep up the fight in what increasingly seems to be a losing battle with the ruling political establishment.

Along with this process of mellowing and moderation, the debate about the intellectuals, their attitudes, their commitment or lack of it, and their relations with the powers that be became less urgent and considerably less heated. It also tended to be conducted outside of Egypt. However, Cairo somehow continues to maintain its centrality in Arab cultural affairs, and a conference on the subject of the intellectuals was held there in mid-1987. The subject of the conference was "The Intelligentsia, Society and Government in the Arab Homeland."

The participants in the conference were a motley crowd of academics, lawyers, and political intellectuals from various parts of the Arab world;

but few of them, if any, could be described as belonging to the Left. There were no clashes, confrontations, or recriminations, which used to be a permanent feature of such discussions in the 1960s and 1970s. According to summaries of the proceedings published in the Cairo weekly *Al-Ahali,* the organ of what is considered Egypt's radical left, the one participant who referred to "the crisis of the Egyptian intellectual" was Ahmad Sadiq Sa'ad, who argued that this crisis was "one of the components of the crisis of the culture and the society." He also found that in one of its dimensions, the crisis of the intellectuals had its roots in the free officers' revolt of July 22, 1952, which he claimed took away the helm of leadership from the intellectuals. The result was that they found themselves confronted by tasks they were incapable of performing, which in turn resulted in their estrangement and alienation.

One of the participants, 'Adil al-Hawwari, read a paper titled "Egypt's Intellectual Elite in the Old Regime, 1923–1952," in which he drew an analogy between the Egyptian liberal elite and its counterparts in the West. To the question as to why liberal thought in Egypt failed to play the same role in the country's fortunes that Western liberals had played in Europe, his answer was that liberalism in Egypt was not sui generis, in that it constituted no "genuine expression of the deeper undercurrents in the evolution of the Egyptian bourgeoisie, nor did it initiate or lead real revolutions to put an end to feudalism." In the realm of the intellect, too, Egyptian liberalism was wanting. It did not lay the foundations for rational thought, and thus ultimately failed to effect that cultural renaissance which in Europe led to a radical change in age-old values and relationships.

Another paper devoted to the Egyptian scene dealt with "Liberal Thought in the 1970s." Its author, Salah al-Din al-Mansi, defined the social basis of contemporary liberal thought as follows:

1. The economic class that adopts liberal slogans in Egypt today is the capitalist class in its various forms and strata. Since this class professes liberalism "in order to defend its interests rather than those of the society as a whole," its policies and teachings tend to be right-wing.
2. The class structure of this liberalism consists of the remnants of the old classes—large landowners and capitalists—and the bureaucrats who have exploited their public positions to amass wealth for themselves, as well as all those Egyptians who have managed to get rich through embezzlement, shady commercial and financial transactions, illegal trading in foreign currency, and drugs.

3. At present, the main liberal elements in Egypt are the New Wafd Party and certain factions of the National Party.

Al-Mansi's final thoughts on the subject were that, since it is basically right-wing in orientation and seeks to preserve capitalist interests and maintain a free-market economy rather than the defense of political freedom for all, "liberal thought now, despite its apparent bloom, carries the elements of its future crisis."

All in all, the Cairo gathering avoided controversial issues and had virtually nothing substantial to say about the crisis of the intellectuals, the role of the intelligentsia in contemporary Egyptian and Arab society, and relations between the intellectual and the regime. One of the Egyptian participants, Sa'd al-Din Ibrahim, gave his paper the intriguing title "Bridging the Gap between the Intellectual and the Authorities." However, at least one respondent to the paper—which was subsequently published in an Egyptian periodical—objected that what was needed was bridging the gap not between the intellectual and the regime but between him and the masses, between the cultural elite and the society as a whole, and between members of the intelligentsia and the classes they are supposed to represent.[33]

Strange as it may sound, the real debate on the Arab intellectual and the intellectual's role in society and politics now rages mainly outside the boundaries of the Arab world, in those places of exile in the West in which Arab intellectuals of the Left—mainly Egyptians, but including a good number of Lebanese, Iraqi, North African, and Syrian writers and men of letters—have chosen to live and work. One of these is Ghali Shukri, whose thoughts on the subject were cited earlier in this chapter. In a series of articles published in the Paris-based Arabic weekly *Al-Watan al-'Arabi,* Shukri raises a number of fundamental questions concerning the status of the Arab intellectual and his role. One of these questions—which Shukri leaves unanswered—is whether "there is in reality anything like Left and Right in our political life in the first place, so that we might be justified in classifying our intellectuals as belonging to the Left or the Right?" Perhaps, Shukri reflects, "the very constitution of Arab societies did not allow the formation of class structures that would in turn make it possible for an Arab intellectual to belong to the Left, the Right or Center."[34]

In a sense, however, the question that continues to be the most pressing of all is that of commitment. Is commitment on the part of the intellectual healthy? Is it necessary? Is it useful to the individual and the society? Or does it hamper the work of the intellectual? These and other related questions were discussed by several Arab thinkers and academics in a symposium published in the Left-oriented Arabic periodical *Al-Mustaqbal al-'Arabi* in the spring of 1984. Only one contributor, a professor of sociology at the University of Tunis, Al-Tahir Labib, thought that intellectual commitment and the intellectual's dabbling in politics were detrimental to members of the intelligentsia in that it interfered with their specialized work as academics, men of science, and other professional workers.

The most outspoken among advocates of active commitment was Abu Bakr al-Saqqaf, professor of literature at the University of San'a, who argued that "commitment is something which circumstances dictate to us," and that these circumstances "decree that the combining of intellectual and organizational-political work should be given first priority." Al-Saqqaf deplored the fact that in the 1970s intellectuals in the Arab world deserted political action in favor of other intellectual and academic pursuits, a development which he said amounted to their being absorbed by the state apparatus.

"It was thus," he lamented, "that the intellectual began to justify his passive and often cooperative attitude to the authorities, and was even, at times, observed to take up the role of the executioner." In this, al-Saqqaf was fully supported by Muhammad Barrada, a fellow professor of literature (at the University of Rabat), who argued that the intellectual was powerless in the face of the state's authority and that therefore he or she ought to join what the Italian Marxist thinker Gramsci termed "the collective intellectual," namely the Party, which is the only organization capable of defying the regime. As far as the Arab intellectual was concerned, Barrada perceived two stages of his relations with the political establishment. Prior to political independence, when both the intellectual and the mainstream nationalist movement faced the same [foreign] foe, the intellectual was permitted to act through allegiance to parties and organizations; but after independence was attained, the intellectuals tended to be discarded and put in their place, and their role was entrusted to technocrats and executives.[35]

By way of conclusion, it would be appropriate to say that the crisis of the intellectuals (*azmat al-muthaqqafin*), which was discussed by Nasser's leading spokesman, Muhammad Hasanein Haykal, in the late 1960s, remains as acute today as it was then, although it may have taken on another form or any number of different forms. This is not the least surprising or even unusual. The crisis of the intellectuals—or the crisis of culture as some like to call it—will remain with us in the Arab world and elsewhere as long as it is a reflection of a far larger and more insidious phenomenon, namely the crisis of a whole society and an entire political culture.

Islam on the Defensive

In the foregoing pages, an attempt was made to convey something of the cultural-ideological scene in the Arab world in the years immediately following the war of October 1973. Surveyed briefly were the fields of political ideology (post-Nasserist Egypt); Egypt's national identity; the literary cultural scene; the state of Egyptian culture 1967–1987; and the role of the intellectual (Laroui's secularist program). Virtually nothing has been said about what in a previous chapter was described as the Islamic "offensive."

This was no coincidence, since, in the field of ideology, at least, Arabic Islam's performance during the 1960s and 1970s was extremely poor. To be sure, the decline of the Muslim Brethren in Egypt and elsewhere in the Arab world starting in the mid-1950s did not spell the end of Islamic fundamentalism; yet it was becoming increasingly clear that Islam, as an effective factor in policy as well as in everyday life, was passing through a period of recession. What happened in this field in Egypt, Libya, and Saudi Arabia during this period was plainly in the nature of a reaction rather than an initiative—something that can perhaps best be described as a desperate last-ditch stand with no hope of meaningful long-term success.

Elsewhere in this book, Lord Cromer was quoted as saying of Sheikh Muhammad 'Abduh that he suspected him of being "in reality an agnostic." Almost a century has passed since this observation was made. Yet the difficulty for a believing Muslim of adjusting to life in the modern world seems to remain as acute as it was before. When, in March 1975, Prince Faisal ibn Musa'id assassinated his uncle King Faisal of Saudi Arabia, it was revealed that the assassin's brother, Prince Khalid ibn Musa'id, had been killed by Saudi police some nine years previously while heading a demonstration by Muslim zealots. The demonstration, it transpired, had been staged in protest against the setting up of a television station in Riyadh—on the ground that Islamic law forbids the representation of a human image in any form.

Something of the same religious zeal was the motive force behind two plots to overthrow the Sadat regime during the first half of 1975. The plotters, who planned to set up a government in Cairo that would adhere to the teachings of pristine Islam, appear to have represented a totally new breed of Muslim fundamentalist, one whose zeal surpasses anything Arabic Islam had known in modern times. According to information gathered from the Egyptian press at the time, the plotters were a small group of fanatics with no backing whatsoever from either the masses or the acknowledged religious leadership of the day. For the existing religious establishment, indeed, the group had nothing but scorn, if not worse. They considered their direct ideological precursors and ancestors, the Muslim Brethren, inept failures who shied away from violence and engaged in end-less pontifications about *shura* (consultation), *ijma'* (consensus), and simi-lar theoretical questions. Members of such groups—which included the one responsible for Sadat's assassination on October 6, 1981—were said to have avoided "fellow zealots with past experience" like the plague. The motto of the group was: Recruit three and avoid three! "Recruit the young, the poor and the conscript. Avoid the argumentative, those with past expe-rience among the advocates of Islamic practice, and married men."

The revulsion these groups of zealots felt toward Muslim believers "with past experience" extended to the 'ulema of Al-Azhar. Their members were cautioned not to attend mosques where such men preached at prayers. One of them—who died shortly after being wounded in the course of the attack on the Technical Military Academy in Cairo in April 1974—ex-pressed disapproval of those Azharites who visited him at his deathbed. The leader of the Alexandria ring of the group went so far as to declare that in the new Islamic state he and his comrades sought to set up, the sheiks of Al-Azhar would be employed as street cleaners. He assured his police interrogator that they (the 'ulema) would not object, and that then the country's street cleaners' crisis would be solved. "They are cowards and fear-stricken," he said about these religious savants. "Al-Azhar never was an honorable institution throughout all of its history," he added for good measure.

The zealots had no more respect for the common Muslim. In defense of the conspiratorial, violent road to political change, the leader of the group, Salih Abdullah Sariyya, cited the case of the great Muslim leader and theo-logian Abul A'la Maududi. "There is one by name of Maududi who founded a Muslim league in Pakistan," said Sariyya to his interrogators. "His policy is to seize power through elections; but many years have passed without this aim being attained. The ideal way to establishing the Islamic state in Egypt is that we do what the Communists and others have done and seize power by force in order to reinstate Islam." Asked about the masses and their possible attitude toward his group's plan of action, he replied: "They will support us. All the people will support the Islamic regime. After all, when someone told them the country shall be socialist they acceded de-spite the fact that they had not the slightest idea as to what Socialism meant."

Especially revealing were the notes seized in the room of one of the accused, a student at the Agricultural College born three months before the free officers' revolt of July 1952. "On the one hand," he wrote in one of these notes, "I attended prayers; on the other hand, I went to beaches and the movies. In the end I decided to put an end to these contradictions, and ever since I was enrolled in college I took the path of Islam and stopped frequenting beaches and cinemas." However, the contradictions kept pursuing him, this time in the society as a whole. "We are," he explains, "an Islamic state and we have the Koran—and yet we follow the Charter [of National Action, Nasser's program based on the ideology of Arab socialism] rather than practice the Koran." His analysis of the current state of affairs in Egypt, what he terms "the five fingers of the hand of oppression," is summed up in these "definitions":

Politics: "Intellectual and political tyranny."
Religion: "Backwardness, stagnation and negativism."
Media: "Freedom of speech and information provided they voice no dissent."
Society: "The overwhelming majority follows outworn customs and traditions, while the others are devoid of all values."
Science: "They masquerade as adherents of science, attribute to it more than it can bear, and manipulate it according to their whims and caprices."

Another university student, Muhammad, objects to the regime's adherence to the doctrine of nationalism. "Islam," he noted, "does not recognize the concept of nationality. This doctrine implies that people are defined according to a certain geographical location, a concept which negates Islam and its principles."[36]

Salih Sariyya's was obviously a fringe group of which the majority of believing Muslims would probably disapprove strongly. Col. Mu'ammar al-Gaddafi runs the oil-rich state of Libya uncontested; yet he too has failed to make inroads in this direction. His encounter with a group of Egyptian writers and intellectuals in 1973, in the course of which he made an attempt to expound his own version of Islamic radicalism, shows conclusively that his failure in that sphere was not confined to practical aspects of the doctrine but was evident in the theoretical-ideological sense too.

The encounter took place shortly before the October War, in the course of a visit Gaddafi was making to Cairo to persuade the Egyptians to join Libya in a full-fledged merger. The meeting was held under the benign sponsorship of a sympathetic editor and publicist, Muhammad Hasanein Haykal. In his opening statement, Gaddafi explained that the world's only hope for salvation lay in strict adherence to the teachings of Islam and the prescriptions laid down in the Koran. Present at the meeting were Egypt's leading opinion leaders and men of letters: Tawfiq al-Hakim, Naguib Mahfuz, Husain Fawzi, and Louis 'Awadh; Ahmad Baha al-Din, 'Abd al-Malik 'Oda, and 'Aisha 'Abd al-Rahman; and several others. Haykal acted as moderator.

Armed with Islam as a formidable shield and Haykal as moderator, Gaddafi succeeded in putting some of his critics on the defensive although he himself made not a single point worthy of note. In response to one remark of reproof and insinuation against himself, for instance, Husain Fawzi, a much-respected and dignified man in his seventies, defended himself in these terms: "Sir, I am a believer. I grew up in a wholly Muslim environment and sent my mother and sister [to Mecca] on a pilgrimage when they grew old. I discharge my obligations as an Egyptian citizen and a Muslim and come from a Cairene family of some 200 or 300 years' standing!"

Throughout the deliberations, Haykal kept his cool, remarking every now and again: "It's a highly significant question that is being raised by Gaddafi." On his part, however, all Gaddafi did was mumble things like, "How do we develop our values and improve our condition. . . . No, this question should come later. First we have to agree about Islam. . . . The real problem is this: We are creating Arab unity; we are creating a new civilization which should be part of this unity. We ought to combine the forces of industrial progress and military strength. We stand stronger than life itself."

After enduring much of this, some of the participants at last managed to steer clear of rhetorics and generalities and started a discussion about Islam's place in the modern world and the attitude of the Islamic establishment to reform and change. The most telling remarks were made by Baha al-Din, who spoke directly after al-Hakim had wondered whether Islam was at all capable of adapting to the modern world and, if so, who was to take the lead in such a reform movement.

"Throughout history," Baha al-Din said, "we meet [Muslim] theologians and religious savants twice and consistently—once prior to change, when they rule that it is forbidden, and once after the change had taken place, when they protest that Allah had already envisaged it a long time ago and permitted it." As an example, Baha al-Din cited the subject of the education of women. "For 100 years or so," he said, "[the 'ulema] kept issuing edicts to the effect that education for women was forbidden. However, now that all the ladies have attended school . . . they all proclaim that Mrs. 'Aisha 'Abd al-Rahman [a Muslim scholar also known by the pen name Bint al-Shati] is one of the authorities on the Hadith, Islam's vocal law. Well, why had these edicts not been issued long ago?"

Turning to Gaddafi's standing complaint concerning the corrupting influence on Islam of a whole assortment of Western ideologies, Baha al-Din added: "Disaster befell Islam many centuries prior to the emergence of Communism and Capitalism, and it is not true that it is these ideologies which pose the threat to Islam." According to him, "the challenge we face today does not lie in the fact that we are not sufficiently Muslims. The real challenge is two-fold. One lies in the backward-looking interpretation of Islam and the old rituals, the other in the absence of respect for and appreciation of those modern cultural values which can help us attain progress as a civilized society."

Neither Baha al-Din nor al-Hakim managed to move Gaddafi or influence him in any way. Islam, Gaddafi kept arguing, was the only way to resolve all the contradictions of modern life. "Therefore we must bring all the people to the religion of Allah and thus have done with all contradictory phenomena. Religion has laid down ultimate solutions. Angels used to descend from Heaven. This is no simple matter. How then do we dare to doubt that Heaven itself is linked to Earth?" To this 'Aisha 'Abd al-Rahman, a devout Muslim of the Koranic school, replied with obvious dismay: "When you, O brother Mu'ammar, present Islam as an alternative to these ideologies which clash on our soil, you present an unknown quantity. Views and interpretations of Islam are today extremely disparate. Which Islam are you offering us today?"[37]

To this and similar questions, Gaddafi never attempted to give sustained answers. Nor could he conceivably have done so. Nor, for that matter, could Sariyya and his fellow zealots, or Bint al-Shati—or anyone within sight or hearing distance.

8 | The Shifty Nineties

Fast-Fading Glimpses of Democracy

Three main themes can be said to have dominated Muslim-Arab thinking in the 1990s—democracy, Islamic fundamentalism, and Israel. While these are all interconnected, the subject of democracy and the growth of religious fanaticism often seemed to be twin problems, constantly and materially affecting and influencing each other. Three other subjects that will be dealt with in this concluding chapter are attitudes toward Israel, the status of women, and the plight of the intellectuals.

The year 1990, in which—among other fateful events—Perestroika and Glasnost began to give tangible results in the Soviet Union and the countries of Eastern Europe, witnessed the emergence of certain democratic forms of government in countries extremely disparate geographically, ideologically, and culturally. The 1990s also opened with some good omens for the Arab world and even saw a number of encouraging first moves toward a relaxation of the various forms and degrees of authoritarian, basically one-man regimes in many of the Arab states.

Late in 1990, as the crisis in the Persian Gulf erupted with the invasion of Kuwait by Iraqi forces on August 2—to develop later into a full-scale, destructive armed conflict—two opposing trends became noticeable in the Arab world, one onward and one away from what had seemed to be a slow but promising movement toward regimes with some degree of popular participation and representativeness. Autocratic regimes like those of

Saudi Arabia, Kuwait, and the other Gulf states and emirates found themselves exposed to assaults from so-called "progressive," though essentially
not less authoritarian, Arab regimes and parties such as those of Iraq, Syria,
Libya, the Sudan, Algeria, and Yemen. However, what with pressures both
from outside and from home, authoritarian single-party regimes in these
latter countries were themselves in no mood for a real relaxation of their
grips.

A brief review of the background of these developments, and of the way
thinking Arabs viewed the situation, is in place. After decades of authoritarian, single-party rule, several Arab countries in the late 1980s decided
to change course and follow the relatively recent example of Egypt, proclaiming a democratic, politically pluralistic system of government. These
were Jordan and Iraq in the Arab East and Algeria, Tunisia, and Morocco
in the Maghreb—counting out Lebanon and the Sudan, where whatever
democratic practices there had been came to a virtual standstill.

The causes for this change of course were, in the main, external. The
trend away from one-party rule and toward democracy in Eastern Europe
and the world at large, and the conviction that only political pluralism,
popular participation, and freedom of expression can help societies resolve their problems and material difficulties, could not and did not by-
pass the Arab world. As many an Arab writer and intellectual has pointed
out again and again, with the world becoming "a global village" Arab
regimes simply could not stand aside and be content with the role of an
onlooker—especially those whose economies lay in utter ruin and who
came to realize that the road to growth is through free-market systems and
political pluralism. This realization came, in the first place, when it became fairly evident that authoritarian regimes generally failed to meet the
challenges their societies faced. Even at the cost of sacrificing political freedoms, it transpired, no economic progress and no self-sufficiency had been
achieved. Secondly, there grew an awareness that democracy and political
liberalization, while not ends in themselves, could be effective means for
attaining primary national goals like security and defense.

Other arguments advanced and regularly reiterated by Arab intellectuals and political scientists can be summed up as follows:

1. Democracy provides the only solution to the problems confronting
   the Arabs today, and there is no democracy without political parties.
2. Pluralism and variety is deeply rooted in human nature and are therefore essential to the growth of a healthy society.
3. The multiparty system is good for the regimes, in that it allows people

to air their grievances and frustrations, thus absolving governments from taking all the blame and responsibility on themselves, since more than one party would share in them.

The way to attain healthy, pluralist democratic regimes in the Arab world, it was further argued, was through some kind of new "social contract" based on principles of openness to fresh social and political trends, the rule of law, freedom of expression for all, political participation, and a sharing of authority. None of these lofty goals could be attained, however, unless these four conditions were met: freedom of the press and free access to information; a broadened base of decision making; safeguarded freedom of thought and association; and the formulation of a comprehensive program for economic and social growth.

Arab writers and observers who dealt with this subject were well aware, however, that the drive toward political pluralism and liberalization in the Arab world may in the end come to naught. Past experience in this regard, they explained, tended to show that rulers took the path of democracy and pluralism merely to appease and go along with prevalent popular opinion. Eventually, these rulers chose to back out and took the first opportunity that came their way to reinstate themselves as sole arbiters.

One crucial aspect of the subject of democracy that tended to be ignored by these students and observers was the effect the parallel upsurge of Islamic fundamentalism was likely to have on the trend toward political liberalization and pluralism. This particular aspect of the problem was discussed at considerable length by Arab writers and political scientists. To give one example: In an interview printed in a Cyprus-based Arabic weekly, Tunisian scholar and university lecturer Hisham Je'it blamed the upsurge of Islamic fundamentalism for slowing down the democratic process. The rising Islamic movements, he asserted, were the culmination of a one-hundred-year-long process of radicalization and galvanization. Early Muslim reformists in Egypt, like Al-Afghani and Muhammad 'Abduh, who had been moderates open to new ideas and influences, were succeeded by groups of hard-liners and traditionalists culminating, in the 1930s, in the rise of the Muslim Brethren in Egypt and a revivalist fundamentalist movement led by the Pakistani theologian Maududi. In more recent years, what with the failure of Western ways and modern ideas to take root in the Arab world and the subsequent deep disillusionment with everything foreign to its culture and traditions, the fundamentalist movement in Islam everywhere became increasingly radicalized.

According to Je'it, the dangers inherent in this process of escalation, and in the emergence of radical Islamic movements in countries like Tunisia, Algeria, and Jordan, are ominous. For one thing, these movements can take advantage of the new liberalism to gain influence and seek a greater share in political power—as they were already doing in the countries mentioned above. For another, and far more ominously, fundamentalist Islamic movements could now actually come to power through the perfectly democratic process of a majority vote in fair and free parliamentary elections. The Tunisian scholar concludes with a warning: While democracy is a legitimate aspiration meeting real human needs, its practice requires a number of conditions and circumstances. Apart from a certain measure of order and discipline, he explains, for democracy to be firmly established and stabilized, a minimum of literacy is needed. On this showing, at least, the countries of Eastern Europe are far ahead of the Arab world, where the rate of illiteracy is extremely high and where "our intellectuals are preoccupied with ideological, utopian and often non-worldly subjects and problems," rather than with the day-to-day, down-to-earth business of contributing to the commonweal and to general amelioration of their peoples' lot.[1]

The point made here about the dangers posed to a democracy by the absence of a suitable environment was illuminated by the legislative elections held on November 29, 1990, in Egypt, a country in which parties and parliaments had existed for almost a century prior to the overthrow of its constitutional monarchy in 1952. With all but one of the opposition parties boycotting the elections, controversy was rampant and advocates of participation had their full say against those who called for boycotting the elections, which proved to be the most controversial and contested of the three to be held in Egypt in the space of eight years. While the bulk of what was written on the subject and the pleas that were made were polemical in character, some tended to throw some light on a state of affairs about which little was known to outsiders.

A particularly instructive example of the latter is a long article by a veteran lawyer and political intellectual of the Egyptian left, Jalal Amin. In this reflective article, printed in the opposition Cairo weekly *Al-Ahali* shortly before voting day under the title "Victims of the People's Assembly," Amin explains in very touching terms how he came to be so totally uninterested in anything connected with his country's parliaments and the rather convoluted processes of their election and the numerous plebiscites held in that regard. The writer first relates how many years previously it became clear to him that the Egyptian parliament in its various phases and forms in no way represented the people. It was always used by the government of the day merely to make people believe, at home and abroad, that Egypt enjoyed some form of democratic rule.

Some forty years before, Amin relates, when attending his first year of law school, he was taught about the principle of the separation of the three powers—legislative, judicial, and executive—and was satisfied that such separation provided effective safeguards for freedom and an orderly political system. "This was all of four decades ago," Amin laments. "Since then, Egypt has known one power and one only, the executive, i.e. the government. With unprecedented daring, the government subjugated both the legislators and the judiciary and subjected them to unspeakable insults. . . . The Speaker of the People's Assembly was reduced to the status of a government employee appointed and dismissed at will."

Amin then cites the strange case of the 1990 elections and how they came to be held. The outgoing assembly was elected in 1987, but in May 1990, in response to a complaint made by a concerned citizen, the Higher Constitutional Court pronounced the elections null and void since the elections law, according to which the new assembly had been chosen, was "unconstitutional." When he heard that the government decided to comply with the court's decision and dissolve the House, Amin relates, he welcomed the decision but wondered why the government, having in the past ignored several such verdicts, this time chose to heed the court's findings and its ruling.

Then, not content with this measure of make-believe, the government came up with what Amin claims was merely another trick: It suddenly decided to put the whole matter to popular vote, asking for a yes or no answer to the question of whether the assembly should be dissolved. Why go to the trouble of holding a nationwide plebiscite when there is a ruling by what is supposed to be the highest constitutional instance that the assembly had to be dissolved? What Amin finds especially ironical about all this, he writes, is that the decision to hold the plebiscite was claimed by the government to have been decreed by the principle of the separation of the three powers![2]

In any event, and quite predictably, more than 90 percent of the Egyptians who took part in the plebiscite—held on October 11, 1990—approved the dissolution, and elections were set for November 29. Besides the ruling National Democratic Party, however, only one more party of any significance—the National Progressive Unionist Alignment Party, better known as the Alignment—participated in the elections. What happened was that, ten days after the plebiscite was held, four of the five parties of the opposition announced they were boycotting the elections. It took observers by surprise that the boycott was joined by the New Wafd Party, a center grouping that generally supported the government in its domestic and foreign policies and that had supported President Hosni Mubarak in his adamant stand against the Iraqi ruler and Iraq's annexation of neighboring Kuwait—an issue that was becoming of crucial significance.

Complaints that the Egyptian authorities and the ruling party were consistently interfering with the voting process, charges of ballot rigging, bribes, intimidations, and corrupt practices had been made by the opposition in the past with singular regularity. Safeguards were demanded for fair elections and, above all, for the abrogation of emergency regulations, imposed as far back as 1981, immediately following the assassination of President Sadat on October 6 that same year. The charges and complaints continued to be made, and the government continued to ignore them. The boycott of the 1990 elections by the four opposition parties failed to make any impression on the authorities or the ruling party, which won a total of 348 seats out of the assembly's 454, not including the ten deputies subsequently named by Mubarak, whom the elections law empowers to appoint.

Of the 10 members of the People's Assembly President Mubarak named, 5 were Copts, including Minister of State for Foreign Affairs Boutrus Boutrus-Ghali. Since only 2 out of the 444 elected deputies were Copts, Mubarak's generous gesture brought the total number of Copts in the House to 7. This is a sad reflection, not only on the position of the Copts in Egyptian society and politics, but also on the inadequacy of the electoral process and the elections law. While the precise percentage of Copts in the Egyptian population has never been verified, official estimates speak of 6 percent, while Copt spokesmen claim their community constitutes nearly 15 percent of the population. Whatever the correct percentage, however, Copt spokesmen claimed that the ruling National Democratic Party was less than fair in including only 2 Copts in its list of candidates. One dissatisfied Copt, writing in *Al-Ahali*, accused Mubarak's party of trying to appease the Muslim fundamentalists by showing so little consideration for the country's Christian Copts—a ploy which the writer characterized as an attempt "to counter extremism by extremism," with the result that the Copts ended up doubly victimized.[3]

The example of Egypt offers perhaps the best illustration of the huge gap separating theory, even actual written legislation, from practice. A passing look at what the constitutions of a number of Arab countries lay down with regard to this particular point is in place.

According to the Lebanese constitution, promulgated in 1926 and last amended in 1947, "All Lebanese shall be equal in the eyes of the law . . . . The legislative power shall be exercised by the Chamber of Deputies." The chamber is "to consist of elected members" chosen by "every Lebanese citizen who has completed his twenty-first year and fulfills the conditions laid down by the electoral law."

The situation on the ground in the early 1990s was quite different, however. To be sure, after fifteen years of civil strife during which all pretense to a democratic system or a representative form of government had been abandoned, there still existed something called a parliament. But since 1975, this shadow of a legislature seldom managed actually to meet or have the required quorum, often because the deputies simply failed to find a place where they could convene unmolested. What is more, the chamber of deputies had been elected back in May 1972, and in 1989, thirty of its original ninety-nine members were no more among the living. According to an agreement reached at the Saudi city of Taif in the autumn of 1989 by all the warring parties, and which has come to be known as the Taif Accord, nine more Muslims were to be added to the chamber, beside the need to elect successors to the thirty dead deputies.

The Taif Accord, which finally was said to be implemented only late in 1990, tried among other things to rectify a situation that was the source of much complaining and bitterness on the part of Lebanon's Muslims. This attempt at giving the Muslims the representation they claimed they deserved was in fact long overdue. In accordance with the country's hopelessly outdated constitution, membership of the chamber—since named the National Assembly—is allotted to the various communities, religions, and denominations as follows: thirty Maronite Catholics, twenty Sunni Muslims, nineteen Shiite Muslims, eleven Greek Orthodox, six Druze, six Greek-Melkite Catholics, four Armenian Orthodox, one Armenian Catholic, and a Protestant. This was calculated to give Christians fifty-three seats and Muslims forty-five, with the two missing seats allotted to "others." Elections to a new assembly, originally scheduled for April 1976, were postponed for twenty-six months; but in January 1978, the term of the house was further extended until June 1980. In December 1987, after four further postponements, the term was extended until 1990.

The Constitution of the Kingdom of Jordan, as amended in 1955, vests the legislative authority "in the King and the National Assembly, consisting of the Senate and the Chamber of Deputies." It further stipulates that the chamber "shall consist of members elected by universal, secret, and direct suffrage," while one-half of the members of the senate shall be appointed by the king.

The elections held in November 1989 were the first Jordan was to have in twenty-two years. Up to that date, little was heard about the Muslim Brethren of Jordan, their organization, or their activities. Their existence was brought to the fore, however, when the results of the elections were announced. Together with a few much smaller Islamic organizations, the Brethren won a stunning thirty-one out of the House's eighty seats. The number of seats occupied by the Brethren alone is twenty-two.

When polling ended and the results were made known, many observers in the Arab world and outside thought the Islamic groups constituted a grave danger to the Jordanian regime and to the throne itself. As in so many other similar cases in his long years as monarch, however, King Hussein was able to deftly weather the storm, somehow making the Brethren and their allies feel at home in the House and keeping them out of harm's reach. Indeed, their chief spokesman, 'Abdul Latif 'Arabiyyat, got himself elected Speaker of the Chamber. Finally, later in the year, the Brethren's position was stabilized further when they were given five cabinet seats, including the education portfolio, thus becoming practically part of the political establishment of the country.

Universal, free, direct, and secret suffrage is guaranteed also in the constitutions of Tunisia, Morocco, pre-Gaddafi Libya, Kuwait, and the Sudan. In all of them, legislative power is said to be vested in the people and their elected representatives, and in the case of monarchies, that power is shared by the king. The same goes, in theory at least, for post-1952 Egypt, where, in effect, some "revolutionary command council" ruled the country uncontested for more than three decades.

The phrase "direct and secret universal suffrage" figures, too, in the constitution of the Algerian People's Democratic Republic, where the National Liberation Front was the sole arbiter until the year 1990, when a strong coalition of Muslim fundamentalists made considerable headway in local elections, a victory which resulted in the proclamation of military rule.

The Algerian Experiment and Its Aftermath

How the twin problems of democracy and Islamic fundamentalism manifested themselves during this period can best be illustrated by Algeria's experience and some of the reactions to it. In December 1991, in the first round of parliamentary elections—the first ever to be held in Algeria since

it gained its independence in 1952—the voters rejected the National Liberation Front, the party in power, and gave 82 percent of the seats to the
Islamic Salvation Front (ISF), an avowedly religious party that pledged to
reinstate the strictly Islamic rules of the shari'a. The ISF was expected to
win the second round of the elections scheduled for January 1992 and gain
a decisive majority. However, the military intervened and declared the elections null and void.

Reactions in the Arab world to this manifestly undemocratic—and un-
Islamic—move varied only very little. It was Saudi Arabia, famously an
Islamic state, that was the first to congratulate Algeria's new rulers on
their success in preventing the rise of an Islamic government there. The
fact was that both governments were now actively persecuting Muslim
activists in their midst.

While this seems to be something of a paradox—especially where Saudi
Arabia was concerned—there are perfectly convincing explanations for it.
To be sure, Saudi Arabia has always styled itself an Islamic state. Since the
early 1930s, when 'Abd al-'Aziz Al Saud assumed the title of King of Saudi
Arabia, the kingdom was governed by the monarch "in consultation" with
a *majlis shura* (consultative council). This is in keeping with the *shura* system of government decreed by Islam, and, like all Islamic practices, is based
on the teachings of the Koran and on Islam's oral tradition, the Hadith. In
this case, the practice originates in the brief Koranic ordinance *amruhum
shura baynahum*—"[The believers'] communal business is to be [trans-
acted in] consultation among themselves" (Koran XLII:38).

Muslim thinkers consider this injunction the fundamental operative
clause of all Islamic thought relating to statecraft. Indeed, as one of Islam's
contemporary thinkers has put it, the clause "is so comprehensive that it
reaches out into almost every department of political life . . . so self-expres-
sive and unequivocal that no attempt at arbitrary interpretation can change
its purport." The "business" (*amr*) in the injunction, he adds, "refers to all
affairs of a communal nature and therefore also to the manner in which
the government of an Islamic state is to be established, that is, to the elective principle underlying all governmental authority." The injunction also,
according to the same authority, "makes the transaction of all political
business not only consequent upon, but synonymous with, consultation;
which means that the legislative power of the state must be vested in an
assembly chosen by the community specifically for this purpose."[4]

That members of the majlis must be elected by means of the widest
possible suffrage, including both men and women, is seen to be evident
from the context of the phrase "among themselves," which is said to refer

to the whole community. The extent of the suffrage, however, and the qualifications to be demanded from the voters and the candidates, are details
regarding which Islamic law provides no clear-cut legislation. This leaves
much to the discretion of the powers that be, a state of affairs that clearly
leaves much room for manipulation.

It has often been argued, for instance, that instead of being elected, directly or indirectly, by the whole community, majlis al-shura might be sufficiently representative if its members were simply nominated by the emir
(the man in authority), who owes his position and authority to a popular
mandate and thus might be deemed to be an embodiment of the community's
will. However, though this view is richly supported by examples from history, it is not accepted universally by Muslim theologians, since the manner in which a legislative body comes into being is counted among the
most important of communal affairs—which in turn are, according to the
ordinance quoted above, to be transacted on the basis of popular consultation. Therefore, it is further argued, the process of constituting the majlis
must in itself be an outcome of consultation, in the widest and most direct
sense of the word. Clearly, in our day and age, such consultation can take
no form other than that of elections during which the merits of the respective candidates are publicly discussed and the votes cast accordingly. Here,
again, the shari'a does not lay down any rules regarding the method of
elections or any other practical aspect of the elective powers. These are,
therefore, matters left for "the community" to decide.

This, of course, is a circular argument from which no convincing practical conclusion can be drawn. "Matters for communal decision" have to
be discussed by an elected majlis, which in turn must be freely elected by
the community as a whole. However, the crucial subject of the *manner* of
the election and other practical aspects of the process are themselves matters for communal decision that are to be decided by consultation that
legitimately can be conducted only by a majlis freely elected by the whole
community.

And so on. The loopholes are as varied as they are numerous, and are of
course duly and systematically exploited by Muslim regimes that claim to
follow the rules of the shari'a to the letter—and the Saudi monarchy is no
exception. Since the early 1930s, answers to questions such as who is to
choose those individuals who are to "consult among themselves" regarding communal and state affairs have been submitted by various spokesmen
of the regime; but none of these answers seemed quite convincing to the
objective observer.

Al Saud's own "consultative council," for instance, comprised heads of tribes and patriarchs of whatever urban families there were in the kingdom at the time—a simple and effective enough practice, considering the overwhelmingly tribal character of the country some sixty years ago. For three decades, until the early 1960s, the system worked fairly smoothly. Following the Arab military coups of the 1950s, which toppled the constitutional regimes of Syria, Egypt, and Iraq, the Saudi monarchy along with the other Arab hereditary regimes felt threatened. When the Cairo-instigated and backed civil war in neighboring Yemen became a symbol of the struggle between traditional and "progressive" trends in the whole Arab area, the Saudis thought the time was ripe for some change. Then, as on many later occasions, a promise was made by the Saudi monarch to the effect that, "Allah willing," a consultative council would be duly set up.

The promise, however, was forgotten once the threat to the regime was lifted, what with Nasser's fiasco in the Six-Day War of 1967 and the withdrawal of Egyptian troops from Yemen. In 1979, and again in 1980, similar promises regarding the constitution of a majlis shura were made by the late King Khaled; but nothing came out of these promises either, despite the fact that Khaled named an eight-man commission to draw up the relevant legislation and prepare for the election of the assembly, for which an impressive building was planned. However, though the building—in marble and glass—was duly finished, it stood empty on a hill overlooking the capital for many years.

More than a decade later, in March 1992, Saudi Arabia's ruling dynasty finally proclaimed the formation of a new consultative council for the kingdom, suggesting broadly that the new body was the nearest approximation to an elected parliament and thus an adequate answer to those liberals and modernizers who had been calling for the institution of some sort of representative government in what was an autocratic monarchy.

Saudi Arabia is not the only Arab state to have a shura council; but all the shura councils in existence so far—in the Sultanate of Oman, Qatar, Bahrain, and the United Arab Emirates—are formed in the same way. Each consists of sixty members, all but one of whom are "selected" from amongst notables, tribal chiefs, and representatives of the country's provinces. The remaining member, who is appointed by the government, heads the council. The council is authorized, first and foremost, to discuss proposed legislation and to question ministers and other government officials about domestic affairs.

This, of course, is a very far cry from the democratically elected body known as parliament. The situation in Saudi Arabia being what it is, however, Fahd and his aides have every reason to be wary about what they promise. For some years now, but especially since the Kuwait crisis and the war, the Saudi establishment has been facing a twofold challenge, posing a grave danger to the monarchy.

On the one side there are what can be called the forces of progress clamoring for far-reaching reform of the system and the establishment of some sort of a Western-type, multiparty system based on representative government. On the other extreme, there are the forces of fundamentalist Islam calling for an Islamic regime based strictly on the shari'a, roughly on the lines of Khomeini's Islamic Republic of Iran.

Of these two challenges, the one that causes the Saudi establishment the most worry is that posed by the fundamentalists, who seem to have grown in number and become more vocal and outspoken since the Gulf crisis. They have been agitating against just about every aspect of the regime and its policies. With no organized, recognized status of their own, these militants conduct their activities mainly in mosques and through bona fide religious societies and charitable institutions, as well as in the many Islamic colleges and universities, where some of them work as teachers and lecturers.

Among other things, the campaign the Muslim radicals conducted against the regime targeted Saudi support of U.S. policies and Riyadh's condoning and partial participation in peace talks between the Arabs and Israel. It was also aimed at the government's financial and banking policies, deemed by the Islamists to conflict with the teachings of the Koran.

An especially stern attitude is taken against Saudi women who work in the field of education and who enroll in institutions of higher learning; the term *prostitute* is widely and liberally used here. Confronted by such dangerous opponents, Saudi Arabia's ruling establishment has understandably relegated the reformists' challenge to second or third place. Mindful of what is taking place in Algeria, Jordan, and the Sudan, the government decided to give priority to action against the extremists and mobilized its own Muslim religious leaders and theologians for the task.

There are, of course, a number of other good reasons why Western-style democracy cannot work in Saudi Arabia. The Saudi political system is the only one amongst the Arab states that does not even claim to be democratic. Indeed, with a royal family so extended as to constitute a class all its own, ruling the land uncontested and enjoying authority on the basis of paternalistic norms of kinship, Saudi Arabia is likely to remain for some time under a government guided by some consultative practices based on tribal chiefs and sheikhs, a semblance of the shari'a, and neo-feudal royal patronage. Indeed, shortly after the new sixty-member shura council was proclaimed, on March 1, 1992, King Fahd went on record as ruling out parliamentary elections in his kingdom, arguing that "the democratic system prevailing in the world does not suit us here in this country." Islam, he added, "is our social and political law; it is a complete constitution of social and economic laws and a system of government and justice."

It was obvious right from the start that the new consultative council, which came after nearly ten years of expectancy, was never meant to be anything like a Western-style parliament. The sixty leading businessmen, academics, jurists, and clergy were all chosen by the king. The procedure is that the council takes a look at measures taken by the government and the municipal councils. If a majority disagrees with any of these, the matter is to be referred back to the king, who will have the last word. Lest anything be seen to be done in haste, however, the sixty dignitaries were to be appointed in installments over a six-month period.

It is worth noting that together with the decision to establish a shura council came the publication of "a basic law of government" that establishes a rule of civil law guaranteeing personal freedom for citizens and expatriates, while stressing that the Koran and its teachings remain the unchanging constitution of the land and the shari'a its everlasting law.

Exactly why democracy as we know it is judged by the Saudi monarch as not suited to Arab traditional societies of the Gulf—and is generally equated by Islamists with Western atheism—is a subject neither goes into. However, a fairly articulate answer to this question comes from the proceedings of a conference held in Cairo late in 1991 to discuss "the *shura* and its role in reform and the awakening of societies." One of the more important participants, the leader of the Muslim Brethren, Sheikh Mamoun al-Hudheibi, said among many other things that the shura system was "an assured guarantee for the health of society and its well-being . . . as it ensures for people dignity and pride and the right to resist oppression and be independent." Shura and freedom are inseparable, he said. "Freedom is *shura* and *shura* is freedom!" To leave no one in any doubt about where exactly he stood, Hudheibi concluded by saying, "The West fights us because it knows that its democracy is a sham and that we give it no credibility."

Another participant, a professor of economics at the religious University of Al-Azhar, Shawqi al-Fanjari, was more careful. "Let's not bother our heads on the subject of the relation between democracy and the *shura*," he told his august audience. "Let me simply say that democracy as delineated by the rules of the *shari'a* is the sum total of the Islamic *shura*."

Equally blunt was 'Atef al-Banna, head of the Center for the Study of Human Rights, the College of Law, Cairo University, who laid it down that there was no discrepancy between the shura and democracy. "Democracy," he said, "was government by the people . . . [but] we object to Western-style democracy because it began as a lay, materialist theory that ignored the religious outlook, violated the rights of minorities, and gave license to everything so that injustice, perversion and sexual permissiveness have become widespread."

These, of course, are strictly religious reflections echoing what the Saudi monarch and Islamists generally have been reiterating. Arab liberals as a whole, including many Saudi intellectuals, academics, and businessmen, expressed deep disappointment at Fahd's announcement, including the claim he made that "momentous events in the recent past made it necessary to develop the country's administrative structure."

It is clear, they complained, that the almost imperceptible "reforms" announced by the king marked the limit of what may be hoped for in that country for a long time to come. With the king's assurance that the new consultative council "amounts to [no more than] developing and modernizing a long-observed system," it is obvious that the road to anything like Western-style democracy is hard and long.[5]

Democracy's Grim Prospects

This gap between written state legislations and actual practice in the Arab world is often remarked upon and deplored, and the merits of "true democracy" are enumerated with nostalgia. Indeed, in the late 1980s the word *democracy* was perhaps the most frequently used in pronouncements made by every Arab writer, commentator, and thinker—and often enough by political leaders as well. It is not important what the ailment or the complaint or the shortcoming happens to be; democracy was said to provide both the treatment and the cure.

More specifically, some of these writers pointed to the phenomenon of Muslim fundamentalists in Egypt and elsewhere in the Arab world resorting to acts of violence and individual murder. The answer to this, they claimed, is democracy. Had there been in these countries some sort of workable democratic system, they explained—one that provides for truly free elections, personal freedom, a free press, and an equitable distribution of wealth—these fanatics would have had other, legitimate and peaceful outlets for their frustrations, and the resort to acts of murder and terror would have been abandoned.

The same goes for a long and varied list of complaints: An absence of distinction, let alone separation, among the legislative, executive, and judicial powers; chronic differences and rivalries between the Arab states; widespread illiteracy; the dearth in literary and artistic creations; discrimination against women, minorities, and dissidents; social injustices. All these long-standing features of life in the Arab world, it was argued, would slowly but surely disappear if stable, honest-to-God democratic systems were introduced.

The emphasis, of course, is on genuine, working democracy rather than what almost all the Arab regimes calling themselves democratic have to offer. The forms of government in the Arab world today can be classified under three general headings: "democratic republics," constitutional monarchies, and nominal theocracies that are often autocratic in character. It is important to note, however, that within all these three categories many of the regimes are authoritarian, and in some of them absolute individual rule prevails. Of these, the most notorious are Iraq, Syria, and Libya (all masquerading as democratic republics), while in Jordan and Morocco, the sole surviving constitutional monarchies in the area, a certain measure of democracy and representative government prevails.

In the other democratic republics—Algeria, Egypt, Tunisia, Lebanon, and Yemen—varying degrees of basic freedoms and formal tools of democratic rule are provided for in written constitutions and laws, and in some cases are actually enjoyed and used by the populace. As of the beginning of the 1990s, Saudi Arabia remains the only Arab country in which a theocratic form of government prevails. The other Arab countries, situated mostly in the Persian Gulf area, are emirates and sheikdoms whose affairs are run in accordance with ancient tribal customs and practices. Among these, Kuwait's was the only regime that had pretensions, even some rightful claim, to a democratic form of government. The rest—the United Arab Emirates, Bahrain, Oman, and Qatar—are ruled according to the old tribal norms and make no claims to democracy even in theory.

Clearly, then, it is impossible to make any generalizations about the state of democracy in the Arab world as a whole, or even in specific groups of states whose affairs are administered, in theory at least, by identical forms of government. The gap yawning between theory and practice is too wide, and convergences and contradictions are too numerous for such generalizations to be made with any measure of safety.

To give one example: While participatory norms are accepted formally in many of these countries—in democratic republics and constitutional monarchies as well as in the one theocracy—the regimes in many of them do not allow these norms to exist in practice. Others, like Saudi Arabia and most of the Gulf emirates and sheikhdoms, insist that democracy is simply not suited to their countries and would not admit its merits even in theory.

The overall picture is one of utter confusion. One can indeed say that the jigsaw puzzle is as difficult to assemble as the Arab area as a whole is difficult to govern. The reasons for this, it must be pointed out, have nothing to do with anything so fanciful as "the Arab character," "the Arab mentality," or "the fanatical nature of Islam." Apart from certain outside factors—including the continued trauma the Arabs feel the establishment of Israel in their midst has caused them—these reasons are attributable in great measure to the problems of change accompanying the ongoing processes of modernization and Westernization. The Arab world in the past several decades has been under great pressure to accept and introduce some profound change. But while radical changes have either been actually introduced or loudly demanded, the political order keeps lagging behind. More significantly, the existing order has proved incapable of managing the deep social conflicts that such changes were bound to engender.

For many Arab intellectuals and political observers, the way out of this predicament lies in a system of government that would embody and institutionalize popular participation. This, of course, is just another way of defining democracy and the democratic process as they are generally understood in the West. The trouble, however, is that very few of the prerequisites of meaningful participation have been provided by the political process—a state of affairs which made for the emergence of regimes with varying degrees of control and coercion, and whose survival is itself a function of such coercion.

This being the situation, political life in the Arab world as a whole remains unstable. It is not as though the will to democratize is lacking, either on the popular or the official levels. What seems to stand in the way to democracy and participation is fear—fear on the part of the existing regimes of what democratization would entail, fear that militant opposition forces would take over, perfectly democratically, and eventually establish some of the worst dictatorships the region had ever known. These fears are by no means unfounded. In Iraq, Syria, and Egypt, constitutional, semirepresentative governments were all toppled during the 1950s, to be replaced by authoritarian one-man or single-party regimes.

Thus, though decades have passed since constitutional rules and provisions were laid down, and despite the fact that numerous changes of regime have taken place in some of the countries involved, the actual situation has changed little, despite the fact that all the coups and revolts claimed, perhaps even earnestly aspired, to replace the hated old regimes by better, more egalitarian, progressive, and revolutionary ones.

Such discrepancies and contradictions notwithstanding, claims continued to be made by Arab rulers that theirs were bona fide democratic regimes. One of the more interesting of these is the version the Kuwaiti sheikhs and emirs propagated of their own form of government. Some time in the autumn of 1990, a few months after Iraqi troops seized his country, the Emir of Kuwait, Sheikh Jaber al-Ahmad as-Sabah, had a meeting with French President Francois Mitterand. According to the London-based Arabic weekly *Sourakia*, the opening part of the meeting went as follows. The interpreter was ready, Mitterand waiting patiently—and thus said the emir: "In the Middle East, your Excellency," he started, stopping briefly for the interpreter to translate. "In the Middle East, your Excellency," he repeated, "there are only two democracies, Lebanon and Kuwait. And look what they have come to!" The interpreter translated, then turned to the president for his reaction. But he had to wait quite a while before Mitterand, embarrassed and not a little bewildered, finally came up with some polite response or other.[6]

What could Mitterand, president of a nation that gave democracy its fullest meaning some two hundred years ago, have told his princely highness? That pre-1975 Lebanon practiced a version of democracy made perfectly to measure to fit the Christian minority and left the Muslim majority grumbling and embittered—and that the fifteen-year-long civil strife that was presumably coming to an end in those very days was nothing but the cumulative outcome of forty-five years of a regime run by a handful of Maronite feudal-type warlords and chieftains? Could Mitterand, again, have told the exiled emir that his highness had himself dispersed his own parliament, for what it was, four years before, leaving the emirate without even that semblance of democratic government? That he, his guest, remains the sole arbiter to the emirate and the exclusive owner of the land, its oil, its trees, and whatever else that in a democracy belongs rightfully to the people? That his highness is a ruler no one chose except his own extended family, and that he is there at the helm thanks only to some biological coincidence?

Ironically, though, in the context of the environment and the political culture in which he functions, the emir had quite a point. True, his government had suspended parliament in July 1986, sixteen months after it was elected; but the regime and its apologists maintained that the reasons were strictly external and had to do with the war between Iraq and Iran, which at the time was in its sixth and most decisive year, and when the Iranians were threatening Basra, Iraq's outlet to Shat al-'Arab and the Gulf and just next door to Kuwait.

Not that the National Assembly, Kuwait's parliament, was representative of the inhabitants of the emirate in any meaningful sense. According to the Kuwaiti elections law, only males whose forebears were residents there before 1920 and who are twenty-one years of age or older are entitled to vote—a rule which according to reliable estimates renders more than 90 percent of the population disenfranchised. Out of a population of nearly 1,800,000 and some 826,000 potential voters, only about 63,000 can actually exercise their right to vote.

Later in 1990, nearly five years and one more Gulf war after their parliament was dispersed, the rulers of Kuwait were biding their time in Saudi Arabia awaiting the restoration of the country's "legitimate government." Members of that government and other representatives of the regime—sheikhs and emirs to a man—seldom deigned to speak about their plans for the future, after they had been restored to power. Instead, they spoke, in vague general terms, about such things as peace and reconciliation and the fact that they bore no grudges against those of their subjects who might have been misled into some naughtiness or misdemeanor.

For decades now, perfectly democratic rules and provisions have figured in every written constitution in the region, formulated by some of the best minds in the field. Nevertheless, the actual situation remained the same—no truly representative government of any kind has been seen and no real separation of powers achieved. If anything, where changes were effected, these were always for the worse, and, of the three powers, the executive has always had the upper hand, manipulating both the legislature and the judiciary any way it chose.

Several observers and students of the Arab scene, Arabs as well as Westerners, have tried to fathom the reasons for this failure on the part of the Arab states to adapt themselves to the democratic system of government. Needless to say, deep socioeconomic, political, cultural, and historical factors lie at the root of this state of affairs—factors that are often ignored or dismissed as irrelevant by theorists, well-wishers, and planners of all kinds. One of the few students of the area who addressed himself to this subject is Charles Issawi, acknowledged authority on the economic history of the Middle East. Some years ago, Issawi set out to examine what he called "the economic and social foundations of democracy" and to relate them—or the lack of them—to the subject of democracy and its fortunes in the Arab world.

Taking as a yardstick those countries in the West, chiefly in Western Europe and North America, where democracy is practiced, Issawi reaches the conclusion that "democracy does not thrive in the Middle East because the economic and social basis which it requires is as yet non-existent." That basis, he adds, embraces the following aspects: size of territory and population, level of economic development, distribution of wealth, industrialization, homogeneity of language and religion, degree of education, and habit of cooperation association. It is Issawi's basic assumption that for democratic institutions to develop, and for the democratic spirit to flourish, two conditions seem necessary: "the community must be bound by a strong social solidarity; and at the same time it must contain enough diversity to produce tension between its constituent parts."

In practically all these spheres, Issawi implies, the Arab world is at a disadvantage. What is needed, he asserts, "is a great economic and social transformation which will strengthen society and make it capable of bearing the weight of the modern state." Mere constitutional or administrative reforms, or just a change in government machinery or in personnel, he emphasizes, would not be enough— "not even the adjustment of an obsolete political structure to bring it in line with a new balance of forces reflecting changing relations between various social classes."[7]

Other explanations have been advanced for the shortcomings of Middle Eastern democracies. One of these used to be the standard popular explanation offered by Arab nationalists and local patriots, who argued that no real democracy could develop in countries such as Iraq, Syria, Egypt, Jordan, and Lebanon as long as British and French armies of occupation were the determining factors in all political matters, and "as long as the population continued to be preoccupied, not to say obsessed, with the problem of its relations with the foreign power."

Another explanation, current in the West, is that democracy is a plant of slow growth, which gradually developed over several centuries in the congenial climate of Europe and North America and which could not possibly be expected to thrive when suddenly transplanted to an alien Eastern soil which, since the dawn of recorded history, had bred nothing "but the thorns and thistles of despotism." The absence of democratic traditions, Issawi explains, and of the historical customs, habits, and attitudes required to make democracy work, "was one of the first aspects of the East to strike nineteenth-century Europeans—and no one has expressed this better than Lord Cromer." He then quotes Cromer's dictum: "Do not let us for one moment imagine that the fatally simple idea of despotic rule will readily give way to the far more complex conception of ordered liberty."[8]

A third explanation, also cited by Issawi, has been prevalent both in the West and in the Middle East. It is that Middle Easterners generally "are incapacitated, by their extreme individualism, from achieving the degree of cooperation required for the successful functioning of democracy." Middle Easterners, it is argued, tend to develop "intense loyalty to certain small units, such as the family, the clan, the tribe, or the religious sect, but they do not seem to be able to transcend these groups and feel towards any larger body, for example the city or the nation, enough devotion and responsibility to subordinate their individual selfish propensities to some common goal." Issawi goes all the way back to Ibn Khaldun, the fourteenth-century Arab historian and keen social observer, who wrote in his famous *Introduction* (*Muqaddimah*): "Every Arab regards himself as worthy to rule, and it is rare to find one of them submitting willingly to another, be it his father or his brother or the head of his clan, but only grudgingly and for fear of public opinion."[9]

It is interesting to note that, while arguments regarding these shortcomings in the standards of traditional ways and political forms originated mostly in the West, Western-oriented reformers and revolutionaries in the Arab world have reiterated them since the late-nineteenth century, and in several cases tried to emulate the ways of the West. However, Western-style democracy and parliamentary forms proved unworkable and, as the experiences of almost all Westernizing Arab politicians were to show, raised numerous problems and, in the end, proved to be these politicians' own undoing. The examples of Iraq, Syria, Egypt, Libya, and Algeria are the first to come to mind.

Democracy is, of course, government by the people—by the people as a whole, rather than by any section, class, or interest within it. The fact that almost all Third World regimes, including those of the Middle East and North Africa, claim to be "democratic" springs from the confusion regarding who is it that takes the decisions and in whose interests these decisions are taken. In these regimes, however, political decisions are considered democratic if they further, or if they are perceived as furthering, "the interests of the people," even though they might be made by some revolutionary command council or the central committee of some political party that happens to have seized power, or have been established by a group of politicians and army officers, though by plainly undemocratic means.

This distinction is usually reinforced by another, even more problematic one. Democracy, it is habitually argued by men at the helm and by their apologists, is not one of a piece. There is bourgeois, or capitalist, democracy; economic democracy; and social democracy. Capitalist democracy, they argue, is a sham; it is a device used to prevent the emergence of democracy at the economic and social levels, which is what really matters. Since "true democracy" can come about only when conditions for it are well prepared, there is need for "directed democracy" on the political level.

This argument, in many different ways, has been advanced by practically every Arab regime that lacks even the bare formalities of democratic rule—in Nasser's Egypt from the 1950s through the 1970s; in Gaddafi's Libya; in the Saudi monarchy; in Ba'thist Syria and Iraq; in the Sudan, Yemen, and—at different times and in different periods—in virtually every Arab state.

All these plainly undemocratic regimes do not merely make claims to "true democracy"; some of them have also taken it upon themselves to propagate new and rather novel theories purporting to furnish effective answers to the shortcomings and ailments they attribute to Western capitalist democracy. A book carrying the sensational title *The Nasserist Solution to the Crisis of Democracy* was published as late as 1975, eight years after Nasser's debacle in the Six-Day War and five years after his death. And this, not to mention Col. Mu'ammar al-Gaddafi's *Green Book,* in which the Libyan ruler lays the rules for an entirely new version of democratic government totally free of the ills and malaises of democracy as it is practiced in the West.

In the early 1990s the belief was widespread, in the West as well as in many Arab quarters, that after the armed conflict in the Persian Gulf was over many Arab regimes would have the sense to turn to some sort of democratic rule and genuine popular participation and representation through parliaments freely elected by secret ballot. Several observers of the Arab scene, however—including some of the more astute Arab writers and commentators—tended to draw a different kind of scenario. Rather than turning to genuine democratic ways for a solution to their problems, these observers argued, Arabs might well be swayed by a massive wave of Islamic fundamentalism. To prove their point, they cited the cases of Jordan, Algeria, Sudan, and Tunisia, as well as other Arab countries, where they claimed the signs were unmistakable.

Some of these bleak scenarios have in fact been partially enacted. Much still depends, however, on the manner in which the many outstanding problems confronting the Arab world—chief among them, perhaps, are Islamic fundamentalism and peace negotiations with Israel—are to be resolved. To be sure, the post-Gulf war years have been overshadowed by the image of one man, Saddam Hussein. As luck would have it, however, the Iraqi leader proved to be just another aspirant to leadership of the Arabs who was to fail them. Not only was he no match for the formidable forces arraigned against him; the choice he offered his would-be followers was an impossible one.

A dictum attributed to Muhammad, the founder of Islam and its prophet, goes as follows: "After me, there will be caliphs; and after the caliphs, emirs; and after the emirs, kings; and after the kings, tyrants."[10] The prophecy embodied in this hadith—the sequence of emirs-kings-tyrants—has proved to be the common pattern of politics in the various Arab successor states to the much-maligned Ottoman Empire. Events in the Arab world in the late 1980s and the early 1990s were no exception. With Saddam Hussein masquerading as the rebel, the reformer, and the savior—as against the evil neo-feudalist kings and sheikhs of Kuwait, Saudi Arabia, and the other Persian Gulf states—what the Iraqi leader was actually asking his fellow Arabs to do was to face a ponderous choice: back to the age of the emirs or forward to the era of the tyrants.

Attitudes toward Israel: From Demonology to Normalcy

On the subject of Israel and the Israeli-Arab conflict, the 1980s and early 1990s witnessed vast changes in Muslim-Arab thinking. Signs of such change started to appear in the early 1970s, shortly following the Six-Day War of June 1967. That war can be said to have marked a radical if gradual change in Arab attitudes toward Israel both on the popular and official planes. The effects also became apparent in Arabic writings on the subject of Israel and the Arab-Israeli conflict. A more sober, more realistic stance began to appear and a kind of normalcy tended to replace the largely demonological perception of the Jewish state. Israel, in short, began to appear in Arab writings as part of the global order of things, a phenomenon—hostile and objectionable, to be sure—but a state among many other states with which one has to deal in the wider context of world politics and using the generally accepted means of diplomacy and war and hard bargaining.

That such an approach was possible or even conceivable, that writers and intellectuals in the Arab world began to risk giving expression to such sentiments, was of course due largely to the fact that the official Arab attitude of outright rejection and lack of realism turned out to be little short of disastrous, and the various Arab regimes were shown to be helpless and totally unable to cope with the situation. Two examples of this newly acquired candor are worth citing here in some detail.

Fi Muwajahat Isra'il (Confronting Israel) is the title of a book published in Cairo in 1969 and written by an Egyptian university lecturer of marked

Marxist leanings, Isma'il Sabri Abdullah. Calling for "a balanced view" of Israel, the author devoted his introductory chapter to an attempt at demolishing what he termed the "partial views" of the Zionist phenomenon. He listed three such "wrong and dangerous approaches to Israel." The crudest and most illiterate of these, he asserted, was "the racial approach," which has it that the Jews constitute an evil race bent on an attempt to corrupt and dominate mankind by means of money and sex. This view, which Abdullah said was based on the so-called "protocols of the elders of Zion," stood in direct opposition to the values of Arab civilization, which rose and flourished under the principle that faith and religious observance, rather than racial origins, are the sole yardsticks by which a man's worth ought to be measured.

The most dangerous aspect of the racist approach to Israel, Abdullah adds, "is that it represents a total acceptance of the Zionist enemy's point of view itself." Zionism, he explains, "is founded on the idea that the Jews constitute a distinct race," a superior race, to be sure, but taking the other extreme of considering the Jews an inferior or evil race does not make any difference: Both views consider the Jews a distinct race and are thus erroneous.

The other two "partial views" of Israel Abdullah sets out to refute are that Israel was "a tool of the imperialists" and the analogy the Arabs were in the habit of drawing between Israel and French Algeria. The two main grounds on which this latter view of Israel is rejected by the author are, first, that while the French settler in Algeria was a Frenchman living there, the Israeli settler in Palestine held no other passport. Thus, he had to fight it out with his or her back to the sea for sheer survival. Second, unlike the French in Algeria, the Israeli did not live in a country whose majority of inhabitants belonged to another nationality; the Israelis have chosen to live within boundaries in which they constitute a clear majority.

In the final section of his book, Abdullah makes a brief reference to the subject of "Israeli nationality." Some intellectuals, he writes, though they reject the idea of a "Jewish nationality," claim that during the two decades of Israel's existence there developed in that country a distinct Israeli nationality unrelated even to the rest of Jewry. He is highly skeptical of this perception. "The main obstacle to the formation of a distinct Israeli nation is the Zionist link," he argues. "Israel cannot become a nation unless it finally ceases to consider itself the homeland of the Jews. The concept of an Israeli nationality inevitably negates Jewish nationalism; it can crystallize and assert itself only insofar as the idea that the Jews form a single nation declines and withers away."[11]

Sabri Abdullah's book was published two years after the Six-Day War and four years before the Yom Kippur War of 1973. Following this latter armed conflict in which the Arabs achieved a significant if rather partial victory, the general tone of Arab writing on Israel became more realistic and as "balanced" and "normal" as it was possible to expect, considering the quality of what had been produced during the previous twenty-five years or so. The most outstanding of the books published on the subject in the mid-1970s—and what can justly be considered a landmark and a break-through—was Muhammad Sid-Ahmad's *Ba'dama taskut al-madafi'* (After the guns fall silent), published in Cairo in 1976. The book's central thesis was that the Yom Kippur War, together with a new world constellation created by détente, had served to change the very basis of the Middle East conflict. For the first time in thirty years, Sid-Ahmad argued, there now obtained a certain measure of parity, or "commensurability," between the Arabs and Israel that was likely to allow for compromise and peace.

"For the first time," he elaborated, "the Arabs proved that they possessed a measure of Israeli 'quality' on the battlefield. So, too, certain features of the Arab 'quantity,' such as petroleum, gave the Arabs a qualitative edge. . . . Conversely, Israel no longer has the capacity to compensate for this advantage with some 'qualitative' endeavor; it could threaten to resort to the ultimate weapon, the nuclear bomb, but to do this would be akin to Samson destroying the Temple and burying himself in the ruins."

From this basic change, Sid-Ahmad construed a number of conclusions, the most striking of which was that, a military solution being absolutely out of the question, the Arabs would be well advised to contemplate a "functional role" for Israel in a post-settlement Middle East. He drew an analogy with Lebanon which, he said, "was prosperous to the extent that it was both complimentary to and different from the surrounding Arab environment." It was in this sense, he explained, that Lebanon had a functional role in the region, and there was no question that Israel would one day acquire a similar role. However, Israel cannot acquire such a role—or any kind of role for that matter—"as long as it does not convince the Arab countries that it is no longer the embodiment of a project alien to their destiny or directed against them."

To be sure, "Israel can claim that it has always declared its readiness to perform such a role and that it was the Arabs who consistently and obstinately refused. In reply the Arabs can point to Israel's activity in Africa and prove that it aimed less at 'cooperation,' 'complementarity' or, *a fortiori,* at 'integration' than it did at 'domination.' And certainly Israel's aims as regards the Arab world are more ambitious than its aims *vis-à-vis* Africa."

A special "functional role" can then be allotted to Israel. Before going on to specify the nature of such a role, Sid-Ahmad makes an interesting attempt to probe the real reason the conflict had gone on for so long. Do the Arabs reject Israel because it is a Jewish state implanted in the heart of the Islamic world? Is the conflict basically national, one between Arab nationalism and Jewish nationalism? Is it, alternatively, a conflict over territory? In various degrees of emphasis Sid-Ahmad's reply to all these questions is in the negative. After all, he points out, not all Muslim countries boycott Israel—witness Iran and Turkey. Then, as far as the "national" character is concerned, he argues that the Arabs should not accept this premise, implying as it does that "all Jews constitute a national entity"; by accepting such a premise, the Arabs "would be adopting the basic Zionist thesis which justifies the establishment of a national home for the Jews in a land usurped from the Arabs."

As to the territorial argument, Sid-Ahmad's stand is that, since dislodging Israel completely from all territory the Arabs consider to be theirs is totally out of the question and any attempt to realize this aim could provoke a third world war, it is evident that there is (among the Arabs) "a more or less tacit acknowledgement that the existence of Israel within secure and recognized borders is unavoidable after the Arabs recover their occupied territories and after the establishment of some Palestinian entity."

This being the case, Sid-Ahmad asks: "What will then stand in the way of this acknowledgement evolving into an acceptance that Israel play a role in the region?" His answer, put briefly, is that the Arabs fear "that Israeli 'quality' is a challenge to Arab 'quantity.'" One "decisive reason" why all Arab countries have refused any intercourse with Israel, he explains, is that "they fear Israeli technological and economic supremacy over the region. Even if a territorial settlement is concluded this would still remain a stumbling-block."

Here, however, Sid-Ahmad comes to his central argument concerning the "new reality" he believes has emerged—namely that "certain aspects of Arab 'quantity' have acquired a 'qualitative' value." The proven ability of the Arabs to wage a highly efficient war and the use of Arab oil and Arab capital, he explains, "have shattered Israel's economic and technological supremacy." After the Yom Kippur War, "Israeli quality could no longer neutralize Arab quantity." And since, accordingly, Arab quantity could now hold its own against Israeli quality, it has become possible, for the first time, to envisage "some kind of match between Israeli technological know-how and Arab capital." Such a state of affairs is quite conceivable since, for one thing, "capital seeks technology just as the investment

of technology requires available capital"; and, for another, "Israel has always striven for this complementarity on which it bases its concept of
inter-regional relations in the year 2000."[12]

However, while thus advocating the renunciation of the use of force and
recognition of Israel within its pre-1967 borders, Sid-Ahmad's ultimate
vision is that "the Zionist enterprise will perish at its zenith," and that
"the very instant of its completion will signal its extinction." This vision,
which the author admitted could prove defective since "history seldom
unfolds with digressions and imponderables," is based on the premise that
the Zionist enterprise will not be able to survive the pressures of Israel's
surroundings, into which ultimately it will have to integrate itself.[13]

It was only a little more than a year after the publication of Sid-Ahmad's
book that the late Egyptian president, Anwar el-Sadat, made his historic
visit to Jerusalem in November 1977 on a spectacular peace mission. The
visit, and the ensuing negotiations, were widely hailed in Egyptian intellectual and literary circles, with such prominent writers as Tawfiq al-Hakim,
Husain Fawzi, and Naguib Mahfuz publicly giving it their blessings. The
mission was opposed, however, by left-wing and diehard Nasserist elements—including, oddly enough, Sid-Ahmad himself.

After the Egyptian-Israeli peace treaty was signed in April 1979, Israel
ceased to be the distant, outlandish, and rather esoteric subject it used to
seem to Arab authors and observers and in a way became part of the everyday political-intellectual concerns. This is true not only where Egypt is
concerned—in which Israel's presence was becoming too conspicuous to
ignore—but also in the rest of the Arab world, where the fact that the
largest and most powerful Arab state had made peace with "the Zionist
enemy" left a strong and lasting impression.

Thus, insofar as writing on Israel is concerned, developments since the
late 1970s have had the somewhat paradoxical effect that books devoted
wholly to Israel, Israeli society, and politics or to Zionism and "the Zionist
scheme" became progressively fewer and harder to come by. Instead, Israel
began to figure in all kinds of books written about a wide range of subjects
and treated largely in the contexts of more general issues—the peace process, the occupied West Bank and Gaza Strip, the fate of the Palestinians;
Zionist settlement past and present, alleged Israeli inroads into and "infil-
tration" of Egyptian academic and intellectual circles; and Israeli espio-
nage activities, mainly in the past.

For over a decade following the signing of the peace treaty with Israel,
Egypt remained the only Arab country to maintain and promote peace
with the Jewish state. There are, in fact, a number of very good reasons

why Cairo has always shown such a keen interest in the success of the peace talks between Israel and its immediate Arab neighbors. Not least of these is the fact that for nearly half a century Egypt found itself subjected to fierce Arab fire of all kinds and from all directions.

The list is long and almost inexhaustible. During the first Arab-Israeli War in 1948–49 there were unending accusations by Transjordan and Iraq concerning the Egyptian army's ineffectiveness and/or inaction. In the heyday of the Baghdad Pact in the mid-1950s, Nasser's Egyptian regime was savaged by the Iraqis and their Arab allies. The same happened following the spectacular dissolution of the Egypt-Syria merger in 1961; in the aftermath of the 1967 Six-Day War; and in the wake of Sadat's visit to Jerusalem in 1977, the Camp David Accords, and the peace treaty with Israel. Finally, in the early 1990s, during the Kuwait crisis and the Gulf war, both Baghdad and Amman pointed an accusing finger at Cairo and its conduct.

On each of these occasions, fierce controversies erupted, touching at times on Egypt's very "Arabness" and reminding Egyptians of their Pharaonic origins! Following the signing of the Israeli-Egyptian peace treaty in 1979, for instance, the veteran Egyptian politician and newspaper editor, Ahmad Abul Fat'h, argued in a long and bitter rejoinder to Arab accusations of betrayal that "the people of Egypt, too, have rights." He then went on to remind his Arab readers that Egypt had until then fought four devastating wars, all aimed at promoting the Arabs' cause and in the course of which tens and even hundreds of thousands of innocent lives were lost, the Egyptian economy lay in utter ruin, the Egyptian people were impoverished to the point of hunger, and Egyptian girls were compelled to work as domestic servants in various Arab countries "as well as to render certain other services well known to the Arabs."

A writer in another of Cairo's leading dailies gave this heading to his article dealing with the arguments advanced by the so-called "rejection front" against a partial peace agreement with Israel: "He who wants to fight is welcome to do the fighting here in Sinai!" Another writer, Foumil Labib, wrote in the Cairo weekly *Al-Musawwar* in response to an open letter addressed to Sadat by a prominent Syrian Ba'th Party functionary — who also happened to be Syrian President Assad's brother, Rif'at — defending Sadat's decision to change Egypt's name from the United Arab Republic to the Arab Republic of Egypt.

Rif'at al-Assad, described by Labib as "the well-known Ba'th millionaire," had lamented that whereas until Sadat's assumption of the presidency Egypt had preserved her Arab name, things took a different turn owing to the new regime's "particularism and Egyptianization." Labib's rejoinder, undoubtedly reflecting official opinion, stressed the following points:

1. Talk about Egypt's change of name marks a return to an old Ba'th allegation concerning "Pharaoism" (*fir'awniyya*)—a charge that had created a "complex" with the late president Nasser, who consequently decided to delete the name "Egypt" and replace it with "Arab." "We," Labib declared, "have now cured ourselves of that complex. We do not disown our Egyptianness, because we don't intend to disown our distant past and its glories, of which we feel quite proud." Nasser, Labib explained, had surrendered Egypt's name in pursuance of Pan-Arab leadership. Sadat, in contrast, "does not seek leadership; what he wants is to liberate Arab lands and ensure the well being of the Egyptians."

2. The man who revived Egypt's name also happened to be the man who decided to fight and who attained the victory of October 1973. "Who knows? Perhaps the name 'Egypt' has some magic for the soldiers fighting at the front." After all, Egypt has a unifying influence on its citizens—in contrast to the general run of Arab countries, which are torn by narrow communal and denominational rifts.

3. Egypt has always been open to proposals for Arab unity and Arab unification; but she does not wish unity to be a mere slogan. One of the factors that led to the collapse of the tripartite union between Egypt, Syria, and Libya in recent history was "Syria's insistence on enjoying certain economic privileges that tended to impoverish her partners." Here Labib reminds Assad of what he claims to be a saying of Syrian coinage: "Libya pays, Egypt leads and Syria gets the trophy."[14]

Another call for the normalization of relations with Israel came from a somewhat unexpected source. In 1994, a book appeared in Paris titled *Hassan 2, La memoire d'un roi: Entretiens avec Eric Laurent.* The book, comprising a series of long interviews with a French journalist, was translated into Arabic and serialized in several leading Arabic dailies before it came out in book form under the title *Mudhakirat malik* (A king remembers).

Two chapters are devoted to the Arab-Israeli conflict. In one passage, asked when he first started to take an interest in the conflict, Hassan says it was the Suez War of 1956. He then recalls how, as someone for whom "the centuries-old coexistence between Arabs and Jews in Morocco was one of the mainstays of this country," he often spoke his mind on the subject to the amazement and shock of his Arab listeners.

On one such occasion, he recalls, in the course of a visit he paid to Lebanon in 1958 or 1959, he attended a dinner party in his honor with a number of Lebanese intellectuals. "With utmost sorrow," he says, "I told them: 'To put it bluntly, the Arabs will never be able to settle this problem. Had I had to decide, I would have recognized Israel and integrated it into the League of Arab States.' My God! What a chorus of shouts followed this statement."

Pressed further, the king said it was the Arabs who had done harm to the Arab cause: "Had they accepted the UN partition resolution in 1947, we would never have reached the state of affairs in which we find ourselves today."

Turning to the Palestinians, Hassan tells his interviewer that several Arab regimes were trying at that time to promote their Pan-Arab ambitions by riding the Palestinian bandwagon, knowing full well that they were unwilling and unable to do anything to help. In 1968, he recalls, he told the PLO leadership he met with at Agadir: "I am eager to cooperate, but you will never be able to destroy Israel. Stop deluding yourselves. . . . If you carry on like this you will be merely wasting the time of Arab leaders!"

Responding to a remark that back in 1970 he was the first Arab leader ever who met a leading Jewish personality with close ties to the Israeli government—the late president of the World Jewish Congress, Nahum Goldman—the king says: "Yes, for it never occurred to me to refuse to meet with someone just because he was a Jew. And no wonder. My position no doubt springs from deep-rooted Moroccan traditions and from my country's history. Morocco's Jews always lived with its Arabs in full amity; they all belong to this land. "

On that first encounter with Goldman, Hassan has this to say: "Actually I met a man who I discovered was open and extremely sensible and moderate—a person quite different from what I had expected. . . . He displayed a great deal of acumen and fairness. Rather than starting our talk by complaining, we started directly on prospects for the future."

Throughout this part of *A King Remembers*, in almost every utterance he makes, King Hassan II finds occasion to refer to his country's long record of Muslim-Jewish coexistence. "On the whole," he tells Laurent, "Jews lived side by side with Arabs peacefully and amicably—certainly without the kind of tragedies that were staged in the West's arena." There is, indeed, a hint of a genuinely cultural-anthropological approach here, even when the subject at hand appears to be purely political in character. One example is the king's first encounter with Moshe Dayan, who, in his capacity as foreign minister, met Hassan twice in 1977 on a secret mission in preparation for the momentous peace initiative launched by Sadat. Knowing that Dayan had grown up in an Arabic-speaking environment, Hassan relates, "I told him he must speak to me in Arabic. 'But I haven't spoken Arabic for a long time now,' he answered. I insisted, and he relented—and we conversed in Arabic half or perhaps even three-quarters of the time. True, his Arabic was generally wanting . . . but this link which bound us together helped create an atmosphere of confidence."

On a more practical plane, possibly the one revelation the king makes about this first encounter is the one regarding Dayan's position on the status of the Golan Heights: "As soon as we took our seats, I said to myself that my first question should be one to enable me to measure his pulse and probe his mentality. So I opened by saying: 'General, what is your position on the Golan?' 'The Golan is Syrian,' came the answer after a minute of reflection. Upon which I said: 'Now we can talk.'"

The Moroccan monarch's memoirs include a good deal of criticism of the way the Arabs conducted themselves throughout the years of conflict with Israel. At one point, for instance, the king tells Laurent that the Israelis "could hardly be blamed for firing the first shot in the Six-Day War of 1967. Considering the perpetual danger to Israel's existence and the pompous rhetoric that characterized pronouncements made by Arab leaders, the Israelis were justified in their fears and suspicions."

On the causes of that war, Hassan says: "In my opinion the Arabs had fallen victims to a trait which is at once one of their highest virtues and their single most important shortcoming—i.e., their grandiloquence." What were people to say, he asks rhetorically, upon hearing someone like Ahmad Shuqeiri (the late self-styled leader of the Palestinians) declaring, "We shall throw the Jews into the sea; we shall burst the wombs of pregnant women, extricate the babies and crush them with our feet?" Nevertheless, he did not believe Israel would strike, "used as it must have been to its neighbors' annoying threats and sloganeering."[15]

Women's Liberation—and Men's

Assia Djebar, a well-known Algerian writer, recently depicted the current state of Middle Eastern women in metaphors borrowed from two Western works of art. In the early 1830s, Eugene Delacroix visited Algeria after spending a month in Morocco. Upon his return to Paris he painted his *Femmes d'Alger dans leur apartement*. The Algerian women are depicted in "a luminous light but at the end of a long dark hall," the implication being that the figures represented were somewhat enigmatic prisoners in a harem world inhabited largely by women.

More than a century later, Pablo Picasso painted a paraphrase of the Delacroix work with the doors of the hall open and sunlight streaming in. Djebar sees in these paintings two views representing two periods, and she concludes: "Let us hope that it is Picasso's vision that is the vision of the future . . . [and that], with the door open in bright sunlight, as Picasso painted it, we can search for and find a concrete and permanent liberation of women."[16]

Many a modern Arab woman would no doubt join in Djebar's prayer. However, a characteristic feature of contemporary literature produced by women in the Arab world has been that, unlike their fellow feminists in the West, they do not concentrate on problems exclusive to their gender. Speaking generally, indeed, Arab attitudes toward the subject of women's liberation suffer from glaring inconsistencies. More than one Arab writer and social scientist have remarked on the wide gulf that lies between the contemporary young educated Arab male's intellectual image of his women friends and associates and his actual behavior toward them. With all his modern, liberal views and education, he remains under the impact of the age-old belief that a woman outside the safe walls of the home is in mortal danger of losing her chastity, that she has no business "exposing" her charms in Western dresses unless she means to sell them or give them away. Moreover, a woman who would give herself, even to her beloved, out of wedlock automatically disqualifies herself as a wife.

This disparity is paralleled by another, no less pronounced one: Young men and women, going through the same educational process, attending the same universities, and absorbing the same modern Western notions about woman and her place in society, emerge from their training with widely disparate attitudes and expectations. In many cases the result is disappointment and disillusionment.

Side by side with this, there have been some instances of "hard-core" women's liberation ideas propagated by a younger generation of Arab women writers and professionals. For the first time, a book on woman and sex in Arab society, *The Hidden Face of Eve*, was published by an Egyptian woman doctor in the 1970s. Nawal el-Sa'dawi, writing about her own experiences, set out in her book to slaughter a good number of sacred cows, chief among them the notion of "honor" in Arab society and its equation with chastity. After describing some of the devices used to restore the appearance of virginity to girls whose misfortune was to have been led astray by unscrupulous suitors, Sa'dawi asked whether a girl who lies in this way should be considered more honest than one who loses her virginity in one ill-conceived premarital affair.

In other chapters of the same book, Sa'dawi resorts to the latest notions and concepts used in the current literature of women's liberation in the West, including such terms as "male chauvinism," "master and slave," and "education and repression." In addition, she calls for an immediate end to all manifestations of "departmentalization" of men's and women's interests, even in such innocuous matters as women's magazines and special pages in newspapers devoted to women—fashion, home decoration, food, swimwear.

Another radical though less outspoken Egyptian feminist is Laila Abou Saif, a Western-educated woman who tells her own story in a moving autobiography, *A Bridge through Time*. It is a revealing and highly readable personal memoir, and is in its own way also a feminist manifesto. The author, born in 1941 and educated in English-language schools and colleges, writes with feeling about life in her social milieu and of Egyptian women struggling to set themselves free from centuries of rigid tradition and emerge as equal human beings—modernized, educated, and fully aware of their rights and their place in society.

Laila Abou Saif is of course aware that this is bound to be a long and arduous struggle. She begins her book with a few words about her grandmother, Om Abdou (Abdou's Mother), "who derived her identity and her being in that small village in Upper Egypt" from the name of her son. "She had a name, my mother's mother. It was Asma. But everyone referred to her as Om Abdou." Om Abdou's second husband, Mikhail, a widower in his sixties when he married twenty-five-year-old Asma, was distant, busy only with his farming and marketing. His wife was not allowed to sit at meals with him.

One day, after *khawaja* Mikhail ordered his morning coffee, Asma, acting upon some unexpected impulse, asked for some for herself as well. "Millennia of male supremacy grew red with indignation as the blood rose to the *khawaja*'s face," but Om Abdou's gaze did not waver. Many years later, as she told the story, "she recalled her feeling of pride as the coffee was brought in for the two of them."

That scene must have taken place some time in the mid-1920s. Almost six decades later, as she was finishing typing her memoir, Laila Abou Saif was not disheartened. "One cannot lose heart in the middle of the fight," she explains. "I am tired, but I am filled with hope that somehow these pages will bring Western women closer to their sisters in the Middle East and the Third World. . . . Egyptian women have achieved so much in the past fifty years, and if social change and revolution are to happen, and it must, it will be at the hands of women. Returning to the veil will not bring about the revolution we so badly need. We cannot face our ancient enemies by hiding from them."

At first glance, this seems like a wild claim and a very tall order. But it is worth paying close attention to the explanation. "There is no hope for Egypt," Abou Saif asserts, "unless the role of women is radicalized. The population problem threatens to devour our country. A new baby is born every twelve seconds, and in 1984 we had a budget deficit of millions of dollars. By the year 2000, there will be 100 million people in Egypt, living within the same boundaries and resources of the past thirty years. Even though the Sheikh of Al-Azhar declared in 1983 that Allah will provide, the infrastructure, even with Allah's help, cannot survive this dizzying baby boom. There's so much women in Egypt can do."[17]

This is only one aspect of the problem confronting modern educated Arab women. There are other, no-less ponderous ones. Some time in the 1910s, Emeline Pankhurst, the British suffragette and fighter for women's rights, submitted a rather novel formulation of the subject of women's liberation. "We have," she declared, "to free half of the human race, women, so that they can help to free the other half."

In one formulation or other, this has been the theme of the fast-growing feminist movements in the Arab world in the 1980s and 1990s. As Ghada el-Samman, a well-known Syrian writer and columnist, put it, "It is dangerous for women in my country to aspire to become mere eunuchs; a woman must remain a woman. . . . What is needed is not merely equality between the sexes but the liberation of both woman and man in a society which enslaves both. For the truth is that there is a dialectical relationship between the two: Behind every imprisoned woman lurks a suppressed man, and behind every prostitute there is a miserable man who suffers from lack of meaningful human relationships."[18]

Not all Arab feminist activists would go along with this appraisal. Arwa al-'Amiri, director of the Woman Studies Center in Amman and head of the psychology department at Amman University, believes that a separation between the subject of women's liberation and reform of the society as a whole is possible, even essential. It is true, Al-'Amiri explained in an interview published in 1990 in the weekly *Al-Kifah al-'Arabi*, that Arab men as well as women are exploited and oppressed by the system, and that both suffer from the absence of freedom of expression and of movement. "When I am back in the house from work, however, I find the same kind of situation—ruler and ruled, exploitation inside the family, where the man is the owner and the woman performs the domestic chores with no remuneration. In short, there is a condition of slave-master relationship within the family itself."

Asked whether social class—beduin, peasant, townsman—played a decisive part here, Al-'Amiri said she did not think so. "Man's superior status has prevailed throughout the world for the last four millennia," she explained. "I therefore believe that political change alone won't be enough." In speaking of the emancipation of women, she added, the issue tends to seem as if it were one calling for a change mainly in the status and conditions of women, when in reality it calls for a change in all walks of life—children and the way they are raised, man and his attitude toward equality and reciprocity. "What is needed is a radical change in all strata of the society," she asserted.[19]

Not that the overall status of Arab women anywhere is satisfactory. In an interview published in the London-based Arabic daily *Al-Hayat,* Lebanon's first lady, Muna al-Hrawi, complained that "feudalism" reigned supreme in her country, and that this bars women from holding political positions there. Mrs. Hrawi, who was speaking to the paper's Paris correspondent while on a private visit there, added that a certain woman member of the Lebanese parliament got there only because she replaced her late husband. "A woman has to go into mourning to get a parliamentary seat," she lamented.[20]

Now Lebanon is considered the most advanced of the Arab countries of the Middle East, and if this was what the position of women there was like in the early 1990s, then little can be expected in other parts of the Arab world. From Morocco and Algeria in the west to Yemen and Saudi Arabia in the east, articulate women complain of discrimination, social inequalities, obsolescent laws and customs, and a variety of other restrictions that render their position way inferior to that of their menfolk.

And with good reason. In Egypt, the first Arab state to grant women the right to be represented in parliament and in local councils, the situation of women in that sphere has worsened considerably. Two landmark laws, one passed in 1956 granting women the right to be elected and another, passed in 1979, making it mandatory to allot women a fixed percentage of seats, remained in effect until the mid-1980s. The result was that in the 1984 parliamentary elections thirty-seven seats were won by women. In 1986, however, the Higher Constitutional Court decided to abrogate the 1979 law on the ground that it violated the principle of equality as embodied in the constitution! The result was that in the 1987 elections only fourteen seats were won by women, as against the thirty-seven they had in the previous house. It was then that President Mubarak intervened and named four women members, out of a certain number of seats the law allowed him to name personally.

A more recent example—also from Egypt—concerns the legal status of women seeking divorce from their husbands. A new law passed in May 1992 decreed that a court order granting a woman divorce could not be actually implemented before all hearings of claims against it had been considered by the court and rejected. This meant that a woman who had filed for divorce and duly got the order would now have to wait, possibly for years, before she could look for a husband. As told by Nafeesa 'Abed, woman's page editor of the Cairo weekly *October,* it was only "by a miracle" that this particular article of the law was annulled through the intervention of Fawziyya 'Abdel Sattar, chairperson of the Legislative Committee of the People's Assembly.[21]

Some years ago, a Lebanese writer—a male—remarked that, while people generally say that there were 100 million Arabs, the fact is that there are only 50 million of them, since in Muslim society the female population is not allowed to assume social responsibility.

This dictum is quoted with approval by Fatima Mernissi, the author of a book on male-female dynamics in Muslim society. Mernissi, a professor of sociology at the University of Rabat, asserts that Muslim men have always had many more rights and privileges than Muslim women, "including even the right to kill their women."[22]

Complaints about the position of women in the Arab world today generally come from women writers and columnists. The author of a book published in Amman in 1996 titled *The Problems of Women in Literature and in Life,* for example, dwells on the image of woman in contemporary Arabic letters. Arab male novelists and authors, she writes, while they tend to be influenced by the latest in intellectual trends and sociopolitical ideas, their attitude toward women remains as it was when Arab society was in its darkest eras of decline, when women were held in subjugation, ridicule, and slavery. In a chapter titled "Towards a Better Understanding of Woman's Problems" the author, Munira Shareeh, writes: "Many people believe that what women advocate—equality of rights with men, the right of a woman to determine her own private affairs, a share in the affairs of state and the social process—is no more than a temporary explosion of feelings . . . on the part of women passing through life crises or ones who are generally not normal."[23]

Shareeh is a literary critic. In contrast, Fatima Mernissi approaches her subject from a deeper sociological perspective. As she sees it, the plight of women in contemporary Muslim society is due partly to what she terms "Muslim sexuality." One of the distinctive characteristics of this sexuality, she asserts, is its "territoriality," which reflects a specific division of labor and an equally specific conception of society and power.

"The territoriality of Muslim sexuality," she explains, "sets patterns of ranks, tasks, and authority. Spatially confined, women were taken care of materially by the men who possessed them, in exchange for total obedience and sexual and reproductive services. The whole system was organized so as the Muslim *umma* [nation] was actually a society of male citizens who possessed, among other things, the female half of the population."[24]

A bleak enough picture, to be sure. Is it a true reflection of the status Islam as a faith allots its womenfolk? Not at all—if we are to go by what the Koran and the Hadith tell us. One particular story incorporated in the Hadith is worth citing here.

The story indicates that several of the women in the first Muslim community were what we today would term feminists. One of them, who had taken part in a number of Muhammad's battles, was bold enough to ask the Prophet why, in the Koran, Allah always addressed himself to men and neglected the women. According to the story, God himself, recognizing the justice of the complaint, henceforth addressed himself to the faithful of both sexes (*muslimun was-muslimat, muminun wa-muminat*).

This does not mean that Islam grants women full equality with men. Like Judaism—and mostly in identical spheres—Islam would seem to discriminate against women: Menstruating women are "impure" or "polluted"; daughters are apportioned only half the inheritance allotted to their brothers; in cases where a male witness to a business transaction is unavailable, two female witnesses are required; and women's subordinate economic status is represented as an unalterable fact of life.

These and a number of other areas of inequality and discrimination against women have, of course, ready enough "explanations" periodically supplied by various apologists. In the case of witnesses, for example, we are told that women are less familiar than men with business procedures and thus are liable to make mistakes. In the matter of divorce, again, it is argued that in pre-Islamic times women had no divorce rights whatsoever, whereas the Koran embodies a number of laws that significantly enhance the status of women—compared to that they had previously.

In recent years, a number of Arab writers—including women and feminists—have developed a novel approach to the subject. Fatima Mernissi, whose work is quoted above, draws a clear distinction between sexual inequality in Islam and in the Christian West. According to her, a candid and articulate feminist, sexual inequality in Western culture is based on a belief in women's biological inferiority. "This," she writes, "explains some aspects of Western women's liberation movements, such as that they are almost always led by women, that their effect is often very superficial, and that they have not yet succeeded in significantly changing the male-female dynamics in that culture."[25]

Islam, in contrast, does not recognize such innate inferiority in women. "On the contrary," says Mernissi, "the whole system is based on the assumption that women are powerful and dangerous beings. All sexual institutions (polygamy, repudiation, sexual segregation, etc.) can be perceived as a strategy for containing their power."

According to Mernissi, this belief in the power of women is likely to give the evolution of the relationship between men and women in Muslim settings a pattern entirely different from the Western one. If, for instance, there are any changes in male-female status and relations in Muslim society, these changes "will tend to be more radical than in the West and will necessarily generate more tension, more conflict, more anxiety and more aggression." This is because, while the women's liberation movements in the West focus on women and their equality with men, in Muslim countries such a movement "would tend to focus on the mode of relatedness between the sexes and thus would probably be led by men and women alike."

In the long perspective, Mernissi is essentially quite optimistic about the chances Muslim women have to improve their lot. Because men can see how the oppression of women works against men themselves, she writes, "women's liberation [in Muslim society] would assume the character of a generational rather than sexual conflict."

She goes so far as to assert that this phenomenon could already be observed "in the opposition between nationalists and old traditionalists at the beginning of the century, and currently it can be seen in the conflict between parents and children over the dying institution of arranged marriage."[26]

Intellectuals Under Stress

Intellectuals have always been a subject of controversy in the Arab world, and the intellectual's role in society and politics remains at issue among the educated classes there. The eruption of the Gulf crisis with the invasion of Kuwait by Iraqi forces in 1990 served only to intensify the debate, with some academics and writers taking sides in favor of this side or that.

In Egypt, especially, intellectuals came under heavy fire—and from all directions. Groups and circles opposed to Iraq's move attacked those who showed sympathy or even leniency toward Baghdad, while they tried to defend their stand as best they could, considering they were swimming against the tide and against their country's position.

More interesting and instructive have been the sharp exchanges between the intellectuals themselves. Mutual recriminations and accusations were thrown around, and Julien Benda's famous work on "the treason of the intellectuals" was presented as proof and justification for the critics' stand. Things came to such a pass, indeed, that 'Abdul 'Azim Ramadhan, a respected Egyptian historian, found fit to introduce an article he wrote on the failure of the Arab Left with a disclaimer. He announced that he had never worked for, or been associated with, any Kuwaiti institution, academic, governmental, or journalistic—the implication being that in opposing Baghdad's seizure of the emirate, he had no ax to grind.[27]

The subject is also tackled in calmer and more academic ways. "Defined in any way one chooses, the Arab intellectual is part of the Arab predicament," says Sa'deddine Ibrahim, professor of sociology at the American University of Cairo and one of the more active and outspoken Egyptian intellectuals writing and lecturing in the 1990s.

"As intellectuals," Sa'deddine adds in an interview published in the Cairo weekly *Rose el-Yusuf,* "we may have erred sometimes, perhaps most of the time. Perchance we lacked courage and thus betrayed our people, being their vanguard and consciences; perhaps we failed in our analyses and our perceptions of our present condition, allowing this to blur our vision and paralyze us. It may be, too, that we have traded our integrity for a livelihood, freedom for social justice, independence for material growth, traditionalism for modernity . . . Perhaps, perhaps. . . ."[28]

On the tricky subject of relations between the intellectual and the powers that be, Sa'deddine is far more wary. Writing in the learned Arabic quarterly *Al-Fikr al-'Arabi* not long ago, he wondered what an intellectual ought to do when he finds himself disagreeing with what the regime asks him to do. His answer: "Let him excuse himself, politely and without undue fuss in the media."

In furnishing such an easy way out, however, Sa'deddine seems to be strangely unaware of the assumption implicit therein—namely, that for a ruler to be in a position to ask an intellectual to do his will implies that the latter has been safely "establishmentized."

This, in fact, is the thrust of the argument made by Mahmoud Amin al-'Alim, an Egyptian intellectual of the Left, in an article in the same issue of the quarterly. "The majority of Arab intellectuals today," al-'Alim writes, "have, consciously or subconsciously, become court poets, apologists for monarchs, and have used tools for justifying, guiding and helping pass policies and measures imposed by the present Arab regimes and give them a false air of legitimacy."

Not that Sa'deddine is not aware of all this; he is only much more careful. "As a rule," he tells his *Rose el-Yusuf* interviewer, "government does not heed what intellectuals say—which is part of the former's problem, rather than the latter's." The intellectuals, he adds, are not called upon "to draw an Arab strategy for the future." What they ought to do is just "to visualize situations in the far future"—visions that become blueprints and strategies.[29]

Viewing them in this way, the Egyptian academic finds that Arab intellectuals have done their bit, as witness the multitude of blueprints and strategies they have proposed since the late 1960s in the economic, educational, technological, and military spheres. The trouble, however, has been that "while intellectuals generate ideas, the rulers generate venom." A great gap thus yawns between thinkers and political authority, and Sa'deddine says he himself is trying to contribute toward bridging that gap, in his capacity as organizer of the prestigious Arab Thought Forum.

The Arab Thought Forum, an all-Arab think tank set up and financed by Jordan and acting under the auspices of Crown Prince Hassan, holds frequent conferences to discuss current topics of concern to the Arab world. According to Sa'deddine Ibrahim, the Forum aims at putting to the test some of the ideas of its participants, who usually include men of ideas and people with authority to make decisions in equal numbers. He cites the case of Prince Hassan himself, who, besides being the originator of the idea, is also a man of authority.

Dealing with the same subject, another Egyptian academic, Fuad Zakariyya, comments in an interview with the French News Agency on the extent of "thought control" exercised by governments, especially in the Arab world. Zakariyya, a professor of philosophy at Ein Shams University, says this hegemony over the minds of ordinary men is an outcome of the exclusive control by governments of the education apparatus and the information media. He adds that what the Arab regimes want to see is an obedient citizen incapable of debating their policies or identifying the basic flaws in the system under which he or she lives.

In this state of affairs, Zakariyya says, the responsibility of the intellectuals is indeed a major one. The problem, however, is that governments possess the power to encourage and help disseminate the ideas of certain intellectuals while suppressing those of certain others, so that the latter's voice and the impact of their ideas become marginal at best, heeded by a tiny minority of people holding the same kind of convictions anyway.[30]

While these and related subjects continued to be discussed by the intellectuals themselves in the early 1990s, the debate started to cease to be in the nature of a family affair. The steady radicalization of Islamist movements and the emergence of what has come to be known as Al-Jama'at al-Islamiyya put the largely secularist intellectuals at crossfire, becoming as they did a target for the fundamentalists' wrath. The tragic case of Faraj Fouda is worth telling in the present context.

In the ideological lexicon of religious fanatics, the word *secularist* is almost always equated with *atheist* or *apostate*. As far as one can judge from his own writings, Faraj 'Ali Fouda, the Egyptian author and columnist who was gunned down in a Cairo suburb on June 7, 1992, was no apostate. He was certainly not an atheist, and not only because as a child and youth he was given a strictly traditional Islamic education.

Fouda was, however, an advocate of a modern, Western-style secular state, as opposed to the religious state Muslim fundamentalists demanded. Strictly speaking, Egypt is effectively a secular state, though along with almost all other Arab states—with the exception of Syria and Iraq, where the Pan-Arab Ba'th Party rules—its constitution declares that Islam "is the religion of the state."

This, of course, is far short of what is envisioned by the Islamists, whose spokesmen consider the present Arab regimes, with the possible exception of Saudi Arabia—and more recently Sudan—heretical. The fundamentalists advocate a state run strictly according to the laws and commands of the Koran, the kind of state the Islamic Republic of Iran claims—or aspires—to be.

It was against this fundamentalist "tide" that Fouda set himself and his sharp, pithy pen. While by no means the only one among the Egyptian intelligentsia to see the danger and sound the alarm, he was undoubtedly the most outspoken of all those who fought what he perceived as a threatening avalanche. Consistently and mercilessly, Fouda exposed the leaders and the ideologues of the Islamist groups known in Egypt as *al-gama-'at* and all boasting the name jihad (holy war). He showed them to be forces of darkness—lawless bigots, anti-progress, anti-women, xenophobes, and, above all, incurable hypocrites, to use his own terminology.

It was, indeed, ironic that Fouda's very last column, which appeared in the Cairo weekly *October* on the day he was assassinated, was devoted precisely to this aspect of the fundamentalists' behavior. What he perceived as most hypocritical in their conduct, he wrote, lay in their attitude toward sex and sexuality. He related, for instance, that two months previously he had received a videocassette showing 'Abdel Fattah Murro, founder and leader of The Awakening (the Tunisian Islamist party) having sex in his office with his attractive Tunisian friend *on the prayer rug!*

He also cited some of the antics fundamentalist theologians had thought up: a man should not take a woman's seat on a bus before ten minutes has passed—until, that is, the woman's body heat has had time to cool; a woman doctor should refrain from conducting an autopsy on a man's body; it is forbidden for a girl to undress in front of a male dog; and music is forbidden if accompanied by body movements.

He was quite aware of the difficulty Muslim males encounter, especially the young among them—unemployment, the housing crisis, high dowries, and the sexual urge itself—Fouda wrote. In their desperate search for a peg on which to hang all these problems and needs, he added, they have chosen women. "We feel the sexual urge—and we cry that women should stay at home . . . wear the veil, be punished for 'indecent exposure,' and so on," he wrote derisively. "Woman becomes the peg, and the only explanation for this is that we believe she is weaker, and that as Orientals we are entitled to impose on her anything we wish, and she is duty-bound to comply."[31]

Fouda's most serious charge against the fundamentalists was that they had "abandoned the true teachings of Islam." He also thought that the authorities should adopt tougher measures to stem "the tide." In the course of a meeting that Egypt's President Hosni Mubarak held in May 1992 with a group of journalists and editors, Fouda asked him to initiate anti-terror legislation to curb the extremists.

Fouda—who was by profession an economic consultant—devoted all his political and intellectual energies to fighting Islamic fundamentalism. All his books had two main themes—curbing the Islamist tide and promoting Muslim-Coptic reconciliation and coexistence. Their titles faithfully reflect their contents: *The Terror, The Absent Truth, Before the Fall, The Omen.*

In *The Omen,* Fouda lists some of the fundamentalists' main stands:

1. They do not recognize Egyptian nationalism and national unity.
2. They disown the acts of violence and terror they themselves commit.
3. They are ignorant of Islamic history and distort its true character.
4. They teach that woman's place is in the home.
5. They distort modern civilization and depict it as one of permissiveness, sexual perversion, and AIDS.
6. They portray the Islamist state as a veritable Garden of Eden, ignoring the shameful record of torture and summary executions in the Islamic Republic of Iran.[32]

Fouda's style was pithy and unsparing, and at times perhaps too biting and too personal. Muhammad Sid-Ahmad, a fellow political intellectual and a friend, said after the assassination that, while Fouda's erudition was not in question, his style was characterized by sarcasm—"and, perhaps, there was in it a certain measure of innocence, of naivete."[33]

To promote his views, Fouda made several unsuccessful attempts to be elected to the People's Assembly, Egypt's parliament, advocating the separation of religion and state and adorning his election propaganda material with both the crescent and the cross, representing Egypt's two religious communities. He is said to have enjoyed massive support among Coptic voters. He also applied for a license to form a political party—*Hizb al-Mustaqbal* (Party of the Future)—but his request, along with those of many other individuals and groups, was rejected.

Notes

Chapter 1: The Modernist Movement in Arabic Islam

1. Arnold Toynbee, *Civilization on Trial* (New York, 1948), 212.
2. Quoted in Peter Partner, *A Short Political Guide to the Arab World* (London, 1960), 100–101.
3. Cf. Kenneth Cragg, "The Modernist Movement in Egypt," in *Islam and the West,* ed. R. N. Frye (The Hague, 1956), 149–64.
4. Nadav Safran, *Egypt in Search of Political Community* (Cambridge, Mass., 1961), 1–3.
5. Ibid., 3–4.
6. Nikki R. Keddie, *Sayyid Jamal al-Din "al-Afghani": A Political Biography* (Berkeley and Los Angeles, 1972), 10.
7. Ibid., 10–11.
8. B. Michel and Mustafa 'Abd al-Raziq, *Risalat al-tawhid* (Paris, 1925), xxiii.
9. Sylvia G. Haim, ed., *Arab Nationalism: An Anthology* (Berkeley and Los Angeles, 1968), 37–40.
10. Elie Kedourie, *Afghani and 'Abduh: An Essay on Religious Unbelief and Political Activism in Modern Islam* (London, 1966), 63.
11. Nikki R. Keddie, *An Islamic Response to Imperialism: Political and Religious Writings of Sayyid Jamal al-Din "al-Afghani"* (Berkeley and Los Angeles, 1968), 37–40.
12. Charles C. Adams, *Islam and Modernism in Egypt* (Oxford, 1933), 15–16.
13. Qadri Qal'achi, *Jamal al-Din al-Afghani: Hakim al-sharq* (Jamal al-Din al-Afghani: The sage of the east) (Beirut, 1947), 15.
14. Reported in Jurji Zaidan, *Mashahir al-sharq* (Famous men of the east) (Beirut, n.d.), 1:281.
15. Jamal M. Ahmed, *The Intellectual Origins of Egyptian Nationalism* (Oxford, 1960), 78–79.
16. Mustafa 'Abd al-Raziq, *Muhammad 'Abduh* (Cairo, 1946), 18–25; Osman Amin, "Muhammad 'Abduh," *Al-kitab,* January 1946, 332–38.
17. For a fuller account of Afghani's influence and the circumstances of the two men's encounter, see 'Abd al-Raziq, op. cit., 47–63; Adams, op. cit., 32ff.
18. 'Abd al-Raziq, op. cit., 92–101.

19. Adams, op. cit., 62–63.

20. Ibid., 80–81.

21. Muhammad 'Abduh, *Al-Manar* 8 (1896):892–93; reproduced in Rashid Rida, *Taarikh al-ustadh al-imam* (Cairo, 1931), 1:11–12, and quoted in Malcolm H. Kerr, *Islamic Reform: The Political and Legal Theories of Muhammad 'Abduh and Rashid Rida* (Berkeley and Los Angeles, 1966), 108–9.

22. Horten's study, published in German in 1917, is summarized in Adams, op. cit., 104–7.

23. 'Abduh, as reported by Rida, op. cit., quoted in Adams, op. cit., 61.

24. Albert Hourani, introduction to Ahmed, *The Intellectual Origins of Egyptian Nationalism*, , ix.

25. Quoted in Adams, op. cit., 168.

26. Amin, in Frye, op. cit., 171–74.

27. Ibid., 177.

Chapter 2: Egypt in the Wake of Modernism

1. Ignaz Goldziher, quoted in Charles C. Adams, *Islam and Modernism in Egypt* (Oxford, 1933), 1.

2. Peter Partner, *A Short Political Guide to the Arab World* (London, 1960), 103.

3. Summarized in Adams, op. cit., 181.

4. Quoted in Adams, op. cit., 184.

5. Adams, op. cit., 219–20.

6. Malcolm H. Kerr, *Islamic Reform: The Political and Legal Theories of Muhammad 'Abduh and Rashid Rida* (Berkeley and Los Angeles, 1966), 15.

7. Ibid.

8. Ibid., 15–16.

9. Jamal M. Ahmed, *The Intellectual Origins of Egyptian Nationalism* (Oxford, 1960), 44.

10. Ibid., 45.

11. Quoted from *Sir taqaddum al-ingliz al-saksoniyyin,* published in 1894, in Ahmed, *Intellectual Origins,* 45.

12. Cf. Ahmed, *Intellectual Origins,* 45–46.

13. 'Abd al-Rahman al-Rafi'i, *Mustafa Kamil,* quoted by Ahmed in *Intellectual Origins,* 77.

14. Ibid., 78.

15. Ibid., 78–79.

16. Ahmed, *Intellectual Origins,* 52–53.

17. Ibid., 55.

18. Quoted by Albert Hourani in *Arabic Thought in the Liberal Age, 1798–1939* (London, 1962), 221.

19. Quoted by Ahmed from a lecture delivered at Dublin University in op. cit., 47.

20. Adams, op. cit., 231.

21. For a summary of Amin's first book, see Adams, op. cit., 47–49.

22. Quotations from al-Sayyid's works are from Ahmed, op. cit., 85–112.

23. A summary of 'Ali 'Abd al-Raziq's controversial book is given in Adams, op. cit. Ahmed also offers a summary, op. cit., 117–18.

24. Ahmed, op. cit., 118.

25. G. E. von Grunebaum, *Islam: Essays in the Nature and Growth of a Cultural Tradition* (London, 1955), 198–99.

26. Nadav Safran, *Egypt in Search of Political Community* (Cambridge, Mass., 1961), 142.

27. Grunebaum, op. cit., 200.

28. Adams, op. cit., 253–54.

29. Safran, op. cit., 129–30; Adams, op. cit., 255.

30. Ahmed, op. cit., 118–19.

31. Safran, op. cit., 153–55.

32. Adams, op. cit., 256–58.

33. Safran, op. cit., 168, 179–80.

34. See Grunebaum, op. cit., 208–16, for a summary of this section.

35. Safran, op. cit., 179.

36. Grunebaum, op. cit., 199.

37. Kerr, op. cit., 107.

38. Partner, op. cit., 100–101.

39. W. Montgomery Watt, *Islamic Philosophy and Theology* (Edinburgh, 1962), 177.

40. See Safran, op. cit., 1–4.

Chapter 3: Islam Takes the Offensive

1. Hasan al-Banna, *Mudhakkirat Hasan al-Banna* (Memoirs) (Cairo, ca. 1949), 62.

2. Werner Caskel, "Western Impact and Islamic Civilization," in *Unity and Variety in Muslim Civilization*, ed. G. E. von Grunebaum (Chicago, 1955), 346–47.

3. Ishak Musa Husaini, *The Moslem Brethren: The Greatest of Modern Islamic Movements,* 2d ed. (Beirut, 1955), 9–10. For a brief history of the movement, see Christina Phelps Harris, *Nationalism and Revolution in Egypt: The Role of the Muslim Brotherhood* (The Hague, 1964), 177–94; Caskel, op. cit., 344–47. The best and fullest account is in Richard B. Mitchell, *The Society of the Muslim Brothers* (London, 1969), 1–162.

4. Quoted in Caskel, op. cit., 345–46. The literature of the Brethren themselves is scattered in booklets and pamphlets mostly undated. Al-Banna's main works are *Mudhakkirat; Da'watuna* (Our mission) (Cairo, 1947); *Min khutab Hasan al-Banna* (From Hasan al-Banna's speeches) (Cairo, n.d.); and *Rasayil Hasan al-Banna* (Hasan al-Banna's letters) (Cairo, n.d.). See bibliography in Mitchell, op. cit., 232–36.

5. Husaini, op. cit., 15, 17.

6. Harris, op. cit., 226–37, for the Brethren's fortunes since the assassination attempt on Nasser. Also Mitchell, op. cit., 151–62.

7. Quoted by Husaini, op. cit., 61–62.

8. Quoted in Caskel, op. cit., 347.

9. *Da'watuna*, summarized in Husaini, op. cit., 65–66. See Mitchell, op. cit., 264–70, for the Brethren's teachings on nationalism, Arabism, and Islamism.

10. Elie Kedourie, "Pan-Arabism and British Policy," *Political Quarterly*, April–June 1957, 142–43.

11. This passage from the Brethren's Prayer is quoted in Husaini, op. cit., 65.

12. Quoted in Husaini, op. cit., 62–63.

13. M. M. Pickthall, *The Meaning of the Glorious Koran* (New York, 1953), LX:8. All citations from the Koran are taken from this work.

14. Ibid., II:136–37.

15. Ibid., LX:9.

16. Ibid., XVII:34, IX:4.

17. Ibid., IX:7.

18. *Nahwa al-nur* (Towards the light). This memorandum, addressed to the rulers of various Muslim countries in 1936, was eventually published in booklet form in Cairo and Amman in 1950. For an ample summary, see Harris, op. cit., 169–74; Mitchell, op. cit., 15.

19. *Nahwa al-nur*, containing the Fifty Demands, cited in Husaini, op. cit., 66.

20. Husaini, op. cit., 66–67.

21. Ibid., 68.

22. *Nahwa al-nur*, 22–25, quoted in Husaini, op. cit., 69–70; see also, French translation in *Orient* 1, no. 4 (1957): 53–55.

23. Quoted in *Al-ikhwan wal-irhab* (The brethren and terrorism) (Cairo, 1954).

24. Quoted in Husaini, op. cit., 39.

25. Summarized in Husaini, op. cit., 41–42.

26. Ibid., 42–43.

27. Quoted in Husaini, op. cit., 45. More on the life and opinions of Hasan al-Banna in his early days is furnished in Anwar al-Jundi, *Qayid al-da'wa* (Leader of the mission) (Cairo, n.d.). Also, Mitchell, op. cit., 1–34.

28. Harris, op. cit., 230–31.

29. Muhammad Naguib, *Egypt's Destiny* (London, 1955), 150–51.

30. Harris, op. cit., 233. Other material consulted: J. Heyworth-Dunne, *Religious and Political Trends in Modern Egypt* (Washington, 1950); Hasan al-Banna, "La nouvelle renaissance du monde Arabe et son orientation," *Orient* 2, no. 2 (1958): 139–44; Yaacov Beham, "Tenu'at ha-ahim ha-Muslimim be-mitzra-yim," *Ha-mizrah he-hadash* (Jerusalem) 3, no. 4 (1954): 12.

Chapter 4: The Secularist Response

1. Elie Kedourie, *Nationalism*, rev. ed. (London, 1961), 58–59.

2. Muhammad al-Ghazzali, *Min huna na'lam*, 5th ed. (Cairo, 1950); English translation by I. R. al-Faruqi, *Our Beginning in Wisdom* (Washington, 1953). These passages are taken from Professor E. I. J. Rosenthal's more literal trans-

lation in his book, *Islam and the Modern National State* (Cambridge, 1965), 110–11.

3. Hasan al-Banna's remarks are quoted from Z. I. Ansari, "Contemporary Islam and Nationalism," *Die welt des Islams* n.s. 7, no. 1–4 (1961): 3ff.

4. Al-Kawakibi's work on the subject is summarized in Sylvia G. Haim, "Islam and the Theory of Arab Nationalism," originally published in *Die welt des Islams* (1956) and reprinted in Walter Z. Laqueur, ed., *The Middle East in Transition* (London, 1962), 272–73.

5. Quoted in Albert Hourani, *Arabic Thought in the Liberal Age, 1798–1939* (London, 1962), 272–73.

6. See ibid., 273, for a general outline. There is a useful chapter on al-Kawakibi in Khaldun S. al-Husry, *Three Reformers* (Beirut, 1968), 55–112.

7. H. A. R. Gibb, *The Arabs* (London, 1940), 4.

8. Zeine N. Zeine, *The Emergence of Arab Nationalism,* rev. ed. (Beirut, 1974), 137, 138, 130–31.

9. 'Abd al-Rahman al-Bazzaz, *Islam and Arab Nationalism* (Baghdad, 1952). English translation by Sylvia G. Haim in *Arab Nationalism: An Anthology,* ed. S. G. Haim (Berkeley and Los Angeles, 1962), 172–88.

10. G. E. von Grunebaum in "Problems of Muslim Nationalism," in *Islam and the West,* ed. Richard N. Frye (The Hague, 1957), 15–16.

11. Ibid., 22–23.

12. Quoted from al-Husri's writings in William L. Cleveland, *The Making of an Arab Nationalist* (Princeton, 1971), 126. See also Sati' al-Husri, *Al-'Uruba awwalan* (Arabism first) (Beirut, 1955), 99–114.

13. Cleveland, op. cit., 153, 154.

14. Abd al-Rahman 'Azzam's lecture was presented at the 14th Annual Conference of the Middle East Institute in Washington on May 5, 1960. Text in William Sands, ed., *The Arab Nation: Paths and Obstacles to Fulfillment* (Washington, 1961), 1–14.

15. Sands, op. cit., 6–11.

16. Salah Khalaf's statements are taken from a report in the East Jerusalem daily *Al-Quds,* February 27, 1979.

17. G. E. von Grunebaum, *Islam: Essays in the Nature and Growth of a Cultural Tradition* (London, 1955), 185.

18. Hazem Zaki Nuseibeh, *The Ideas of Arab Nationalism* (Ithaca, 1956), 57–64.

19. *Al-Adab,* November 1955, 873–78, 949–51.

20. Ibid., March 1957, 265–71.

21. *Ma'a al-qawmiyya al-'Arabiyya* (With Arab nationalism) (Cairo, 1957).

22. Ibid., 162.

23. Ibid., 165.

24. *Al-Adab,* July 1957, 676–80.

25. Nuseibeh, op. cit., 57–58.

26. Abdullah al-'Alayli, *Dustur al-qawmiyya al-'Arabiyya* (The constitution of Arab nationalism) (Beirut, 1941); quoted by Nuseibeh, op. cit., 58–59.

27. Abdullah 'Abd al-Dayim, "Insaniyya la 'alamiyya" (Humanism, not internationalism), *Al-Adab*, September 1955, 713–16.

28. 'Abd al-Latif Sharara, *"Beina qawmiyya wa-qawmiyya"* (Two types of nationalism), *Al-Adab*, October 1955, 857–59.

29. *Al-Adab*, April 1957, quoted by Naji 'Alloush in *Al-Adab*, August 1957, 771–72.

30. *Al-Adab*, June 1957, 587–91.

31. *Al-Adab*, September 1957, 885–88.

32. Albert Hourani, "The Decline of the West in the Middle East," *International Affairs*, April 1953; quoted by Nuseibeh, op. cit., 101.

33. For a summary of these works, see Nissim Rejwan, *Nasserist Ideology: Its Exponents and Critics* (New York and Jerusalem, 1974), 60–65.

Chapter 5: The Shock of 1967

1. *Al-Adab*, July–August 1967, 2–3.

2. *Al-Adab*, October 1969, 1–3.

3. Salah al-Din al-Munajjid, *A'midat al-nakba* (The pillars of the disaster) (Beirut, 1967).

4. From an interview in *Al-Dustur* (Amman), December 22, 1967.

5. Kamal Yusuf al-Haj, *Hawla falsafat al-Sahyuniyya* (On the philosophy of Zionism) (Beirut, 1967).

6. *Al-Adab*, July–August 1967, 35.

7. Sadiq Jalal al-'Azm, *Al-naqd al-dhati ba'd al-hazima* (Self-criticism after the defeat) (Beirut, 1968).

8. Al-'Azm, in *Mawaqif*, November–December 1969. Reprinted in his *Dirasat yasariyya* (Left studies) (Beirut, 1970), 179–91.

9. Al-'Azm, *An-naqd*, 27–69.

10. Ibid., 69–86.

11. Ibid., 87–92.

12. Ibid., 130–46.

13. Sadiq Jalal al-'Azm, *Naqd al-fikr al-dini* (A critique of religious reason) (Beirut, 1969).

14. Ibid., 8.

15. Ibid., 10.

16. Ibid., 13, 15.

17. *Al-Nahar*, December 22, 1969.

18. *Saut al-'Uruba*, December 24, 1969.

19. Ibid., December 31, 1969.

20. *Al-Adab*, January 1970, 89.

21. *Al-Hawadith*, December 26, 1969.

22. Abd al-Jalil Hasan in *Al-Adab*, March 1970, 11–12, 89–90.

23. Shukri Muhammad 'Ayyad's paper is reprinted in *Al-Adab*, May 1969, 3–6.

24. Muhammad Kamal Husain, *Al-wadi al-muqaddas* (The sacred valley) (Cairo, 1968).

25. Abd al-Jalil Hasan, in *Al-Katib*, November 1968, 84–91.

26. Shukri 'Ayyad, op. cit., 4.

27. Ghali Shukri, *Al-Tali'ah*, May 1969, 101–10.

28. Ibid., 103.

29. Salah 'Isa in *Al-Adab*, April 1971, 5–6.

30. Muhammad al-Naqqash in the Beirut daily *Al-Sha'b*.

31. Suheil Idris in *Al-Adab*, December 1971, 2.

32. *Al-Iza'ah wal-televizyon*, April 4, 1969.

33. All of Mahfuz's three stories are collected in *Taht al-mazalla* (Under the awning) (Cairo, 1969), 3–16, 17–32, 285–321, respectively.

34. Naguib Mahfuz, *Hub taht al-matar* (Love under the rain) (Cairo, 1973).

35. Sa'd al-Din Wahbi, *Sab' sawaqi* (Seven waterwheels) (Cairo, 1969).

36. *Al-Musawwar*, April 4, 1969.

37. Constantine Zureiq, *Al-Adab*, July–August 1967, 45.

38. Costi K. Zureiq, "The Essence of Arab Civilization," printed in *Middle East Journal* 3, no. 2 (1956): 125–39.

39. Ibid., 126.

40. Ibid., 135.

41. Costi Zureiq, "Arab Nationalism and Religion," originally a chapter from his *Al-wa'y al-qawmi* (On nationalist consciousness) (Beirut, 1949). English version by Sylvia G. Haim in *Arab Nationalism: An Anthology* (Berkeley, 1962), 167–71.

42. Ibid., 169–70.

43. Zureiq, *Al-Adab*, July–August 1967, 5.

44. Constantine K. Zureiq, *Palestine: The Meaning of the Disaster* (London, 1956). A translation by Bayly Winder of Zureiq's *Ma'na al-nakba* (Beirut, 1948). All quotations are taken from this translation.

45. Constantine Zureiq, *Fi ma'rakat al-hadara* (In the battle of civilization) (Beirut, 1964).

Chapter 6: Patterns of Disillusionment

1. Jacques Berque, *The Arabs: Their History and Future* (London, 1964), 42–43.

2. For a résumé of al-Malayka's views and those of her critics, see Nissim Rejwan, *Nasserist Ideology: Its Exponents and Critics* (New York and Jerusalem, 1974), 135–41.

3. Frantz Fanon, *The Wretched of the Earth* (Harmondsworth, 1972), 66.

4. "Historical Notes on Ideological Aspects of Culture in Germany and Russia," in A. L. Kroeber and Clyde Cluckhohn, *Culture* (New York, 1960), 404–5.

5. Muhammad Kamal 'Ayyad, "Mustaqbal al-thaqafa fi al-mujtama' al-'Arabi" (The future of culture in Arab society), in *The Arab World: Essays and Studies* (Cairo: Cultural Department of the Arab League, 1953), 143–67.

6. Taha Husain, *Mustaqbal al-thaqafa fi misr* (The future of culture in Egypt) (Cairo, 1937).

7. Ahmad 'Abbas Salih, in *Al-Katib*, January 1965, 7.

8. Ruth Benedict, *Patterns of Culture* (New York, 1953), 19–20.

9. Muhammad Wahbi, *Azmat al-tamaddun al-'Arabi* (The crisis of Arab civilization) (Beirut, 1956).

10. Ibid., 9–11.

11. Ibid., 14–16.

12. Ibid., 31–40.

13. Ibid., 100–110.

14. Ibid. 124–46.

15. Ibid., 151.

16. Muhammad Wahbi, *'Uruba wa insaniyya* (Arabism and humanism) (Beirut, 1958).

17. Ibid., 21–25.

18. Ibid., 25–26.

19. Ibid., 30–37.

20. Muhammad Wahbi, "Mushkilat al-'Arab al-siyasiyya mushkilat akhlaq" (The Arabs' political problem is a moral one), *Al-'Arabi* (Kuwait), March 1963, 33–38.

21. Wahbi, *Azmat,* 20–21.

22. Hisham Sharabi, *Muqaddimat li dirasat al-mujtama' al-'Arabi* (Introductions to the study of Arab society) (Beirut, 1975).

23. Hisham Sharabi, "Political and Intellectual Attitudes of the Young Arab Generation," in *The Arab Middle East and Muslim Africa,* ed. T. Kerekes (London, 1961), 47–61.

24. Hisham Sharabi, *Al-jamr wal-ramad: Dhikrayat muthaqqaf 'Arabi* (Embers and ashes: The memoirs of an Arab intellectual) (Beirut, 1978).

Chapter 7: October and After

1. Tawfiq al-Hakim, *'Awdat al-wa'y* (The return of consciousness) (Beirut, 1974).

2. Tawfiq al-Hakim, *'Awdat al-ruh* (The return of the soul) (Cairo, 1933).

3. al-Hakim, *'Awdat al-wa'y,* 5–6, 19–21.

4. Ibid., 21–22.

5. Ibid., 38–39.

6. Ibid., 39–40, 58–60, 66.

7. Ibid., 60–61. For a less personal, more systematic critique of the Nasserist experiment, see the series of three articles by Fuad Zakariyya, "Jamal 'Abd al-Nasser and the Egyptian Left," in *Rose al-Yusuf* (Cairo), April 14, 21, 28, 1975.

8. Muhammad Hasanein Haykal in an interview published in the Beirut weekly *Al-Sayyad,* quoted in *The Jerusalem Post,* September 5, 1974.

9. Muhammad 'Oda, *Al-wa'y al-mafqud* (The lost consciousness) (Cairo, 1975).

10. Ibid., 282–85.

11. For a summary of a previous debate on the same subject, see Rejwan, *Nasserist Ideology,* 58–59.

12. "Hiyad Masr" (Egypt's neutrality), *Al-Ahram* (Cairo), March 3, 1978.

13. *Al-Akhbar* (Cairo), March 23, 1978.

14. *Al-Ahram,* May 12, 1978.

15. *Al-Ahali* (Cairo), March 22, 1978.

16. *Al-Ahram,* April 20, 1978.

17. Ibid., May 13, 1978.

18. Ibid., May 11, 1978.

19. Sa'd al-Din Ibrahim, ed., *'Urubat Masr wa hiwar al-sab'inat* (Egypt's Arabism and the debate of the seventies) (Cairo, 1978).

20. Al-Hakim's appeal was reported in *The Jerusalem Post,* January 3, 1975.

21. Talal Rahma, "On Arab Culture after October: A Crisis of Creativity or a Crisis of Inflation?" in *Al-Hawadith* (Beirut), November 22, 1974, 98–99.

22. Ibid., 98.

23. Ibid., 99.

24. Ibid.

25. Salah 'Isa's article appeared in *Al-Adab,* October 1971, 71–75.

26. Abdullah Laroui, *The Crisis of the Arab Intellectual: Traditionalism or Historicism?* (Berkeley, 1976), a translation by Diarmid Cammell of Laroui's *La crise des intellectuels Arabes: Traditionalisme ou historicisme?*

27. Ibid., 153–54.

28. Ibid., 154.

29. Ibid.

30. Ibid., 155–56.

31. Ibid., 171–72.

32. Ibid., 174.

33. All quotations and summaries from the Cairo conference are taken from the full-page report published by *Al-Ahali* (Cairo), June 24, 1987.

34. Ghali Shukri's reflections are quoted from an article in *Al-Watan al-'Arabi* (Paris), July 19, 1987.

35. The symposium in its entirety was printed in *Al-Mustaqbal al-'Arabi* (Beirut), April 1984.

36. Information on the group and their trials is based on reports printed in the Egyptian press. See Nissim Rejwan, "The Moslem Plotters," *The Jerusalem Post,* June 27, 1975.

37. Ibid.

Chapter 8: The Shifty Nineties

1. Hisham Je'it, *Al-Ufuq* (Limassol), July 10, 1990.

2. Jalal Amin, *Al-Ahali* (Cairo), October 24, 1990.

3. *Al-Ahali* (Cairo), December 14, 1991.

4. Muhammad Asad, *The Principles of State and Government in Islam* (Berkeley, 1961), 44–45.

5. Nissim Rejwan, "Leave It to the Imam?," *The Jerusalem Post,* August 7, 1992.

6. *Sourakia* (London), November 19, 1990.

7. Charles Issawi, "Economic and Social Foundations of Democracy in the Middle East," in *The Middle East in Transition,* ed. Walter Z. Laqueur (London, 1958), 33.

8. Ibid., 36.

9. Ibid., 38.

10. Quoted by Bernard Lewis, *The Political Language of Islam* (Chicago and London, 1988), 43.

11. Ismail Sabri Abdullah, *Fi muwajahat Isra'il* (Confronting Israel) (Cairo, 1969).

12. Muhammad Sid-Ahmad, *Ba'dama taskut al-madafi'* (After the guns fall silent) (Cairo and Beirut, 1976).

13. A few of the more representative books published in Arabic following the Israeli-Egyptian peace treaty are summarized in Nissim Rejwan, "Arab Books on Israel: From Catastrophology to Normalcy," in *Books on Israel,* ed. Ian S. Lustick (New York, 1988), 91–106.

14. Ahmad Abul Fat'h and Foumil Labib are quoted in Nissim Rejwan, "Egypt's Stake in the Peace Process," *The Jerusalem Post,* November 28, 1991.

15. A comprehensive summary of King Hassan II's memoirs appears in Nissim Rejwan, "Grandiloquence: The Arabs' Undoing," *Midstream* (New York), January 1995, 39–40.

16. Quoted in Nissim Rejwan, "Arab Women's Long Road to Liberation," *Midstream* (New York), October 1988, 15.

17. Abou Saif's book is summarized in Rejwan, "Arab Women's Long Road," 16–17.

18. *Al-Usboo' al-'Arabi* (Beirut), November 11, 1991.

19. Al-'Amiri's interview is quoted in Nissim Rejwan, "Challenging the 'Master-Slave' Relationship," *The Jerusalem Post,* June 16, 1990.

20. *Al-Hayat* (London), June 27, 1992. Quoted in Nissim Rejwan, "Arab Women's Status: More Downs than Ups," *The Jerusalem Post,* July 28, 1992.

21. Ibid.

22. Quoted in Nissim Rejwan, "Women's Liberation as Men's Liberation," *The Jerusalem Post,* October 16, 1992.

23. Ibid.

24. Fatima Mernissi, *Beyond the Veil: Male-Female Dynamics in Muslim Society* (London, 1975), 169–70.

25. Ibid., 12–13.

26. Ibid., 176–77.

27. Quoted in Nissim Rejwan, "Intellectuals at Cross-Fire," *The Jerusalem Post,* December 28, 1990.

28. Ibid.

29. Ibid.

30. Ibid.

31. Fouda's column appeared in *October* (Cairo), June 7, 1992, 23.

32. Summarized in Nissim Rejwan, "Death of an Islamic Secularist: Faraj Fouda's Literary Legacy," *The Jerusalem Post,* June 19, 1992.

33. Ibid.

Index